AF684230

ALTERNATIVE REALTIME CAREERS

A GUIDE TO CLOSED CAPTIONING AND CART FOR COURT REPORTERS

BY GARY D. ROBSON

Alternative Realtime Careers
A Guide to Closed Captioning and CART for Court Reporters
By Gary D. Robson

Copyright © 2000 by Gary D. Robson and the National Court Reporters Association. All rights reserved. No part of this book may be reproduced or transmitted in any form or by any means, electronic or mechanical, including photocopying, recording, or by any information storage or retrieval system without express written permission from Gary Robson and the National Court Reporters Association.
Printed in the United States of America.

Printing History:
June 2000: First Edition.

Limit of Liability/Disclaimer of Warranty: The author and publisher of this book have expended their best efforts to assure the accuracy of the information contained herein. Neither the author nor the publisher, however, make any representation or warranties with respect to the accuracy or completeness of the contents of this book, and specifically disclaim any implied warranties or merchantability or fitness for any particular purpose, and shall in no event be liable for any loss of profit or any other commercial damage, including but not limited to special, incidental, consequential or other damages. Under no circumstances is any information in this book to be construed as legal advice, and all information is subject to change. This book is not recommended for use as a hangover cure. Possible side effects of using this book include blurry eyes, confusion, dizziness and uncontrollable finger movement when watching television. No baby harp seals were harmed in the production of this book. The typesetting and word processing for this book were done using all recycled electrons.
Trademarks: All brand names, company names and product names used in this book are trademarks, registered trademarks, service marks or trade names of their respective holders.

ISBN 978-1-881859-51-2
LCCN 00 132076

Dedication

This book is dedicated to my children, Heather and Douglas. I thank you both for your patience while I worked on this book when I probably should have been playing games or riding the horses with you.

Special thanks are due here to my wife, Kathy, for her assistance and inspiration — sometimes when she didn't even realize she was helping.

Writing a book is not a solo act. The National Court Reporters Association provided people to do proofreading, typesetting, layout, photography, drafting and to handle a million details from getting an ISBN to picking the right paper. I had to do most of those things myself on my last book, and it makes me appreciate all of their hard work even more.

And finally, to Peter Wacht, the editor of the *Journal of Court Reporting,* who believed in the project and made it happen. Thanks, Pete. It wouldn't have come together without you.

Table of Contents

About the Author

Gary Robson has been involved in the captioning industry since 1989 and was awarded the Andrew Saks Engineering Award by TDI (Telecommunications for the Deaf Inc.) for his "outstanding contribution to improving the visual accessibility of information."

In addition to his software engineering work in captioning and court reporting, he wrote *Inside Captioning* (1997, CyberDawg Publishing), the definitive guide to the captioning industry, and co-authored *The Court Reporter's Guide to Cyberspace* (1996, CyberDawg Publishing), a 350-page guide to telecommunications, data transfer and the Internet for court reporting professionals.

Gary is a contributing editor for the *Journal of Court Reporting* and captioning columnist for *Newswaves for Deaf and Hard-of-Hearing People*, and has written numerous articles on the conjunction of captioning, court reporting and computers on subjects ranging from captioning for city governments to speech recognition. Many of those articles are available online at his Web site (www.robson.org), including the comprehensive Frequently Asked Questions About Closed Captioning.

He has given seminars and panel discussions on closed captioning for many groups, including the International Television Association, the United States Department of Education, TDI, the National Court Reporters Association, state and local court reporting associations, and various legal groups. He has also been an instructor for the NCRA

Certified Legal Video Specialist and realtime workshops.

Gary was a computer-aided transcription instructor for a California community college, with a teaching credential in computer and related technologies. In 1987, he founded Cheetah Systems with his wife, Kathy, a CSR, RPR and CRR who does city council and television news and sports captioning. He has been a principal designer for all of Cheetah's captioning, CAT and legal software, as well as the Gemini ergonomic stenotype machine. He is currently the Chief Technology Strategist for VITAC Corporation, the largest closed captioning company in the United States.

Gary has written numerous software programs (including a minicomputer operating system), designed seven integrated circuits, run a manufacturing facility, started four electronics companies (three of which are still operating), written software manuals and worked on just about every microcomputer from the original Altair 8800 to the latest PCs, Macintoshes and Unix machines. He was a contributing editor for *VLSI Design* magazine (a chip-design publication), a member of the editorial board for *Silicon Systems Design* magazine, a book reviewer for *IT Solutions* (the magazine of UniForum), has given seminars on using computers for chip design in the United States and France, and consulted for the U.S. Department of Defense on IC design systems.

Gary set up the groundbreaking realtime captioning of Vice President Al Gore's speech on CompuServe in 1994; realtime captioning on the Internet for the Discovery Channel in 1995; and realtime captioning on America Online and the World Wide Web in 1996. He has taught numerous captioning and realtime seminars, both solo and with his wife, Kathy.

You can contact Gary via e-mail at gary@robson.org.

Introduction

What Is This Book About?

This book *is* all about taking your realtime court reporting skills and applying them to new markets, stretching and enhancing your skills while serving a whole new audience.

This book is *not* a primer on writing style. It does not espouse or endorse any particular theory and offers remarkably few hints on how to write anything. If you're looking for books on steno theory, there are a lot of good ones out there already.

In *Alternative Realtime Careers*, we will explore closed captioning and CART both from a technological point of view and from a business point of view. We'll cover everything from marketing to equipment, from laws to customer communications.

Why Would a Court Reporter Care?

Do you have no interest in realtime whatsoever? Are you perfectly happy translating your work after the fact and editing it later (or simply handing it off to a scopist or notereader)? Then this is not the book for you.

If you are a court reporter currently using realtime every day, do you enjoy your job? Do you feel challenged and rewarded by what you do? Then your only reason for reading this book is to satisfy your curiosity and expand your knowledge.

If, on the other hand, you are a skilled realtime reporter who feels burned out by the legal system, or if you are searching for a new challenge in your life, this book is much more. It is a tutorial on what may be your new career.

CART and captioning bring you up close and personal with people who really *need* what only you can do. Your realtime skills can have a profound effect on people. My wife, Kathy, had worked as a court reporter for 10 years when she began doing live captioning of city council meetings. She realized, of course, that she was giving deaf and hard-of-hearing people a chance to understand and participate in government proceedings from which they had always been excluded. Just what that meant was hammered home when a deaf man came up to her during a break, took her hand and said, "You've changed my life."

Does that bring a tear to your eye? How about the deaf mother crying and hugging the captioner because she was actually able to understand what was happening at her daughter's wedding?

Oh, I can't promise that every day in the captioning and CART business will bring such visceral rewards. I can't promise that it will *ever* happen to you. There will still be days that you'll feel like a piece of furniture, but CART and captioning will give you the opportunity to feel that you're contributing in a whole new way, and I guarantee it will stretch your skills to the limits.

Chapter 1

The History and Theory of Realtime

Where Did Realtime Come From?

The concept of using shorthand techniques to take down words quickly isn't new. It's been under development for over 2,000 years. Ask most court reporters when realtime translation was invented, and they'll guess it was the 1980s. They'd be two decades late.

You don't need to know any of this to caption or write CART, but it is fascinating nonetheless, so let's take a walk through the last two millennia and see where today's realtime technology came from.

63 B.C. Marcus Tullius Tiro, a freed slave who became Cicero's secretary, develops shorthand techniques to record speeches on wax-covered tablets with a metal stylus. Known as *notae Tironianae* ("Tironian notes"), his system was used to record speeches by Cicero, Cato and Julius Caesar. It remained in use for about 1,000 years.

1180 A.D. A monk named John of Tilbury develops a shorthand system for English, which he later used in the court of King Henry II.

1588 Another English cleric, Timothie Bright, patents the first of the modern English-language shorthand systems and publishes *Characterie: An Arte of Shorte, Swifte, and Secrete Writing by Character.*

1602 John Willis creates his shorthand system. His basic principles of geometric symbols and standard spellings are to be used in most shorthand systems developed during the next 200 years.

1620 Thomas Shelton publishes his shorthand system, later adopted by Samuel Pepys, who used it in his famous diary to describe such events as the great fire of London and the great plague.

1672 William Mason publishes his shorthand system.

1772 Shorthand is officially recognized in England when Thomas Gurney is appointed shorthand writer to the British Houses of Parliament, using his own variant of William Mason's system.[1]

1786 Samuel Taylor devises an English-language shorthand system that is later adapted to a number of other European languages.

1789 Thomas Lloyd uses shorthand to report the first Congress of the United States.

1834 Franz Xaver Gabelsberger creates a German-language system based on cursive writing that is soon adapted to several other languages.

1837 A 24-year-old Englishman named Isaac Pitman invents a phonetic system he calls "the first scientific shorthand system," which is still used today.

1852 Isaac Pitman's brother, Benn, introduces Pitman shorthand to the United States.

1868 The first shorthand machine is built.

---

[1] *As an interesting side note, Charles Dickens worked as an early "court reporter" using Gurney's writing system to record sessions of Parliament.*

1879 The first patent for an American shorthand machine is given to Miles M. Bartholomew.

1888 A 21-year-old Irish inventor named John Robert Gregg develops a shorthand system he calls "light line phonography," which is still used today.

1893 The first American edition of Gregg's system is published.

1897 George Kerr Anderson's shorthand machine, which produced one word per stroke rather than one letter per stroke, is used to report President McKinley's inaugural address.

1914 At the National Shorthand Reporters Association[2] annual convention, a group of reporters enters the National Speed Contest using a new "stenotype" machine developed by Ward Stone Ireland. This contest provided the participants with various categories of material, given at very high speeds, and was graded on the accuracy of the transcription. The "machine writers" (court reporters using Ireland's machine) sweep the contest.

1924 American Emma Dearborn introduces Speedwriting Shorthand, based on longhand letters. It never becomes a factor in court reporting.

1947 Emerson Romero develops the first "captioning" of movies. His process consisted of making text-only frames and splicing them into the film.

1949 J. Arthur Rank captions a movie in London, showing the captions on a smaller screen in the lower left-hand corner of the main screen. An operator had to manually insert each caption slide into a second projector.

---

[2] *The National Shorthand Reporters Association is the old name of the National Court Reporters Association.*

Clarence O'Connor and Edmund Boatner organize Captioned Films for the Deaf (CFD).

Deaf and hard-of-hearing people enjoy the first color open-captioned film — *America the Beautiful.*

1958 Malcolm (Mac) Norwood becomes the first chief of media services for the CFD until his retirement in 1988.

1959 The Captioned Film Act (Public Law 85-905) provides federal funding for the CFD to open caption feature films.

1960s IBM and the United States Central Intelligence Agency create the first computer-aided transcription system, whose goal is fast translation and transcription of data in other languages using a monstrous mainframe computer.

1962 The Captioned Film Act is amended to provide CFD with $1.5 million for training, production, acquisition and distribution of educational media and to provide for research into educational media for the deaf.

1970 The National Bureau of Standards begins researching the possibility of transmitting a standard time signal in the vertical blanking interval (VBI) of the TV signal. The project is eventually abandoned, but it brings about the idea of putting data in the VBI and leads ABC to suggest putting captions there.

1971 First National Conference on Television for the Hearing Impaired is held in Nashville, Tenn.

The Caption Center at WGBH is established as the first TV captioning agency.

1972 A demonstration of closed captioning is held at Gallaudet University, where ABC and the National Bureau of Standards show captions embedded in a broadcast of the *Mod Squad.*

The first nationally broadcast open-captioned program, *The French Chef, with Julia Child*, airs on PBS.

The BBC announces Ceefax Teletext service, which will lead to captioning (the British call it "subtitling") in seven years.

1973 PBS begins broadcasting *The Captioned ABC News*, a late-night, open-captioned rebroadcast, with commercials replaced by stories of special interest to the nation's deaf and hard-of-hearing community. More than 190 PBS stations carry the program, which airs for nine years.

StenoComp is founded by Herbert Avram, Patrick J. O'Neill and William Eisner to commercialize the CAT system they developed for the IBM/CIA project. The first to purchase one of the systems was a deposition firm owner in Los Angeles, Calif., by the name of Frank O. Nelson, who later became President of NCRA.

1975 PBS files a petition with the Federal Communications Commission to reserve a segment of the TV signal for transmitting captions.

1976 The FCC reserves Line 21 of the vertical blanking interval for transmitting closed captions.

1978 StenoComp files Chapter 7 bankruptcy.

1979 EEG Enterprises builds the first Line 21 caption encoders.

NCI (National Captioning Institute) is formed.

First program is captioned ("subtitled") on the BBC using Ceefax Teletext.

1980 The first home caption decoder (NCI's TeleCaption) becomes available.

First closed-captioned TV program airs. For ABC, *The ABC*

Sunday Night Movie; NBC, *The Wonderful World of Disney;* and PBS, *Masterpiece Theater.*

First captioned TV movie is *Force 10 From Navarone.*

IBM becomes the first company to caption a TV commercial.

1981 The International Year of Disabled People

Captioned home videos become available. Among the first: *Close Encounters of the Third Kind, Chapter Two* and *The China Syndrome.*

1982 First realtime captioning system is developed (InstaText, by TSI).

First realtime captioning goes on the air during the Academy Awards, with Marty Block of NCI performing the captioning.

ACC (Australian Caption Centre) opens.

First captioned television program shown in Australia — *The Barchester Chronicles.*

NCI begins regular realtime closed captioning for ABC's *World News Tonight.*

First live sporting event captioned — the Sugar Bowl (college football).

CCDA (Canadian Captioning Development Agency) is formed.

1983 Line 21 realtime captioning hits Canada with the World Conference on Captioning in Ottawa.

1984 PBS broadcasts *The Voyage of the Mimi* with English and Spanish captions, marking the first dual-language captioned series.

TSI, producer of the only realtime captioning system, files Chapter 7 bankruptcy.

1985 American Data Captioning (later to become VITAC) opens its doors.

The Kellogg Company becomes the first corporation to fund captioning of a TV series (*Family Ties*).

1986 First tests of video description of *Mystery!* take place in Boston.

CPC (Computer Prompting & Captioning) develops a teleprompting system that outputs closed captions at the same time as the prompter text.

Xscribe Corporation introduces the XCS-1 realtime captioning system, which swiftly replaces the Jacquard-minicomputer-based InstaText system throughout the industry.

1987 Subtitled Videos Project established to provide access to video titles in Australia — over 800 videos are captioned in the following 10 years.

1988 PBS conducts a national test of DVS (descriptive video service) during the entire season of *American Playhouse.*

1989 In March, public TV stations throughout the country run the *American Playhouse* episode "Stand and Deliver" with Spanish translations on the Second Audio Program channel. It becomes the highest-rated pledge special and the second-highest-rated program in the history of KCET, Los Angeles.

The rock group Living Color produces the first closed-captioned music videos. The group's producer, Ed Stasium, has a deaf daughter.

1990 Television Decoder Circuitry Act of 1990 is signed into law.

Americans with Disabilities Act passes.

Cheetah Systems releases the PC-based CAPtivator Online realtime captioning system.

1991 The ACC (Australian Caption Centre) creates the NWPC (National Working Party on Captioning).

The United States House of Representatives begins captioning its floor proceedings on C-SPAN.

1992 Canada Caption Inc. is formed to raise money to fund captioning in Canada.

Hillsborough County, Fla., becomes the first county to realtime caption all county supervisor meetings.

Fremont, Calif., becomes the first city in the United States to realtime caption all city council and school board meetings.

1993 Television Decoder Circuitry Act takes effect.

"The Clinton Inaugural: A PBS Special" is closed-captioned and described. The program is the first live broadcast accessible to blind and visually impaired people through Descriptive Video Service.

TRIPOD Captioned Films established to open-caption first-run movies on 35mm film and make them available to show in movie theaters.

The Corporation for Public Broadcasting and WGBH establish the CPB/WGBH National Center for Accessible Media.

1994 Information Superhighway speech by Vice President Al Gore becomes first captioned public event in cyberspace.

1995 *Live! with Derek McGinty,* by Discovery Communications, becomes the first regular weekly show to be captioned in cyberspace (performed on America Online and the Internet by Cheetah Broadcasting and Caption Colorado).

The Closed Caption FAQ (frequently asked questions) goes online. As of this writing, it now contains over 100 questions and answers and resides at http://www.robson.org/capfaq/.

1996 The Society of Motion Picture and Television Engineers (SMPTE) forms a working group for captioning standards on MPEG digital video, which is used on DVDs.

1997 Bill Clinton's second presidential inauguration becomes the first to be simultaneously captioned live on television and the Internet.

Microsoft announces the Synchronized Accessible Multimedia Interchange (SAMI) format for closed captioning of multimedia presentations on CD-ROM and the Web.

1998 The Telecommunications Act of 1996 officially takes effect, so the clock starts ticking on mandatory closed captioning.

Activision releases *Zork Grand Inquisitor,* the first computer game with full closed captioning.

Real Networks introduces "RealText" for captioning Internet broadcasts that use streaming audio and/or video and its G2 player.

1999 Stenomask reporters demonstrate viable realtime translation using speech recognition technology. Jim Bouck becomes the first certified RVR (realtime verbatim reporter).

2000 First milestone in the Telecommunications Act, requiring five hours per day of captioning on new English-language programs by all broadcast networks.

2003 The Telecommunications Act requires at least 30 percent of all "old" (first aired in 1997 or earlier) English-language programs to be captioned.

2006 The Telecommunications Act requires 100 percent of all "new" (first aired in 1998 or later) English-language programs to be captioned.

2008 The Telecommunications Act requires at least 75 percent of all "old" (first aired in 1997 or earlier) English-language programs to be captioned.

2010 The Telecommunications Act requires 100 percent of all "new" (first aired in 1998 or later) Spanish-language programs to be captioned.

2012 The Telecommunications Act requires at least 75 percent of all "old" (first aired in 1997 or earlier) Spanish-language programs to be captioned.

One of the most fascinating things about a history timeline like this is seeing how events of long ago still affect our day-to-day lives. As an example, there is still a symbol developed for Tiro's shorthand system over 2,000 years ago that you see every single day — and it still has the same meaning! The venerable ampersand (&) represents *and* or its equivalent in hundreds of languages.

How Does Realtime Translation Work?

You don't need to understand how your car's engine works to drive to the store, but you'd better know what's going on under the hood if you intend to be a race car driver. You need to be able to attune yourself to every nuance of the engine's behavior to squeeze every last bit of performance from it. You must be able to predict how it will perform through experience and by knowing how it sounds and feels.

Similarly, a typical court reporter doesn't need to understand how a CAT system does its translation. It happens, and that's enough.

A good realtime writer, however, needs to understand the underlying behavior of the system well enough to predict how it will act under new and different circumstances. You can't go back and fix problems later — what matters is how your text appears *now*, as you are writing.

Steno Translation Theory

When you press a set of keys on your steno machine, the stroke is sent to the computer.[3] The computer takes that stroke and looks it up in your translation dictionary, where it will get one of four results.

THE STROKE ISN'T THERE

In this case, the system will generate an untranslate. In the old days, this would appear as raw steno on your screen, like {TKPWRAEU} for *gray*. Today's CAT and captioning software will phoneticize untranslates in an attempt to guess what you meant. In this example, it would recognize TKPW as G, and AEU as a long A, so it would produce GRA, GRAE or GRAY, depending on how your system is set up. We'll discuss that more later.

THE STROKE IS THERE AND UNAMBIGUOUS

Much of the time, your stroke will be recognized by the system with only one possible interpretation, so the system will translate the stroke and output it. This does *not* always mean that the stroke translates into an English word. Dictionary entries can be word parts, editing commands, punctuation, formatting information and more.

This book will not spend any time on writing theories and what steno should be used to produce what words. There are many good books on that subject already. Instead, this book will focus on all of the other things that a dictionary entry can contain.

---

[3] *That's not strictly correct, but it's close enough. In actuality, "instant" steno machines like the Transcriptor X, MeritWriter, StenoWriter, TurboWriter and Gemini do send the stroke to the computer as soon as your fingers lift off the keys. "Polled" machines like the Stentura, SmartWriter, StenoRam and Vision wait for the computer to ask for the stroke, which means in realtime mode the CAT software must be constantly asking (or "polling") the machine for steno. That's one reason why some machines feel slightly more sluggish than others when you're writing realtime.*

THE STROKE IS AMBIGUOUS

Sometimes, two dictionary entries will have the same steno. This is known as a conflict. CAT systems have many ways of showing conflicts, but they all consist of a string of entries (usually words) with separators — maybe something like {appear/a peer}. In normal court reporting, you go back later and choose the appropriate entry.

In captioning or CART, you don't want conflicts to appear at all. Some reporters take care of the problem by having their CAT software automatically resolve the conflict, but the appropriate solution is to remove the conflicts from your writing style and from your dictionary.

Using automatic conflict resolution when you're captioning is like using cruise control on a racetrack. *You* need to be the one in control. Some CAT vendors have used the term "artificial intelligence" in reference to their automatic conflict resolution. It isn't even close.[4] Some day, perhaps, there will be true artificial intelligence in CAT systems, but that day is far in the future.

THE STROKE IS PART OF A LONGER ENTRY

This is the most complex of the four cases. Let's say you have a two-stroke entry in your dictionary: TKPWRAEU/SRAOE for *gravy*. You write the first stroke, and the dictionary finds that it could be the word *gray* or it could be the first stroke of the word *gravy*. What is the system to do?

The program has several choices. The first is to go ahead and output the word *gray*, then when the second stroke is entered, back up and change it to *gravy*. This works, and it lets you see exactly what's going on. Unfortunately, it's ugly and distracting to the people watching your screen.

---

[4] *Today's automatic conflict resolution uses grammatical and statistical analysis to watch how you resolve the conflict manually. Do you always pick the first choice if the conflict follows a noun? Do you always pick the second choice if the conflict is at the beginning of a sentence? Once the program has adequate historical information, it begins resolving the conflict for you. Common conflicts may be preprogrammed, so the system comes out of the box understanding {their/they're/there} or {two/too/to/2}. This is a far cry from true artificial intelligence, which would be able to actually* understand *the sentence in context well enough to respond to it.*

The second choice is to hold the stroke and output nothing until it has an unambiguous translation. This works very well, but can be disconcerting to beginning realtimers. A common question in training is, "I wrote a period at the end of the sentence, but I don't see anything. What's wrong?" Most likely, you have FPLT defined as a period and FPLT/FPLT defined as a colon. The program is waiting to see whether you're going to write the second FPLT before it outputs anything. The solution to this problem is a "force" stroke (your software may call it something different). This stroke causes the system to immediately translate anything being held back.

The third choice is a combination of these with a delay added. The system holds back for some period of time waiting for you to resolve the ambiguity. If you don't, it outputs it as is. This delay can also be used to give you time to correct errors, so that if you write a stroke incorrectly, you can use the asterisk to remove it, then rewrite it, and the people watching your realtime never see the error. Captioning systems that use this delay mechanism usually allow each captioner to set his or her own delay factor, and most captioners set it for somewhere between 0.4 and 0.9 seconds.

There are captioning systems that have an "editing window" that all realtime passes through before it is output. This gives you plenty of time to correct errors, but delays the captioning longer. Usually, this is unacceptable in a broadcast environment where things are moving very quickly, but can work well in a seminar or other live event where a couple of extra seconds don't hurt as much.

WHY WORD-BOUNDARY PROBLEMS HAPPEN

The translation software always looks for the longest possible match, scanning forward. For this reason, you must be careful about putting phrases in your dictionary.

For example, you might, with the best of intentions, decide that any time you write about the *Washington Post*, it should be italicized. That's absolutely correct. What happens, however, when someone mentions turning on the television after a Redskins game and catching the Washington post-game show? You got it. The system would interpret it as "*Washington Post* game show," which would mean something else.

Worse yet, that person may mention that the postal workers in Washington have gone on strike. That would produce the "*Washington Post* all worker strike," or something similar. Yuk.

Your alternatives? You can try to anticipate all of the longer phrases, like "Washington post-game," and put them all in your dictionary. This is a losing proposition. You'll never get them all.

You can leave the phrase out and manually add the italics. That works well if *Washington Post* is mentioned infrequently, but you won't want the extra two strokes (italics on and italics off) if it comes up frequently.

You can phrase it completely differently, so that it doesn't form a word-boundary problem or conflict. This works great as long as you remember the phrase. Before creating too many briefs, take a look at the bloopers in Chapter 4 to see how they can come back to bite you.

You can put the phrase in your dictionary and use a null stroke (described later in this chapter) to break it up when those longer phrases come up. It works, but you have to be incredibly alert and very quick to detect and correct them in time.

As always, there is no universal solution. Pick what works best for you and stick with it.

Globals

This is an area where terminology varies greatly from one software package to the next. I've attempted to find some universal terms that mean the same thing no matter what software you use, but they don't appear to exist, so the words you read in this section won't necessarily match what you find in your user's manual.

Since the earliest CAT systems, court reporters have had the ability to change one word or phrase to another, either in a single location or "globally" throughout the file. Performing the substitution throughout the file was known as a "global change," which later was shortened to "global."

There are two very different types of globals, and each software package supports them slightly differently. This simple feature that has existed since the dawn of CAT can have a great effect on your productivity if you learn to use it well.

TEXT GLOBALS

Virtually all word processors can perform a text global. This feature may be called "search and replace," or "global replace," or "global change," or "replace all," or simply "replace." It takes one string of text and replaces it with another.

A text global makes no change to your translation dictionaries and does not take steno into account. If you change *Mohammar Ghaddafy* to *Moamar Kaddafi* throughout your document, it makes no difference if you had 10 different ways to write *Mohammar Ghaddafy* in the first place.

Some systems treat text globals like word processors do: They apply text globals immediately and then forget about them. Others store them in "global tables" so that they can be applied to incoming realtime.

If your system can hold text globals in a global table, then there's an easy way to deal with speaker identification. Let's say that your main speaker ID for "speaker number one" is STPHAO, and that you usually stroke it twice. You'll want to have extra dictionary entries to cover you in case of drops (e.g., SPHAO or STPHA) or drags (e.g., STKPHAO or STPHRAO). Many reporters stroke this ID twice so that a single drop can't make a word (e.g., TPHAO translating as *new*).

This can be a lot of entries! STPHAO involves six keys. That's six entries to cover the six possible drops, three to cover the possible left-bank drags, one for accidentally hitting the number bar, and the correct stroke, for a total of 11. If you stroke STPHAO twice, the number of entries blooms to 121, and that doesn't even consider multiple-key drops or drags.

With a global table, you can define all 121 of those to be the speaker ID for "SPEAKER1," and at the start of each job, text global SPEAKER1 to the person's name. Voilà! With no changes to the dictionary at all, you've added 121 speaker identification strokes.

Your system may have other ways to accomplish this same goal. Some can perform global changes within the dictionary itself, and others can use a template or fill-in-the-blank form at the beginning of a job to set up the speaker identifications.

An Embarrassing Digression

When my wife, Kathy, first began captioning city council meetings, I would often sit with her and assist in whatever way I could during the meeting. We had a system worked out for names. The city required any member of the public who wished to speak to fill out a card, which was handed to the clerk. The clerk would give me the cards, and I'd collect the names. Usually, Kathy would be able to put them into her dictionary during a break.

One evening, there was a discussion about adding a new sister city in India. Dozens of people came to speak, and most of them had Indian names, which were not in Kathy's dictionary. The agenda item was approaching fast with no break in sight. I wrote all the names, put a two-letter abbreviation in front of each one and propped the sheet up in front of Kathy. Then I entered a text global for each one, changing the two-letter abbreviation into the name. This didn't require me to guess how she would write the name. She could just fingerspell the two-letter code.

As an example, *Darshan Singh* would be entered as DS, or *Kanwarjit Jaipuriyaar* as KJ. The captions, in addition to being broadcast on cable TV, were also being displayed on a big television near the speaker's lectern and shown on small monitors in front of each council member. All were impressed by the flawless handling of the long, complex names.

Do you see this coming? Without thinking, I entered *Avtar Nagawan* as AN.[5] I watched the names translating beautifully and leaned back to relax. A quick kick from Kathy brought me back to reality. She had written "This is an exciting evening," and it had translated as "This is Avtar Nagawan exciting evening." Oops! As I scrambled to remove that global

[5] *These are not the actual names of the people who were there that evening, although they are similar.*

(a multistep process at the time), every time she stroked the word *an*, it translated as *Avtar Nagawan*. The mayor was amused. Kathy was not.

Options and Codes

Most systems offer options to their text global command. The most common is "case sensitive." Had we been doing CART (which usually uses mixed upper- and lowercase) rather than captioning (which usually uses all caps) in the city council chambers, I could have specified that AN be globalled, but not *an* or *An*. Before using this option, think about capitalization at the beginning of a sentence.

For example, if you find out that you've been writing *Green* as someone's last name, and it should be spelled *Greene*, a case-sensitive text global is just the ticket. It will fix all references to the name without affecting the color, right? Wrong! Take this example:

Q. What is your last name?

A. Green.

Q. And what color is your car?

A. Green.

There is no way that a global can catch and correct that situation. When editing a court transcript, you could use another common text global option that allows you to verify each change before it is made. In realtime, however, you'd have to come up with a way to write the name and the color differently.

STENO GLOBALS

On most systems, a steno global is another name for adding something to your dictionary. Unlike the text global, which takes effect after the translation process is complete, a steno global is a part of the translation process.

On some systems, when you're using a text global, people reading your screen will see the word appear as translated first, and then the global will apply a moment later. This can be very disconcerting. With a steno global, that won't happen because you don't have a two-step process.

Editing on the Fly

Today's CAT systems allow you to do quite a bit of editing from the stenotype keyboard as you write. Some captioning systems have equivalent capabilities, but not all by a long stretch, and few people do extensive editing when doing CART work.

When you're writing CART, you're likely to have people looking at your computer screen and having windows pop up, or words appearing and disappearing, which can be very disconcerting to the viewer. If you have a way to display the realtime on another computer, then by all means edit your heart out on the main system, but you should avoid having your main CART screen show anything but a smooth flow of realtime text.

In captioning, the problem is slightly different. Once caption text has been sent to the encoder, your options for editing or erasing it are very limited. There is a backspace code for the encoder, but it works slowly and produces a *very* obvious correction. Also, it can only back up on the current line. Once you hit the end of a caption row and it scrolls up, the text is immutable. You can erase the whole screen, but you can't edit a completed row after it scrolls.

The only way, then, to edit captions before they go out is to delay the text. You can experiment with this, but it is usually an unacceptable solution.

What Makes a Good Captioner or CART Writer?

Realtime writers are highly skilled with machine shorthand. This is a given. But is that skill what sets a captioner or a CART reporter apart from most court reporters? Generally not.

The Realtime Attitude

The single factor most likely to create a good CART reporter or captioner is attitude. You have to care about your work product and care about the people you're working for.

There's reciprocity there, too. The people you're working for care about you. For many captioners and CART reporters, the personal relationship with the people they serve in the deaf community sparks a fierce devotion to constantly improving their skills. It isn't unusual to attend realtime writing seminars and clinics and see reporters with 10 or 20 years of experience sitting there picking up tips and changing the way they write.

To be successful in CART and captioning, you must want your writing to be perfect. You must also keep up with the latest equipment. This can be a frightening prospect for a technophobe, but it's mandatory. You have to be able to work with whatever equipment is available, and if your system breaks down, you'd better be prepared to deal with it.

It's a compulsion.

Your Objective

As a court reporter, you've been trained to produce verbatim transcripts. As a stenocaptioner or CART reporter, your job is to make sure people who can't *hear* what's going on can *see* what's going on. That usually does not include a transcript.

Interacting With Your Audience

A court reporter is an objective third party — an officer of the court. Court reporters are not supposed to interact with the attorneys on the record, offering to change or clean up the transcript to suit them.

Captioners and CART reporters writing for large audiences maintain a bit of this detachment. CART reporters working one-on-one, on the other hand, interact with their audience directly and constantly. Good CART reporters realize that they are acting as interpreters. They'll ask the person they're writing for, "Did you get that?" If they see errors in their writing, they'll write some dashes and go back and fix them.

This is not an impersonal relationship. It may be short — just the duration of the job — but the relationship between the CART reporter and the client is like that of a seeing eye dog and a blind person. You are their ears.

Realtime Control of Format

Today's CAT and captioning systems allow a lot of control over how the text looks. You can use italics, bold, underline and even change colors on some systems. Learn to use this to your advantage.

For example, if you are captioning or writing CART for a large audience in an auditorium, you may want to write what the main speaker says in white, but put questions from the audience in yellow. If done consistently, this can help a deaf person understand who is speaking, even if the speaker ID has scrolled off the screen.

Broadcast captioners don't have as much flexibility. Generally, there are stylistic guidelines imposed by the customer or by the captioning firm. That doesn't get them off the hook, though. In fact, on-air captioning has another level of complexity.

MOVING THE CAPTIONS AROUND

Captioners must make sure that their captions aren't covering anything important on the screen. If you are writing a newscast with your captions showing at the bottom of the screen, and the station or network puts a graphic at the bottom, you need to either raise the captions a line or two or bump them all the way to the top, so that the graphic is visible.

This can be a difficult process. Remember that you can't stop writing while you do this. Having a key defined on your computer keyboard to move the captions up to the top of the screen is good, but it requires you to take your hands off the steno machine. Much better is a set of steno strokes that move the captions. We'll discuss that in more detail a little later in this chapter.

Football games are egregious examples of this. They put a little graphic in the corner of the screen that shows the current score, as well as some other statistics. As I watch *Monday Night Football,* that little graphic moves around on the screen. My heart goes out to the poor captioner who has to move the captions away from the graphic while trying to write two announcers at once, but it has to be done.

KNOWING WHEN TO STOP

Sometimes, the screen speaks for itself. When the meteorologist puts a map on the screen with temperatures for all the local cities, it is pointless to cover part of the map with captions that would just repeat the same information anyway.

At times like that, you want to stop writing and have a stroke that clears the screen completely. That can be done in both CART and captioning, and some reporters use it when they write a particularly nasty blooper. Be aware, though, that clearing the screen in the middle of writing can be jarring and distracting and should be reserved for only a few special cases.

Writing in All Caps

Why is it that virtually all captioning in the United States is in all capital letters? It certainly seems counterintuitive. I've heard it claimed that all caps are easier to read. Numerous studies have shown exactly the opposite. In fact, if all caps were easier to read, you would probably be reading this book in all caps right now.

Is there a reason? Yes. In fact, there are several.

The primary reason is historic. Remember that the TV signal only contains the codes for the characters. It is up to the decoder in, or connected to, your television to actually draw the captions. The character set in the early decoders was very crudely drawn, and many of today's decoders aren't much better. This didn't have much effect on the capital letters, but it was murder on lowercase.

Lowercase letters differ from uppercase letters in two critical ways: They have smaller detail and they use descenders. A descender is a part of a letter that goes below the line, as you see on lowercase j, g, y, p and q. Since there isn't any extra room in the character set, these early decoders couldn't actually put anything below the line, so they shoved the whole letter up. This led to captions that looked like this (note the way the *g* and *y* are pushed up):

Ugly Text

Rather than subject people to such ugliness, captioners simply represented everything in uppercase.

The second reason is practical. When you're writing realtime at speeds in excess of 240 words per minute, getting all the words right is difficult enough, without the added trouble of making sure capitalization is correct. In all caps, you don't have to distinguish between *Bill* and *bill* or Dr. *Green* and the *green* car.

The speed issue is partially historic as well, as today's state-of-the-art captioning systems go a long way toward helping the stenocaptioner handle capitalization; and today's stenocaptioners are better trained and better equipped than they were 10 years ago. Still, inertia leads us to do things the easy way.

A third reason doesn't apply much to the United States, but it can still be a factor. The character set used in captioning is quite limited when it comes to accented letters. Not all of the accent marks are available (there is no umlaut [dieresis], for example, like the ü in Münich or the ë in Noël), and the accents aren't available on all of the letters (there's an à, but no ò). In addition, there are no accent marks available on uppercase letters at all (the only exception is the Spanish ñ, which is available in both upper- and lowercase).

In French, this works out fine, because accents aren't typically used on the uppercase letters. Captioning in all caps, therefore, relieves the captioner from the burden of putting accent marks on the vowels. Unfortunately, this overlooks one thing: The Line 21 captioning standard is used in North America; it is not used in France. French is spoken in Quebec, but the Quebecois *do* use accents on the capital letters. Oh, well ...

This doesn't mean that lowercase letters are never used in the United States. There are several common applications for them, such as indicating that someone is speaking quietly or whispering. We will probably see increased use of mixed-case captioning as time goes on and caption decoders improve their text quality.

Dictionaries

You can lose your CAT software, your steno machine and your notebook computer and still go on simply by borrowing someone else's. Your dictionary, however, is the heart and soul of your system, and you can't work without it.

Back up your dictionary frequently. As an old college professor of mine used to say, "This will be on the test." In this case, however, the consequences of failing the test are far more serious. We'll discuss specifics of how to back up dictionaries later in this chapter.

WORD PARTS

Too many reporters rate the quality of their dictionary by its size. They think that a 100,000-word dictionary is automatically better than a 50,000-word dictionary.

In actuality, the number of word parts (common root words, prefixes, suffixes, etc.) is far more important than the number of words. If you have a good set of word parts, then you should be able to put a word like *bunk* in your dictionary and have a whole slew of new words (e.g., *bunk, bunks, bunked, bunking, bunker, bunkers, debunk, debunks, debunked, debunking, debunker, debunkers,* etc.).

Not only does that approach keep the dictionary size down (which is a good thing), but it forces you to be consistent in how you handle your prefixes and suffixes. Having "smart" word endings on your CAT system helps.

Kathy's dictionary was originally built by a scopist. When Kathy got her first CAT system, we took a look at her dictionary in the CAT system's dictionary editor and discovered that there were a lot of unneeded entries. As an example, even though she always wrote endings like *-ing* and *-ly* in a separate stroke, there were over 1,000 *-ly* words in the dictionary. By adding the suffix and removing all of the *-ly* words, the dictionary was reduced in size by 1,000 entries, which helped translation speeds, and the addition of the suffix meant it actually handled *more* words than before.

Make sure you also have a stroke to attach any two words, so you could further expand your list without having words in your dictionary like *bunkhouse* or *bunkmate* (this will be discussed in more detail later in this chapter).

When building word parts, don't forget to include parts of names. Most people, if asked to list common prefixes and suffixes, wouldn't think to include entries like *Mc-, Mac-, O'-, -ville, -ton, -town, -vich, -son, -vale* or *-ich,* but if you settle on a way to write them and add them to your dictionary, you'll be glad of it.

In these days of online mania, don't forget the prefixes *e* and *e-* (as in *e-mail, eTrade, e-commerce* and so on) and the suffix *.com,* which, just in case you've spent the last few years in a cave, is pronounced "dot com." While you're at it, make sure you have *.net, .org, .edu, .mil* and *.gov* in there, too.

SPECIAL REALTIME AND CAPTIONING ENTRIES

The strokes I'm going to describe in this section should exist in any serious CAT or captioning software, but they won't necessarily use the same name I use in this book. What I call "kill-space" may be called "attach" or "delete space" or "combine" in your program. The name isn't important. What it does is. If you don't already have these in your dictionary, look them up in your software manual and see how they are defined in your program.

Kill-space (Attach)

One of my first exposures to how a broadcast captioner works came when I was speaking at a convention. Kathy DiLorenzo of VITAC was going to be captioning for me. When we were introduced, she asked the spelling of my name.

After I answered the question, she went on to another subject. I waited for a moment, and then asked her if she was going to put my name in her dictionary. Surely she didn't have *Robson* in there already?

She replied that she wrote *Gary* and *Garry* differently, so that was easy. For Robson, she could write the word *rob,* a kill-space and the word *son.*[6] This was captioning, and she was writing in all caps. If it were, however, mixed case, she could still have done it by using a "cap next word" stroke, which we'll discuss a bit later on.

The English language is laden with compound words, and the trend is toward turning hyphenated words into compounds. A decade or two ago, the adjective *realtime* was always written as *real-time.* Today, few people include the hyphen. With a kill-space stroke (Hmm. Should that be "killspace"?), you can put any two words together any time.

Hard Space

The hard space originally appeared as a way to prevent words from being separated at the end of a line. For example, a hard space after words like *Mr.* or *Dr.* will automatically move them to the next line if the word that follows won't fit.

Many CAT systems now handle *Mr.* and *Dr.* automatically, but the hard space is still useful for other titles (e.g., *Sgt., Officer, Senator*) and to prevent short phrases from splitting up (e.g., *et al., à la*).

Since all software is written differently, some programs may use the hard space to solve problems described in the next section as fodder for the null stroke. Check your software manual carefully and understand the uses of these strokes thoroughly.

Force and Null Strokes

Earlier in this chapter, while describing steno translation theory, we discussed the concept of a "force" stroke to make the software translate strokes that it's holding back. You will use this stroke constantly. Make it something that you don't even have to think about. Many captioners use the number bar with the asterisk key, and that is the default setting in some captioning software.

---

[6] *Many captioners, probably including Kathy, have* son *in their dictionary as a suffix, which makes it easy to write names like* Johnson, Ericson, Robinson *and so forth. This, however, is a discussion about the kill-space stroke, so we'll just forget about the suffix entry for a moment, OK?*

The force stroke has a useful cousin — a stroke that does absolutely nothing. I'll call it the "null" stroke, but your software may call it something different. Why on earth would you want a stroke that does nothing? Here are a few examples:

- **Breaking up a word-boundary problem.** If you're writing and you realize that "He put it in sideways" is going to translate as "He put it inside ways." There is something you can do. Write that null stroke after the word *in*, and it won't get translated with the following stroke, thus fixing the problem.

- **Separating automatically joined numbers.** If your system is smart enough to combine consecutive digits with no spaces between them, then how do you write "114 12th Street"? How about by writing a null stroke after the four? If that approach doesn't work on your system, try using a hard space.

- **Breaking up stitching.** Similarly, if you want to write "J-O-H-N D-O-E," a null stroke could prevent a hyphen between the N and the D. Again, your system may use the hard space for this, so experiment with it.

Cap Next/Force Lowercase

There is a plethora of methods for dealing with capitalization. Even captioners who work in all caps aren't immune to this issue. Consider, for example, the name *McDonald.* When converted to all caps, which is more readable: MCDONALD or McDONALD? I thought so. Similarly, even when writing in all caps, it looks better if you refer to the San Francisco football team as the 49ers rather than the 49ERS.

To accomplish this, your system should have a code for dictionary entries that overrides all caps translation and forces a letter or group of letters to be lowercase no matter what. Not all systems offer this capability, so look carefully for it.

If you're not working in all caps, you need more.

You should have a dictionary entry that forces whatever you write next to have an initial capital letter. That way, you don't have to make special dictionary entries for names that are also common words, like *Brown* or *Green.* You'll want to have a way to write very common names differently, though, so it won't take two strokes to write the name *Sue.*

This "cap next word" stroke can save you with many types of proper names, like cities (*Pleasant Hill, Happy Valley*), bodies of water (*Eagle Lake, American River*) and other geographical features (*Rocky Mountains, Lookout Point*).

You can also build this code into dictionary entries for titles, so that anything following *Mr.* or *Ms.* is automatically capitalized.

A corresponding stroke to force the next word lowercase helps, too. You may have *Jack* and *Smith* in your dictionary as names, but a metal-worker could refer to himself as a smith, and he'd lift his car with a jack. Again, common words that are also common names should be written differently.

Change Attributes

It's the little things that distinguish a good captioner or CART reporter from a great one. If I mentioned my hometown newspaper, the *Boulder Daily Camera,* would you be able to write it in italics in realtime? If it were your hometown newspaper, it would already be in your dictionary as a phrase (although see the *Washington Post* example earlier in this chapter during the word-boundary discussion), and your italics codes would be built into the phrase.

Make sure you have strokes to start and stop italics, bold, underlining, superscript, subscript and any other character formatting options you have. Sometimes these formatting changes are little things. Sometimes they're not. I don't think many people care whether you write *49th* or 49th, but if you're writing CART for a college chemistry class, $C_{12}H_{22}O_{11}$ is *much* more readable than C12H22O11 (especially since the letter O and the zero look a lot alike).[7]

---

[7] *For the terminally curious,* $C_{12}H_{22}O_{11}$ *is sucrose, or common table sugar.*

Make sure, also, that you have a stroke that turns off all attributes and returns the text to its normal color (white, in the case of captioning). It can get tough to keep track of what's turned on and what's not, but one stroke to turn it all off is easy to remember.

Change Screen Position/Line Length

Here's an issue that's irrelevant for CART, but very important for captioning. In CART, your text is by itself on a screen, and it typically fills the whole screen. Moving the text around or shortening the lines as you write accomplishes little.

In captioning, however, your text shares a screen with a video picture. Your realtime is expected to increase comprehension, which will not happen if it covers something critical.

Ideally, you should define a set of steno strokes for the most common configurations you use. As an example, if you're doing television work for a station or network that often adds crawls,[8] you should have a stroke to put the captions all the way at the bottom and another stroke that moves them up a line or two to make room for the crawl. If you're doing sports work, you'll also want a stroke that pops the captions all the way to the top of the screen. This is important not only because more of the action happens near the bottom, but because TV sports coverage often includes graphics and text at the bottom of the screen.

If your system won't let you define steno strokes to change the position of the captions, define a keyboard macro to do it. If it can possibly be a single key (no shift, control, alt or holding the mouse button down with your nose), do it. The number pad is a great place because you can get to any key with just a glance or without even looking if you have a second to feel for the raised dot or bar on the "5" key.

Be sure to place the computer keyboard so that you don't have to move your hand too far to hit those keys.

---

[8] *In broadcast parlance, a "crawl" is text scrolling across the screen, typically at the bottom. The most common uses are financial tickers and special alerts.*

Clear Screen

We briefly discussed clearing the screen earlier. Let's take a closer look at the issue. Most CART reporters (and all captioners) have a way to clear the screen after a particularly egregious mistake.

Every captioning system has a different way to define a "clear the screen" or "blank video" stroke. It's sure to be in your manual. Pick some steno that you're not likely to hit by accident, but that you can still write quickly when you need it. A short word stroked twice works well, as long as you can convince yourself that it won't ever come up that way in any other context.

In CART, you're using a regular CAT system. The easiest way to clear your screen is to create an include file with a full page of blank lines. Define it as an auto-include, and it will scroll your mistake off the screen. The beauty of this approach is that it works no matter what display mechanism you're using, even if you're outputting to a litigation-support software package like LiveNote or CaseView. It won't erase it from the transcript, but it will get it out of view fast.

Generally, though, this extreme solution isn't a good idea. The major distraction of wiping out the screen when someone is reading it should be avoided unless the mistake is really horrendous.

Direct Encoder Control

Virtually everything you send out to the caption encoder is placed into Line 21 to be handled later by a decoder. There are a few exceptions, though — commands interpreted directly by the encoder itself.

Generally, the encoder reset command isn't something you'll want to do from the steno machine, but you should know how to send one. When everything in your captioning software looks fine, but no captions are coming out, especially on older encoders, sending out a reset is often all it takes to get things working smoothly again.

The other two common encoder commands used frequently in broadcasting are block and pass.

There are two stages to a caption encoder. The first stage removes any captions that may already be present on the incoming video. The second stage adds your captions. Normally, if you stop writing for a moment, you still want the encoder to block all upstream captions.

If you're captioning a TV show, it's important that you set the encoder to *pass through* those upstream captions when you take a commercial break. Advertisers will not be pleased if they spend the money to caption a commercial and you strip the captions from it!

TAKING CARE OF YOUR DICTIONARIES

Dictionary Maintenance

If your CAT or captioning software has a feature that scans a dictionary for errors, do it often. In some systems, just bringing up the dictionary in the dictionary editor and saving it will rewrite the whole dictionary. This is a good way to make sure nothing's broken.

Invariably, dictionaries grow over time. You want to keep this process under control. Pruning your dictionary is especially important when you start realtime and when you decide to take advantage of new software capabilities. Your writing style evolves over time, and you can get some real surprises when your new way conflicts with decade-old dictionary entries that you never got around to removing.

Obscenities

In court reporting, dealing with obscenities is pretty straightforward: If they say it, you write it. Some reporter friends in the criminal courts have shown me transcripts that would peel paint and wilt flowers.

The world of realtime CART and captioning brings up some new issues on obscenities, though, and they require more careful thought.

When you're performing CART, and people have their eyes glued to your realtime, the last thing you want is accidental profanity.

Should you remove all the obscenities from your dictionary? No, for two reasons. First, in CART, if somebody says it, you should write it. You are the interpreter, not the censor. Second, taking the word out of the dictionary won't prevent it from coming out anyway. I've known more than one realtimer who discovered that their CAT or captioning software is quite capable of using phonetics to build some of our favorite four-letter words.

What you have to do is come up with a way of writing those words that you are *extremely* unlikely to stroke by accident. You can try writing them with an asterisk or double-stroking them. Any approach is fine, as long as you remember it.

Put them in your dictionary. Then, figure out how to deal with the common and/or phonetic ways you could write those words. I've seen a variety of approaches, including:

Replace them with an innocuous word. In other words, just treat them as you would any other misstroke, entering them in your dictionary as some similar-sounding word. The "s" word, for example, could be entered as *hit* or *sit.*

Replace them with nothing. Most, if not all, CAT and captioning systems have the ability to create a stroke that does absolutely nothing at all, often called a null stroke. If yours doesn't, just define the obscenity as a hard space. Either way, that word will simply disappear.

Replace them with a tag. This is probably the least popular approach, but some favor it. Define those words as (bleep) or **** (you can't use asterisks in captioning, but they work in CART).

If you're doing on-air captioning, make sure to ask your employer about profanity. Most have the rule that if it's in the audio it should be in the captions. Verify it. They're the ones writing your checks, so do it their way.

One captioning company contacted the FCC to see what the rules were. The FCC responded that captioners who write exactly what the audio says will not bear any legal liability for doing so. Even if there was an issue, the FCC has no regulatory control over captioners.

Sometimes, the audio will have a swear word "bleeped" out. Make sure you have a stroke in your dictionary defined as (bleep), so that you have a way to write that. Again, common approaches are to stroke it twice or use an asterisk. If you do stroke it twice for the (bleep) stroke, you'll need a different way to write a sentence like, "What was that 'bleep bleep' noise?"

I have often been asked about shows that will have an obscenity in the captions that is not present in the audio track. Is the captioner just going nuts?

Usually, this is the result of a pretaped show being edited right before it is broadcast. The captioner will get a script or an early edit and prepare from that. The producer makes a last-minute decision to tone something down, re-dubs the scene and forgets to tell the captioner. The captioner includes the original nasty word, the captions are added to the final cut, and nobody notices the discrepancy until the show airs.

This is something to be extremely careful about when you are doing live-display (pre-scripted) captioning work!

Backups

Back up your dictionary frequently, and not always to the same disk(s). One reporter thought she was safe because she always kept a dictionary backup. Then one day, unbeknownst to her, a disk error on her computer damaged a portion of her dictionary. At the end of the day, not realizing the dictionary was trashed, she dutifully copied it onto her backup diskette, overwriting the only good copy she had.

A better strategy is to keep a set of dictionary backup disks. No matter whether you back up to floppy, Zip or Jaz disks, or onto tape, the principle is the same: Have a backup disk for each day of the week. That way, even a blown backup can be recovered, and you can go back six passes.

I like to keep backups of critical files — and your dictionary is the most critical file you have — off-site. If a fire were to destroy your computer, it would also destroy the backups sitting in the box next to the computer. Put a copy in your safety deposit box and update it every month. Send one to your cousin in Pasadena (unless you live in Pasadena, in which case you should send it to the cousin in Vermont).

A great way to handle backups is on CD-ROM. They last quite a bit longer than floppy diskettes, CD-ROM "burners" (read/write drives) are becoming quite reasonably priced, and they're easy to store. Do your regular backups on floppy, Zip or Jaz disks, cut a CD-ROM with all of your important files every few months, and *keep the CD-ROM forever.*

Dealing With What Isn't in the Dictionary

For court reporters who don't have anyone watching their realtime, it's easy to deal with words that aren't in the dictionary. Just write what you hear and define the untranslates later while editing the transcript.

In captioning and CART work, it's not that easy. As you write, you must constantly be thinking about what is and isn't in your dictionary and how things will appear if they aren't there.

Remember, in CART and captioning, verbatim isn't critical. Your audience's comprehension of the material is.

PHONICS AND DEAF PEOPLE

If you've written realtime for attorneys using realtime litigation-support software like LiveNote, CaseView or Total Access, then you've had experience with people reading through untranslates and mistranslates. Perhaps a witness mentions his *cologne* in testimony and that word isn't in your dictionary.[9] It might come up as *colon,* or as *call loan,* or as *kolon.* In context, an attorney could look at any of these and realize almost instantly that it should have been cologne.

A prelingually deaf person has no idea how words actually sound, only how they *look.* To you, *cologne* and *call loan* sound the same, especially when spoken quickly. To a deaf person who has never heard the words, there is very little similarity, and his chances of understanding are minimal.

When writing for a deaf audience, it is critical that the words come out correctly. If you have any doubt that the word is in your dictionary, then you must be prepared to work around it.

---

[9] *In the bloopers chapter, you'll see an example of what this particular pseudohomonym can produce.*

FINGERSPELLING

Fingerspelling is a staple of court reporting. It is taught right from the beginning, for use in simple exchanges like:

Q. Please state your name for the record.

A. Jan Tveitaraas.

Q. Would you spell that for me, please?

A. J-A-N.

In CART and captioning, you must have a collection of different fingerspelling alphabets. In addition to the example shown above, you need to be prepared to write things like F.B.I.[10] or NCRA or 401(k). You also need to be able to spell out a short word that isn't in your dictionary.

There are two ways to approach all of these fingerspelling alphabets. Some CAT and captioning systems support one, some support the other and some support both.

The first approach involves creating a whole set of different fingerspelling strokes for each method of stitching letters together. You might use a period (AFPLT, PW-FPLT ...) for one, a comma (ARBGS, PW-RBGS ...) for another, an asterisk (A*, PW* ...) for another, and so on. It could take awhile to get used to them and remember them all, but once you've got it, this method is fast and efficient.

One drawback to this approach is that you may have to come up with a special stroke to stop fingerspelling and go back to regular writing. For example, if you had AFPLT defined in your dictionary as "A.<attach>" (and so on, for the rest of the alphabet), then you might feel you were all set. What happens, then, when you write

{TP-FPLT/PW-FPLT/EUFPLT/AGT}

---

[10] *Yes, I know that FBI is usually written without the periods, but it works really well as an example, so bear with me, OK?*

You expect to get *F.B.I. agent*, but instead you get *F.B.I.agent* (note that there's no space before the word *agent*). You'll have to write that space manually after you spell something.

Some CAT and captioning software, on the other hand, has special dictionary defines for various fingerspelling formats, and the software knows to put one ordinary space after the last spelled letter, unless it is followed by punctuation.

A second approach to spelling alphabets is to use "start spelling" and "end spelling" strokes that define the format. Then you have only one alphabet to memorize and a set of strokes to start stitching, start squishing, start spelling with periods and so forth.

The advantage of this method is that you only have one alphabet to deal with. The disadvantage is that you require an extra stroke to start fingerspelling mode. When you're moving fast, that's a significant consideration.

There's a hybrid solution, too. At least one system allows you to define a single fingerspelling alphabet and then define strokes that modify its behavior. You might, for example, set it up so that it always starts in "squish together" mode. No extra strokes are required to start or end fingerspelling. If you require stitched out letters (L-I-K-E T-H-I-S), you write the "make my fingerspelling stitch" stroke *at any point before you start fingerspelling.*

The best way to set up your personal fingerspelling alphabet(s) is to read your software manual, talk to your software vendor and talk to other reporters or stenocaptioners who use the same software. Obviously, you need to do what works best for you, but you also need to work within the limitations of your tools.

PARAPHRASING

What if a word comes up that you know isn't in your dictionary and it's too long to fingerspell at the speed you're writing? In CART and captioning, unlike court reporting, you fudge it. Igor Balanayavich just becomes Igor (or maybe even "him"). The Ferrari Testarossa becomes the Ferrari (or maybe just the car).

If you haven't picked up on the recurring theme of this book yet, here's another chance: Verbatim isn't critical.[11] Your audience's comprehension is. It's far better to drop or change a few words than to make a sentence totally incomprehensible with untranslates or mistranslates.

Paraphrasing requires a mindset different from verbatim reporting. It also requires concentration. Many reporters, after a decade or two on the job, find themselves on autopilot when they're reporting. The words just seem to flow from their ears to their fingers. It doesn't work that way in CART.

CUSTOMIZING A PHONETIC TRANSLATION TABLE

If all else fails, then you want your phonetic translation to be as close as possible to the correct spelling of the word. The first thing you have to do is forget that it is called "phonetic." Much of court reporting theory isn't phonetic, anyway. You write and resolve conflicts based on how things are spelled in addition to how they sound.

Most CAT software these days allows you to customize the phonetic translation rules. They all come with a standard set, and one program comes with four standard sets you can choose from.

Rule 1: *All reporting theories are not created equal, so all phonetic translation rules shouldn't be either.*

Don't just blithely set forth to use your software in the real world without experimenting with the phonetic translation first. You may be lucky enough to use the theory that the CAT vendor based its default rules on, but your style probably differs enough that you'll want to tweak it out.

Try starting up realtime without loading your dictionary. If your software doesn't allow this, create a new dictionary that has nothing in it except punctuation and use that. Watch how the strokes translate, and make notes of places where the translation could be improved. Try all

---

[11] *This does* not *mean that you shouldn't strive for verbatim. Getting everything that is said helps lipreaders and speechreaders and provides all deaf and hard-of-hearing participants with the same information that the hearing people receive.*

of your standard endings in combination. Try exceptions, too, so you know where *not* to make changes.

Rule 2: *Your phonetic translation table is not a dictionary. Don't treat it like one.*

When you customize your phonetic rules, you're not dealing with steno strokes — you're dealing with *fragments* of steno strokes. The system will deal with those fragments starting at the left side. Let's take an example. Say you have these rules:

Steno fragment	English letters
PH-	M
P-	P
HR-	L
OE	EE
-D	D

Now you write PHROED, which we'll imagine is not in your dictionary. What do you get? I'll bet you expect to get "PLEED," but you won't. The program will start at the left, taking the longest match it can get. The PH becomes M, the R stays R, and you have "MREED."

To correct this, you have to put the longer entry (PHR = "PL") in as well.

The same problem comes up with letter combinations that aren't adjacent. Say, for example, that you use the combination *F to produce a V sound. Is it enough to add *F=V to your list of phonetic rules? If you write HA*F, it will indeed come out as "HAV." What would happen, however, if you wrote H*EF? There's no longer an *F to be found in it, so the phonetic rules would drop the * and give you "HEF" instead of "HEV." To get all the possible combinations, you'd need to do something like this:

Steno fragment	English letters
*F	V
*EUF	IV
*EF	EV
*UF	UV
A*EUF	AVE
O*EF	OVE
O*EUF	OVE

Depending on your particular writing style, you might even add entries like these:

Steno fragment	English letters
*EUFT	IVITY
*FLS	VLES
*FR	VER

Rule 3: *An E can make all the difference.*

That last entry was interesting. When you have a combination of final consonants that rarely go together, putting an E between them in the phonetic translation rules can make the results much more readable. Think about combinations like these:

Steno fragment	English letters
-BD	BED
-PBLGD	JED
-PLD	MED
-FD	FED
-RBD	SHED
-BGD	KED
-TD	TED
-PBS	NED
-SZ	SES

You can probably come up with many more that fit your writing, but don't forget to play around first without a dictionary loaded and make sure you don't have any unintended consequences.

Rule 4: *Don't overlook the obvious.*

Make sure you have all of the standard single-letter rules and also all of your common word endings (at least the ones that are written all on the right side of the keyboard) like *-ment, -ments, -tion, -tions, -ism, -isms* and so forth.

Knowing Your Software

A professional must know his or her tools. That statement is so simple and obvious that most pros consider it axiomatic. A surgeon would never consider using a new piece of surgical equipment on a patient without thoroughly reading the instructions and practicing with the equipment in a benign setting first. You should do the same.

Read your software manual and/or help files. You must know how to make that software perform to the limits. Even if you've been using the same program for years, you may learn something new from a perusal of the documentation. How many software updates have you loaded since you last attended a training seminar or read through the manual?

At a CAT seminar I gave, we were demonstrating programmable keys. The generic term for these is "macros," but virtually every CAT program has a different name (some of these include AccelerWriter Keys, EZKeys, GlobalMagic Keys, HotKeys, Hyperkeys, Powerkeys, Smartkeys and TurboKeys).

One woman in the audience was astounded at all the incredible things we were demonstrating and asked why nobody had ever told her about it before. Only after she was given the page number where several of these functions appear in the manual did she admit that she'd never read it.

Do you want to be competitive? Do you want to make your realtime look its best? Then you need to know your software's capabilities.

"SMART" TRANSLATION FEATURES

Most systems nowadays can do more than just translate your steno exactly as you wrote it. Some call these features "artificial intelligence," but that's just marketing hype.

Whatever you call them, though, these capabilities are very impressive, especially in demos. Sloppy notes turn into very good-looking realtime. Nevertheless, there are two conflicting points of view on smart translation features.

Those who like smart translation say that anything which improves their realtime is a good thing, and they consider these features crucial to their choice of CAT or captioning software.

The opponents (generally the more experienced realtimers) say that smart translation features, especially conflict resolution, are crutches for bad writers. They feel that you should learn to write correctly rather than depending on the software to clean it up for you.

Both sides have valid points. The smart translation features are nowhere near as smart as a human who actually understands what's being written.[12] They not only *might* make mistakes, I can guarantee that they *will* make mistakes!

As an example, let's look at automatic conflict resolution. If we take a look at a conflict like *red/read*, we have an adjective and a verb. They are used in situations that are different enough that a lexical parser can resolve the conflict most of the time by checking parts of speech. If the conflict is followed by an article, it's going to be *read* (e.g., *read the book* or *read an answer*). If it's followed by a noun, it's going to be *red* (e.g., *red car* or *red dog*).[13] Obviously, there are more rules, but a good program should resolve it correctly the majority of the time.

What about *principle/principal?* Both words can be nouns (*principal* can also be an adjective), and there's no way the computer can deal with a sentence like "It's the principal/principle." If the statement is an

---

[12] *Real artificial intelligence would actually understand the words and their context and would be able to deal with situations that weren't preprogrammed or "taught." The smart translation features in today's systems (even the most advanced) use a set of preprogrammed rules and "learn" by mimicking your actions.*

[13] *Yes, there are exceptions to the rule, like in the sentence "I read books yesterday." That's what makes automatic conflict resolution so complex for the programmers. When* red/read *is followed by a plural noun, it could go either way.*

explanation of why you're upset about something, it's probably the *principle* of the thing. If it is a response to the question, "Who hires the teachers here?" it's the *principal*. You know the difference (at least you had better!), but the best your computer will be able to do until we have real artificial intelligence in CAT is a guess based on the frequency of each word.

Conflict Resolution

This is the most contentious of the smart translation features. Most managers who hire realtime captioners ask to see your raw steno notes, not your English text. If you haven't resolved the conflicts in your writing, you're unlikely to get a job at one of the top firms, no matter what your software does for you.

Is automatic conflict resolution for you? Try it out. If you make more mistakes than the program does, then use it. If you can resolve your own conflicts perfectly, then why even turn them on?

Word Endings

On the other end of the spectrum, we have smart word endings. This is something that your software should be able to handle well. Yes, the rules for doubling final consonants, changing Y to IE, and so forth are complex, but context doesn't matter, so the program is dealing with a finite problem.

There are words that end in C and have a K added when you add a suffix that begins with a vowel (for example, *traffic* + *ed* = *trafficked*), but there are so few that all of them can be preprogrammed into the CAT software. The program can make guesses based on rules and frequency of use and verify those guesses using a spelling checker dictionary.

Before taking smart word endings out into the real world, you'll want to test for some exceptions that you might have to enter into your dictionary. For example, the program may always change a Y to IE when adding an S suffix. This is correct in *almost* all cases, but it doesn't apply to proper names (e.g., *Kennedy* + *s* should be *Kennedys*, not *Kennedies*). The program may be smart enough not to change Y to IE on a capitalized word, or it may not.

Numbers

Handling of numbers in CAT software has improved dramatically in the last 10 years. Even if the program can't automatically detect by context when a seven-digit number should be formatted as a telephone number, most CAT software allows you to program in hints.

Work with your CAT system. You may have to make some changes to the way you write numbers to take advantage of all of the number translation features, but this will generally be worth doing. Many of the systems are smart enough now to be able to deal with things like turning "2/THOU/4" into *2004* (or even *2,004*), even though you didn't write the embedded zeros. Check your manual and see if yours can do it.

Untran Lookup

There are a lot of "smart" ways to deal with untranslates. All of them are wonderful features for a scopist, but some are dangerous for a realtimer.

For example, I came up with a system years ago for guessing what an untranslate was by looking at possible drags and drops. In other words, if you wrote an untranslate, it would look through your dictionary and see if it made sense by adding in one more key or by dropping one of the keys. The good news: If it was an actual misstroke, it often found the correct translation. The bad news: If you wrote something correctly, but it wasn't in your dictionary, it could be turned into something completely different rather than phoneticizing it. The feature never made it into the production realtime software.

The worst idea I've seen is automatically running phoneticized words through a spelling checker and choosing the closest alternative word during realtime. Again, this can produce something completely different from what you intended (and mangle proper names) rather than letting the phoneticizing code show approximately what you were trying to write.

Knowing Your Steno Machine

Most court reporters understand the basic workings of their steno machine. If there's a significant problem, they can always send it in to the shop.

I've heard horror stories from scopists about reporters writing all day with a maladjusted key that either shadowed or dropped throughout the entire transcript. In realtime, you'll see problems like this as they come up. It is very important that you understand what's happening, and that you know how to adjust it yourself.

The most important thing to remember is what the adjustments mean. What you see on the paper notes is *not* necessarily what you are getting on your diskette, RAM card or realtime cable. Let's look at the mechanics of a shorthand stroke.

- First, in the starting position, all keys are up.

- You start your stroke. As the keys go down, a mechanical linkage causes each one to push a hammer forward.

- When one of the hammers moves forward past the adjustment point for that key, the electronics in the machine decide that a stroke has begun. At this point, depending on the adjustment, the hammer may or may not have pushed the ribbon against the paper to mark a letter.

- Other hammers may move forward, and the initial hammer may come back. Until *all* hammers have moved back behind their adjustment points, keys continue to be added to the stroke.

- When the machine detects that no hammers are past their adjustment points, it declares the stroke officially completed. An instant realtime machine (e.g., Transcriptor X or Gemini) sends the stroke to the computer. A polled realtime machine (e.g., a Stentura or StenoRam) saves the stroke and waits for the computer to ask for it.

To really understand this sequence, get out your steno machine and your CAT or captioning system. Hook everything up and start realtime. Now press down a key and hold it. Nothing on the screen, right? *While still holding the first key,* press and release several more. Still nothing. Now release the first key and watch the stroke appear on your screen.

Now let's try another experiment. Write a stroke with your left hand, pushing the keys down and *not* letting them back up. Now write a stroke with your right hand, again not releasing the keys. Lift your left hand, and then lift your right hand. Congratulations. You've just made a stack.

Stacking happens when one hand starts down on the keys before the other hand comes all the way up. Changing the thresholds on the keys changes your stacking. This is why a machine adjusted for someone with a light touch will often cause heavy stacking if used by someone with a heavy touch.

The most important single lesson from all this is that changing the adjustments of keys on your steno machine changes the way the electronics of the machine interpret your stroke. It does *not* change what appears on the paper. *Always* adjust your machine when it is connected in realtime.

In fact, you should always adjust the machine when the computer is displaying your raw steno, not just translated English. If you have dictionary entries (or smart software) that compensate for dropped or shadowed keys, you can't adjust them properly.

Chapter 2

Closed Captioning

What Is Captioning?

Just as a caption in a book is the text under a picture, captions on a TV screen are text located somewhere on the picture.

The most familiar use of captioning is in broadcast television, where thousands of hours of captioned programming are shown every week, but captioning appears in many other venues, and the broadcast industry is not the only place where you can utilize your realtime captioning skills.

Who Uses Captioning?

Closed captioning was created so that deaf people could watch television. Many people believe that's the whole story, but nothing could be farther from the truth. Certainly deaf and hard-of-hearing people *need* captioning more than the rest of us, but many others can benefit from captioning.

THE OBVIOUS

OK, let's start with the obvious. Captions allow you to understand what's going on when you can't hear the audio portion of a TV broadcast. Does that mean it serves only deaf people? Of course not.

Even though nobody in my household is deaf or hard-of-hearing, we have had a caption decoder on our main TV set for over 10 years. I have found myself growing increasingly dependent on it in order to maintain comprehension.

The phone rings right as a critical portion of my favorite show comes up. No problem — I've got the captions. The children run through the room laughing and playing just as we find out who the killer was on *Diagnosis: Murder.* No problem — I've got the captions. Someone runs the blender in the kitchen during the answer to *Final Jeopardy.* No problem — I've got the captions.

Captioning is a perfect solution for bars, airports and other noisy environments with televisions. Picture a sports bar with dozens of televisions — each tuned to a different game. Turning up the audio would only create more chaos, while putting captions on each set allows people to enjoy all of the games simultaneously.

KEEPING THINGS QUIET

In addition to the convenience factor for hearing people, when captions are used in a noisy environment, captioning can also be used to *keep* a quiet environment quiet. For example, imagine yourself as a hearing person in a hospital room. You're very tired, and you want to sleep. It's early, though, and the person sharing the room wants to watch the 6 p.m. news.

Without captions, if you tried to sleep while he was watching television, you'd be annoyed because the television is making too much noise. He would be annoyed because he couldn't turn it up loud enough to hear. With captions, he turns off the sound and reads the captions while you sleep peacefully.

Obviously, this concept applies just as well in your own home as it does in a hospital, and it's a use of captioning that really should be advertised.

LEARNING TO READ

At the time we put in our first caption decoder at home, my daughter was two years old. We noticed her interest in the captions from time to time and encouraged it. Obviously, a small child won't be able to read the captions to a complex show, but a little checking determined that shows like *Sesame Street* have captions. Not only that, but the captions are edited to a slow, comfortable reading pace. I am convinced that closed captioning is one of the reasons my daughter learned to read earlier than most children.

A friend with a caption decoder in the house took it even farther. He told his children that they could only watch one hour of television with sound per day. They could, however, watch all they wanted if they turned off the sound and turned on the captions. His children read quite well for their age. I can imagine the debates over which show would be the one they'd watch with sound, though.

Benjamin Rogner, former editor of the *Journal of Court Reporting*, did his doctoral thesis on "Adult Literacy: Captioned Videotapes and Word Recognition." His focus was in teaching adults to read using captioning.

Specifically, Dr. Rogner's test consisted of working with volunteer students in Chicago-area literacy programs who tested below a sixth-grade level in reading tests. He tested whether word-recognition abilities improved significantly if one weekly literacy class was replaced with a TV-caption-viewing session. His findings were that captions do, indeed, help the process.

If you are interested in reading the entire dissertation, it is available on Closed Caption FAQ on the Internet (www.robson.org/capfaq/).

ENGLISH AS A SECOND LANGUAGE

When gathering statistics in 1993, before the Television Decoder Circuitry Act had taken effect, I was quite surprised to discover that over half of the almost 500,000 caption decoders sold by the National Captioning Institute *were not sold to deaf and hard-of-hearing people.* This was a major epiphany. Those of us inside the captioning industry knew how wonderful captioning was, and of course the deaf and hard-of-hearing populace knew. Here was cold, hard evidence that other people knew about it, too.

The largest single group of hearing people that purchased decoders was people learning English as a second language. The captions allow reinforcement of the aural data coming in and serve to tie the written language to the spoken language in the mind of the viewer. Here's how Andrea Shettle of Gallaudet University said it:

> *But closed captions are* not *just for deaf and hard-of-hearing people. While I'm not sure how extensive the research has been, at least some indicates that people who leave their caption decoder on when they watch television improve their reading scores. The National Captioning Institute (NCI) reports that about half of all caption decoders have been sold to foreign immigrants learning English as a second language. Apparently people learning English for the first time find it easier to understand (and learn) idioms and other expressions when they see them in print as well as hearing them.*[1]

I had a chance to informally confirm this myself on a trip to Mexico. I was visiting the Giggling Marlin, a well-known bar in Cabo San Lucas,[2] and noticed captioning on the basketball games that were showing on all four TV sets. I asked the manager, Arturo, whether the captions were on because of the noise level in the bar. He explained that noise was part of the reason, but that all of the locals found it easier to understand and learn English if they could see the words at the same time as they heard them.

---

[1] *The full text of Andrea's article can be found in the closed caption FAQ at http://www.robson.org/capfaq/.*

[2] *The visit was, of course, purely for research purposes, which makes the trip a tax deduction, right? Do you think the IRS will agree?*

Terminology

CLOSED CAPTIONING

What we refer to as "closed" captions are captions that are hidden in the video signal and are invisible without a special decoder. The place they are hidden is called Line 21 of the vertical blanking interval, but we'll learn more about that later in this chapter. Since July 1993, virtually every TV set sold in the United States has had a caption decoder chip built in (see Chapter 10 on laws for details on the Television Decoder Circuitry Act).

A TV set isn't the only place where you can experience closed captioning. An ingenious system called "Rear Window" captioning, developed by the National Center for Accessible Media, allows closed captioning in a movie theater. Unlike subtitling, each individual moviegoer has the choice of whether to view captions or not. The captions are shown backwards on a large display in the back of the theater. Anyone who wishes to see them asks for a display device, which is a piece of glass that mounts on the seat and reflects the captions from the rear of the theater.

OPEN CAPTIONING

Open captions, on the other hand, are captions that have been decoded, so they have become an integral part of the TV picture, like subtitles in a movie. In other words, open captions cannot be turned off.

There are environments where open captioning makes more sense than closed captioning. For example, if you board some commercial airplanes, you'll see the preflight announcements on a TV monitor rather than having the flight attendant standing in front of you demonstrating the seat belt and oxygen mask. There is no practical way for a deaf passenger to get captioning without everyone else seeing it, so these preflight announcements are often open captioned.

Open captions can also be significantly prettier than closed captions. Most caption decoders, especially those built into TV sets, follow the minimum specifications pretty closely. Those specifications call for white letters on black bars on the screen. The text is usually fairly chunky and hard to read, and if there are any colors other than white, they'll only be the six primary and secondary colors. Open captions, however, can be produced in almost any combination of fonts, colors and backgrounds, including translucent backgrounds and even edged and shadowed text that require no background.

SUBTITLING

Subtitling is the term used in the United Kingdom to mean what *closed captioning* means in the United States. In the United States, there's a different meaning implied by *subtitling.* It is used to refer to text "burned into" the picture. Subtitles can't be turned on and off like closed captions can.

If you look at the definition of *open captioning,* you will find it very similar to the way we define subtitling (the U.S. definition). Is there a difference? Yes, but it's a subtle and fuzzy difference.

Generally, if you're speaking of a film in a movie theater, it's called subtitling, especially if the subtitles are in a language different from the audio track. If the text has the Line 21 "look and feel" (white letters on a black background, 32 characters per line, 15 lines per screen ...), then it's called open captioning. There is a gray area in between, where the two terms are essentially interchangeable.

People have a tendency to refer to anything generated by a closed-captioning system as *captioning* and anything generated by Chyron (or equivalent) character generators in a studio as *subtitling.*

ONLINE CAPTIONING

Captioning something "live" is called online captioning. It doesn't matter whether the actual program is taped or live, it's whether the captions are being generated as the material is being shown.

OFFLINE CAPTIONING

Offline captioning is done from videotapes or digital video. Typically, offline caption editors have enough time to prepare and research a script, unlike online captioners, who often have to fly by the seat of their pants.

CAPTIONERS AND CAPTIONISTS

So you're starting a career in captioning. What do you put on your business card: captioner or captionist? Both terms are widely used, although *captioner* seems to be more popular in the United States and *captionist* in Canada.

Personally, I favor *captioner*, because the *er* ending is more common in other professions serving the broadcast industry and the deaf/hard-of-hearing communities, like videographer, reporter, interpreter, signer, producer and writer.[3] The list is even longer if you include *or* endings: news anchor, camera operator, editor and director.

There are, of course, exceptions (e.g., audiologist), but from a purely marketing point of view, I prefer to give people what they expect, and captioner seems to fit the bill better.

Since the term *captioner* is also used for people who perform offline captioning of videotaped material, you may want to distinguish yourself by using a term like *realtime captioner* or *stenocaptioner*.

If you prefer captionist, then by all means go ahead and use it. As I mentioned earlier, quite a few people call themselves captionists, and it doesn't carry any negative connotations.

Where Captions Come From

One of the most common mistakes in the captioning business is confusing *online* captioning with *realtime* captioning. In fact, realtime captioning is but one of the facets of online captioning, and the captioner who truly masters online captioning must understand and master all of these facets.

Realtime

Realtime captioning is the contemporaneous creation of text from speech. Up until very recently, stenocaptioning has been the only way to accomplish this. Computerized speech recognition has now been

---

[3] *Not to mention familiar terms from court reporting, like court reporter, lawyer and stenographer.*

used for realtime transcription with acceptable results, although as of this writing there is only one person in the country who has passed the certification for realtime speech recognition. Speech recognition has come a long way in specialized, controlled environments, but it still requires a system dedicated to a specific person.

The individual has to be trained for the system, and the system has to be trained for the individual as well. Speech-recognition systems simply can't be turned loose on the audio of a TV broadcast or the public address system in a lecture hall and expected to have acceptable results.

Why is this? Because humans *know* when they aren't able to achieve accurate realtime transcription, and they understand the subject matter. When a speech-recognition system gets lost, all it can do is spew gibberish that approximates the phonetic translation of the input. A stenocaptioner is capable of switching, on-the-fly, from verbatim to paraphrasing and still capturing the gist of the subject matter.

Even in the unlikely event that the next decade or two produces a speech-recognition system capable of producing 99 percent or better translation with an unknown speaker and unknown subject matter, the system will not be able to produce a paraphrased transcript of an out-of-control situation. A bold prediction? You bet it is. It is rarely safe in the world of computer technology to declare that something won't be accomplished, especially 10 or 20 years in the future. Given, however, that it is almost 20 years since I began work as an operating systems programmer, I feel comfortable with this particular bold prediction.

Scripts

Live display captioning, also known as scripted captioning, is a live "performance" using a prepared script. The most common example would be stories pulled from a newsroom computer prior to a newscast. The stenocaptioner can load these stories into the captioning system and generate the caption output by feeding these stories out a line at a time. Obviously, if the on-air talent (the anchors) follow the script exactly, then this method produces perfect captions. Most of the time, however, that doesn't happen.

A typical newscast will involve anywhere from 35–60 percent

TelePrompTer captioning, with the remainder being unscripted. Unscripted segments in a typical newscast include all live remotes, interviews, banter between the talent, and often the weather and sports. The remainder of the newscast must be done using realtime captions. Broadcasts such as sporting events have little or no available scripted material.

As we will discuss later in the chapter about captioning-related laws, there are now restrictions on when TV stations are allowed to use stand-alone newsroom computer captioning.

Early stenocaptioners had to reach from their steno keyboard up to the computer keyboard every time they wished to feed a line of script. In some cases, the scripts were actually loaded on a different computer, making the process even more complex (or requiring two people for each broadcast). Nowadays, stenocaptioners can define a stroke on their steno machine to feed scripts or in some cases even use a foot pedal.

Stock Items

There are certain captions which appear so often that they end up programmed as a key on the computer keyboard, such as [applause] or [laughter], or the credits that many captioners display at some point during the broadcast. Modern online captioning systems also allow stock captions to be triggered from the stenotype keyboard so that a stenocaptioner can bring them up without touching the computer.

How you go about accomplishing this will vary from system to system. Some don't support stock items at all. Others allow stock items, but they can only be the same style and position as the realtime being sent.

Stock captions can be used like court reporters use auto-includes: any text that is repeated exactly from one job to the next, such as credits, messages to viewers (one TV station puts up a TTY number every broadcast for feedback from deaf viewers), and sign-on/sign-off messages.

Autofeed

Online captioning systems also have the ability to output a prepared script at a specified reading rate, perhaps in a repeating loop. This can be another solution to the dilemma raised above, during the time between the onset of an emergency and the beginning of realtime captioning. Let's take a look, for example, at what could happen during a flood.

In the newsroom, the assigned individual calls the standby captioner and tells him to get on the air as fast as possible. At the same time, someone is responsible for sitting down at the captioning system and typing a message. Perhaps something along the lines of, "There has been a flood affecting ABC County. We expect to have realtime captions on the air shortly." As soon as the call to the captioning firm is complete, the assigned individual prepares a short script file containing a summary of the emergency and the required action. The action may consist of, say, a list of areas being evacuated.

That script file is then loaded in the captioning system and given a reading speed (160 words per minute is typical). The script is then set to repeat. That message will continue to loop across the screens of the deaf and hard-of-hearing viewers until the realtime captioner gets on the air with actual verbatim coverage of the news.

Electronic Notes (C-Print)

This capability goes by several names, including electronic notes, C-Print, keyboard realtime, realtime minutes and others, all of which basically consist of typing captions in realtime.

Why would anybody use electronic notes instead of realtime? There are a number of good reasons.

Perhaps the most obvious is the emergency broadcast. When disaster strikes, many TV stations have contracts with captioning firms to provide emergency captioning on a standby basis. Typically, there is a time specified in the contract. For example, the captioning firm may guarantee to have someone on the air within, say, 10 to 30 minutes of the emergency.

So what happens in the meantime? Are the deaf and hard-of-hearing viewers left hanging for up to half an hour? Without electronic notes, the answer is "yes." With realtime notes, the TV station can grab any available person, sit him at a computer and have him type a synopsis of what is going on. It may not be fast; it may not be accurate; it may not be complete; but *any* information is better than nothing while waiting for the stenocaptioner to come online.

Where Captions Go

Welcome to the VBI

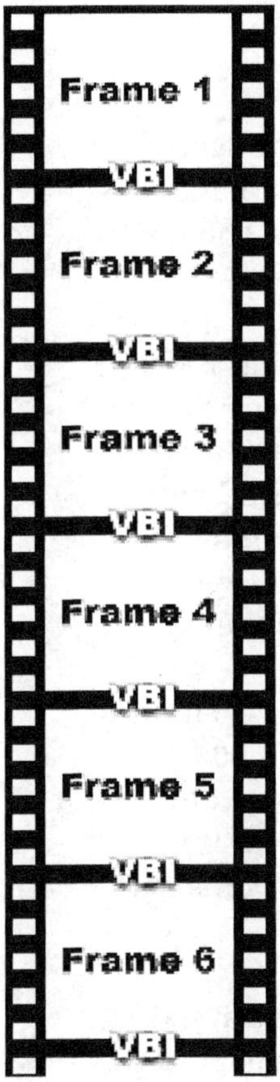

In your TV set, there's a beam of electrons sweeping back and forth across the screen,[4] painting the picture on your screen 30 times per second (25 if you're in a country using PAL or SECAM rather than the NTSC system we use here in the United States).

The electron beam sweeps across the screen once, flashing on and off. Every time it flashes on, you get a dot of color (called a *pel* or *pixel,* which is short for "picture element"). Every time it flashes off, you get black. When it reaches the side of your screen, it has completed one *line* of the TV picture. The electron beam then turns off and zips back over to the other side to start drawing the next line. That time where it is turned off and zipping back is called the *HBI* (horizontal blanking interval).

When this process has been completed 525 times[5] (625 in PAL and SECAM), the electron beam will have drawn a full screen of video (called a *frame*), and the beam will have to return to the top of the screen to start all over again. The time that the beam is turned off and sweeping back to the top of the screen is called the *VBI* (vertical blanking interval).

This whole process is illustrated in the diagram at the left. I know, videotape doesn't have little sprocket holes in it like a film, and you can't actually *see* the frames and the VBI, but I thought it would make a good picture. Bear with me, OK?

---

[4] *If it's a color television, there are* three *electron beams, but I want to keep this reasonably clear and understandable, so hopefully you'll forgive me for skipping those details.*

[5] *Well, actually, since we're dealing with interlaced video here, each frame is split into two vertical sweeps of the electron beam. Each of those sweeps is called a* field, *and we'll be talking about the two fields of Line 21 later on.*

If you have an older television with a "vertical hold" control, you can actually see the VBI. Just maladjust the vertical hold, and you'll see the picture crawl up or down the screen. The black bar between the bottom of one frame and the top of the next is the VBI.

If you look at the VBI on your screen or in the illustration, you'll see that it is more than just one line high. In fact, it is 21 lines high (in NTSC). This is because the electron beam can't snap back to the top in as short a time as it can snap back to the beginning of a line. Since the space is there, however, we do make some use of it.

The most critical information contained within the VBI is the synchronization data that tells the television where line 1 is. This is what allows your vertical hold to be perfectly adjusted every time so that you don't see that black bar wandering up and down your screen.

Line 21, the last line of the VBI, is the home of closed captions. Because of the complexity of reliably placing digital data into an analog TV signal, there is a limitation to how much information can be placed in a line of VBI. Since captioning is critical to many viewers, its designers chose to make the caption signal robust and reliable rather than allowing large amounts of information to be stored there. The result: Two characters[6] (bytes) of information can be stored in each full frame.

That doesn't sound like much, but let's do the math. We have 30 frames per second times two characters in each frame. That gives us 60 characters per second. When measuring words per minute, a word is usually considered to be five letters plus a space, for a total of six characters. This turns our 60 characters per second into 10 words per second, or 600 words per minute.

That still doesn't sound like much? Consider that an average person speaks at between 180 and 220 wpm, which is, not so coincidentally, the speed that you write. Consider also that most people can't read at anywhere near 600 wpm. When we're dealing with text information, those two characters per frame turn out to be more than adequate for captioning purposes.

---

[6] *A "character" in this context is any letter, space, number or other symbol.*

Caption Channels

Since there was a bit of extra room in Line 21, the engineers allowed for two distinct "channels" of captioning, known as CC1 and CC2. These channels have nothing to do with the different broadcast channels that you select. It was thought that the second caption channel could be used for things like a second language or slowed-down (edited) captions for people who can't read as fast. In reality, very little use has been made of CC2, and a lot of decoders and televisions can't even get it.

Captioning is not very costly in the overall view of things. A one-hour show costs hundreds of thousands or even millions of dollars to produce, but under $1,000 to caption. Even this small percentage, however, is paid grudgingly. Very few companies caption their shows willingly, and they are not *about* to create two versions of the captions. The probability of widespread use of CC2 in the near future is pretty slim.

What we haven't looked at yet, though, is that line 21 is split into two "fields." Each of those two fields has the full 600-wpm capacity. CC1 and CC2 live in field 1, and two more captioning channels (CC3 and CC4, of course) live in field 2.

Because captions in the same field interfere with each other and captions in different fields don't, multilingual captioning (where it exists at all) usually uses CC1 and CC3 rather than CC1 and CC2. This has been codified as a recommended practice by the Electronic Industries Association/Consumer Electronics Association committee that oversees captioning, and CC3 is used by CBS for the Spanish captioning of *60 Minutes*.

Other Information in Line 21

TEXT

In addition to closed captioning, Line 21 can also contain text. The text is in four different channels, just like the captions are. Like the captions, however, Text 2, 3 and 4 are hardly ever used. For that matter, Text 1 is very rarely used today.

When you set your television or decoder to display Text 1 instead of CC1, you'll see either a full screen or half screen of text data, as opposed to the one to four lines of captioning overlaying a small portion of the picture. This text can contain anything from a description of the program you're watching to a *TV Guide*-type listing of what's on next.

In fact, since the text fields are usually empty, some creative people came up with something else that could be placed there: ITV Links.

ITV LINKS

Imagine yourself watching television — not too hard for most of us, right? Now imagine that throughout the TV programs and commercials, a small "Internet" symbol appears intermittently in the corner of your screen. When it does, you have the ability, with the press of a button on your remote control, to bring up Web pages containing more information about that program or commercial.

Watching a Dodge truck commercial? That button will take you to the nearest Dodge dealer. The documentary on the history of Silicon Valley just mentioned Steve Wozniak? That button will bring up a description of how he designed the first Apple computer and showed it off at the Homebrew Computer Club. And you can bring the Web pages up while keeping the TV picture in a corner of your screen!

This all sounds like something out of *Star Trek*, but it is real today. The Interactive Television Link (known as an "ITV Link"[7]) concept was created by an innovative Silicon Valley company called WebTV, which produces a set-top box that sits on your TV set and connects to a telephone line. When you're not watching your favorite programs, the WebTV box allows you to use your television to surf the 'Net. In addition to the standard remote control, you also have a remote that looks like a custom computer keyboard with which you can visit Web pages and send and receive e-mail.

WebTV's latest offering, WebTV Plus, finds ITV Links in (you guessed it) the captions of the program you're watching. People without WebTV

---

[7] *Originally, ITV Links were known as Television Crossover Links, or TCLs.*

Plus won't see the ITV Links, because they are hidden in "Text 2," which, as we just discussed, is rarely used for anything else. When viewers activate an ITV Link, information about the Web link is displayed on their television, overlaid on the program they're watching. If they choose to follow the link, WebTV Plus will use the telephone line to dial the Internet and fetch the Web page.

The software to create ITV Links was created for WebTV by Cheetah Systems and VITAC, but other software vendors should soon be adding the capability to their captioning software.[8] These ITV Link software tools are offered as add-ons to Cheetah's CAPtivator software and are now available to anyone wishing to provide ITV Link services along with their regular captioning services.

I know what you're thinking: "Why set up a special service just for WebTV?" Well, it's not just for WebTV. Any producer or advertiser who includes ITV Links in a program or commercial is buying something special: a closer relationship with the viewer and the potential for immediate response. In a TV commercial, ITV Links can take viewers directly to a Web page where they can enter a credit card number and buy the product, without getting out of their chair or dialing a telephone.

During a TV program, ITV Links can provide viewers with a wealth of additional information, right on the network's or station's Web site. The viewers stay around longer, see more advertising and provide valuable demographic information. The program producers find out exactly how many people follow each ITV Link and can even have people in different areas of the country automatically routed to different Web pages. ITV Links are an immensely powerful tool, and anyone can insert them in their commercials or programs *without* paying WebTV (unless they want extra services, like demographically based routing). They *do*, however, need to pay someone to put the ITV Links in their video, and that could be you.

---

[8] *None of the other software vendors that responded to the survey I sent out in late 1999 had ITV Link capability in their realtime captioning software.*

Just like court reporters, captioners need to offer their customers more services than the guy down the street. Customers are attracted to the "one-stop shop," and each service you add is money to your bottom line. The ITV Link software embeds in the captioning software, so if you're already performing the captioning, adding ITV Links to the mix doesn't take that much extra time.

WebTV has offered the ITV Link format as an industry standard, which is likely to be adopted by other manufacturers of "convergence" devices that combine television with Internet access. If you want the technical details, see the EIA-746-A specification or the article entitled "Closed Captions, V-Chip and Other VBI Data" that I wrote for *Nuts & Volts* magazine. This heavily technical article is available on my Web site at www.robson.org/gary/writing/nv-line21.html.

Others can view the future in this business, too. Bill Gates, the chairman of Microsoft, has an uncanny ability to see which way the computer business is going and step in to lead it there (or to make it go the way he wants it to, which accomplishes the same thing). He gave the concept his stamp of approval by purchasing WebTV for over $400 million and making it a key part of Microsoft's convergence strategy.

How can you be a part of the convergence movement? Adding services like ITV Links to your arsenal is a good way to start.

CONTENT ADVISORIES (V-CHIP DATA)

Like ITV Links, parental content advisories (we don't call them "ratings" anymore) are bits of data inserted in the VBI along with the closed-captioning data. Also like ITV Links, you can put them there if you have the software to do it.

The V-Chip is the product of a long political battle. You can't actually rip your TV set open and point at a V-Chip. It's a filtering system that's built into the other control systems in the television, including the menu system, the tuner and the caption decoder. The idea is that parents can set their television to block shows with content that they feel is inappropriate for their children.

The V-Chip system (described in gory detail in EIA-744-A, and in the

Nuts & Volts article mentioned above) supports four different ratings systems. The first is the familiar Motion Picture Association of America system we see at the movie theaters, with G, PG, PG-13, R, NC-17 and X ratings.

The second system is the one designed specifically for television in the United States. The television parental content advisory system works like this:

TV Y **All Children** — This program is designed to be appropriate for all children, especially for ages 2–6.

TV Y7 **Directed to Older Children** — This program is designed for children age 7 and above. It may contain mild fantasy violence or comedic violence. If the fantasy violence is intense, the program will be labeled TV-PG-FV.

TV G **General Audience** — Most parents would find this program suitable for all ages. Minimal violence and sexual content, and no strong language.

TV PG **Parental Guidance Suggested** — This program contains material that parents might find unsuitable for younger children. May also carry moderate violence (TV-PG-V), some sexual situations (TV-PG-S), some coarse language (TV-PG-L) or suggestive dialog (TV-PG-D).

TV 14 **Parents Strongly Cautioned** — Contains some material that many parents would find inappropriate for children under 14. May also carry intense violence (TV-14-V), intense sexual situations (TV-14-S), strong coarse language (TV-14-L) or intensely suggestive dialog (TV-14-D).

TV MA **Mature Audiences Only** — This program is specifically designed to be viewed by adults and may be unsuitable for children under 17. This program contains graphic violence (TV-MA-V), explicit sexual activity (TV-MA-S) or crude indecent language (TV-MA-L).

Ratings may be combined. For example, a show rated TV-PG that contains violence and profanity would be labeled TV-PG-L-V.

There is also a Canadian ratings system supported by the V-Chip and detailed in EIA-744-A. In fact, in true Canadian style, the English- and French-speaking Canadians were unable to agree on a single ratings system, so there are actually two of them in the system. The Canadian English system is:

- E   Exempt
- C   Programs intended for children
- C8+   Children 8 and older
- G   General audience
- PG   Parental guidance
- 14+   Viewers 14 and older
- 18+   Adult programming

The Canadian French system is:

- E   Exemptées
- G   Général
- 8 ans +   Général — Déconseillé aux jeunes enfants
- 13 ans +   Ne convient pas aux moins de 13 ans
- 16 ans +   Ne convient pas aux moins de 16 ans
- 18 ans +   Réeservée aux adultes

XDS DATA

The parental content advisories are actually just one of the types of XDS (extended data services[9]) packets that can be inserted in the VBI. If you're terminally curious, you can get yourself a copy of EIA-766 and see what it's all about, but I caution you that it's mighty dull reading.

In a nutshell, XDS provides a mechanism for TV networks and stations to provide consumer equipment like televisions and VCRs with information like:

- The name, length and start time of current show;
- The type of show, based on a set of category codes;
- Program content advisory (see "V-Chip" above);
- Network name;

---

[9] *Why isn't extended data services abbreviated EDS? Well, it was, but there's this company called EDS (the one Ross Perot used to own) that had other ideas, so now it's XDS.*

- Station name and number; and
- National Weather Service warning codes.

And, of course, there's more. The most exciting XDS packet for most of us is the one containing the current time and date. That means if you pick up the right VCR (ask at the store), it can set its own clock, and you'll never have to stare at a blinking 12:00 again.

For the most part, realtime captioners won't be getting very involved in XDS, because the data gets inserted in so many different places, but you should still stay aware of what's going on, just in case you have an opportunity in the future.

DTV

As the world moves into the digital age, the court reporting and closed-captioning professions must move with it. The word *digital*, as defined in *Random House*, means "of, pertaining to, or using data in the form of numerical digits." What it means to us, however, is video and audio that can be directly manipulated by a computer.

We're already using digital audio in the court reporting profession — every time we use our CAT software to make an audio recording of a proceeding on our computer's hard disk. The sound is turned into a stream of ones and zeros that we can manipulate and synchronize our transcripts to. Digital video is following close behind. Digital audio and video have been around for years, but they are being accepted slowly by the legal and court reporting communities.

Not so with broadcasters. The Federal Communications Commission is putting deadlines on the implementation of digital television. This is the same technology that was previously known as HDTV (High-Definition TV) or ATV (Advanced TV).

DTV offers a dramatically higher-quality picture and changes the shape of the screen to a wider format, like a movie theater. Our current TV sets use a broadcast video format called NTSC (named for the National Television Standards Committee). NTSC defines a video screen with a 4:3 aspect ratio. This means that a picture three feet high would be four feet wide. DTV uses the same aspect ratio as movies,

16:9. With a 16:9 aspect ratio, that three-foot-high TV picture would be five feet four inches wide!

If the whole underlying technology of the TV picture is changing, closed captioning will have to change with it, and that change has been defined. The group that creates technical standards for captioning[10] has released a new standard for DTV captioning, called EIA-708. It makes a number of changes that will make caption viewing better than our current NTSC-based system, which is called EIA-608. The EIA-708 specification is over 100 pages long, so we can provide only a short synopsis of the improvements here.

Viewers at home will be able to control the size of the caption text with a new "caption volume control." People with poor vision can make the captions bigger, people who don't want captions covering as much of the picture can make them smaller, and everyone else can leave them as they are today. This means that captioners will have to place each caption with an "anchor point," determining what part of the caption is locked to the picture. When viewers change the text size, that single point of the caption will stay put as the text grows and shrinks. Captioners will have to think ahead about caption placement and plan for the different sizes in which captions will appear on different televisions.

EIA-708 offers many more letters and symbols, both for multilingual captioning and for American English. There are letters like Ø, Å, ß and many accented letters, as well as some useful symbols, including ©, ¶, ¥, §, typographer's quotes (“” as opposed to ""), and even a CC symbol. Currently, we have to stretch the limits of captioning even to handle languages closely related to English. The EIA-608 character set doesn't have all of the letters and accent marks needed for proper captioning in languages like French, Spanish, German, Italian or Portuguese. EIA-708 provides all of those and more.

Support for multiple fonts and more colors will give us more of the attractive "movie subtitle" look rather than the chunky monospaced

---

[10] *The group is called CEA R4.3 Working Group 1, and as of this writing, I am chairing it.*

white-on-a-black-box look that we've grown used to. TV and decoder manufacturers aren't required to support all the fonts and colors, but the specification defines eight fonts (including proportional-spaced, casual and script fonts). This will allow captioners to dramatically improve the look of the captions, but at the same time, captioners will have to take into consideration how the captions will appear on sets without multiple-font capabilities.

The additional color support means up to 64 different text and background colors. The traditional black box as a background can be replaced by a colored box or done away with entirely in favor of edged or drop-shadowed text. The caption box can also be made translucent (see-through). Again, captioners have more options, but it requires thinking and planning ahead. If you want to define a different color for each member of the news team, it means building special speaker IDs in advance and consistently using them during the captioning. If you are creating captions that will be simultaneously broadcast in both the old (NTSC) and new (DTV) formats, you'll need to make sure that the captions work on both, not relying exclusively on color for information, just as pioneers in color television needed to make sure that their programs would still be clear on a black-and-white set.

Much more information can be included in DTV captions. Currently, if we caption a show in two languages (CC1 and CC2) at 250 words per minute, we've about hit the limit of what can be transmitted. There's no room for text or Internet data like ITV Links. EIA-708 provides room for 16 times as much information.

As you can see, the focus is on giving viewers better-looking information and more control over it. If you get the impression that means more work for captioners, you're right. In the beginning, it will require learning a new environment. As the digital captioning industry matures, the tools of the captioning trade will mature with it, growing more and more sophisticated and handling more of the decisions automatically. Until we know what people prefer and the de facto stylistic conventions settle into place, the pioneers in captioning, just like pioneers everywhere else, will have to "wing it."

The good news is that captions are being taken into consideration now, not added to DTV as an afterthought sometime down the road. Even though DTV is still in its infancy, captions can already be found on some DTV programs.

Luckily for all of us, some of the companies that manufacture caption encoders are now making devices called "transcoders," which accept "old-style" line 21 captions from a captioner and spit out new-style DTV captions.

As the big stations move on to DTV, they will turn their old broadcast frequencies over to others. This means more stations, thus more captioning and more jobs.

The Look of the Captions

Pop-on, Paint-on, Roll-up

Caption text can be displayed on your screen in one of three ways: roll-up, pop-on and paint-on. The first two are by far the most common.

ROLL-UP

This is the style seen during virtually all live (realtime) events. The captions are being generated live by a stenocaptioner or fed from a TelePrompTer, and they scroll up like words on a computer screen. Typically, roll-up captions are positioned at the bottom of the screen, unless they would be covering something there.

You can usually tell the difference between roll-up captions generated by a stenocaptioner ("realtime captions") and roll-up captions from a live display script. Live display captions appear a whole line at a time, while realtime captions appear a word or phrase at a time.

POP-ON

Pop-on captions appear all at once, replacing what was there before. Unlike roll-up captions, there is no scrolling of the prior caption. It just disappears, and the new captions pop onto the screen in its place.

Pop-on captions are used for virtually all prerecorded programs, because they allow much finer control over caption placement and timing than roll-up captions.

PAINT-ON

Paint-on captions look pretty much like pop-on captions, except for two details. First, the prior caption, if any, isn't erased before the paint-on caption appears, allowing it to write over whatever else was there. Second, the paint-on caption doesn't appear all at once, like the pop-on, but "paints" onto the screen a character at a time.

Paint-on captions are used primarily for special effects, as in music videos, or as the first caption of a TV commercial. The reason for using them as the first caption of a commercial is somewhat complex. You want to hear it anyway? OK, here goes:

When a TV station cuts in a commercial, if the first caption is pop-on, it must have time to "build up" in the decoder before it can be displayed. As described earlier in this book, only so much captioning information can fit into a frame of videotape. A long or complicated caption can take one and one-half to two seconds before it is ready to display. By this time, the captions are well behind the audio of the program, and Caption No. 2 will need to be displayed, leaving no time for the viewer to read Caption No. 1.

The solution to this is to begin a commercial with a "blank caption" command, to make sure no previous captions are left on the screen, followed by a paint-on caption as the first caption. This way, the viewer watches the first caption paint onto the screen and has an opportunity to read it as it is being displayed. Caption No. 2 thus requires little or no delay, and the commercial starts much more smoothly.

Text Formats

ITALICS AND UNDERLINING

The captioning character set allows for italics and underlining. Italics are used fairly often. They can set apart the name of the person speaking or be used to indicate that the speaker is off-screen. They can be used for emphasis or for product names.

Underlining isn't nearly as common. It's available, but rarely used.

COLORS

The Line 21 captioning standards allow for some limited control over colors. The background is always black. There's nothing we can do about that. The foreground color, however, can be controlled by the captioning software. There are seven color options: white, blue, red, green, cyan (light blue), magenta (reddish purple) and yellow.

Realistically, the blue on most televisions is too dark to read clearly and easily on a black background, so that leaves six options.

So how come all the captioning you ever see is white on black? Two reasons:

First, captioning with white letters on black is how it's been done for over 20 years. Changing is extra work. If captions are going to be in color, someone has to decide what the extra colors will mean. Will there be different colors to show who is speaking (this is how the BBC does much of its captioning)? Will the color be chosen so that it is artistically pleasing for the background? Will different shows use different trademark colors? Will colors be used for emphasis (shouting is in RED)?

However it is done, it means extra work for the captioners. If it takes longer to caption the show, then the captioners will charge more to do the job. Wouldn't you? So far, few people have felt color captions are important enough to pay for.

There are exceptions, of course. The Disney movie *Pete's Dragon*, captioned by NCI, has wonderfully playful use of color in the captions. Everything said by the dragon, including sound effects, is in green, except where the dragon has been given a belt of whiskey. He then belches fire and his captions appear in red for a while. When they sing about money, the word is green. When they sing about gold, that word comes up in yellow.

All in all, *Pete's Dragon* isn't the best example of the usefulness of color captions, but it's a wonderful example of how they can add to the enjoyment of viewing the video.

Even when there *is* color captioning, you may not be able to see it. Only the built-in decoder chips can show color. TeleCaption decoders and VCRs with caption decoders show all captioning in black and white. The FCC standard for decoders lists color capability as an option, so there is no hard requirement to have it.

Will we ever see regular color captioning on broadcast television? I think so. I saw a show just the other day where the whole show was captioned with white letters until the credits at the very end, where the name of the captioning company was shown in cyan.

It's a start.

FLASHING

Hopefully, by this point in the book, you've discovered that I do not suffer from an excess of journalistic impartiality. Therefore, you won't be shocked by the statement that flashing captions are an abomination.

It is, of course, only my humble opinion, but I believe that captions which flash should be reserved for notification that a major earthquake is about to make California drop into the Pacific Ocean. Even then, I'd look for a way to only make them flash for people in California.[11]

Luckily, we have not been deluged with captioned commercials from Honest Abe's House of Used Steno Machines, where the prices flash green and the rest of the caption flashes magenta. I hope that never happens.

EDGED LETTERS

Several times people have approached me to ask about this. "I saw this television," they start out, "where the captions weren't just white letters on a black background. The captions were superimposed on the picture with black and white edging so that they were easy to read on any color background. How did they *do* that?"

---

[11] *It's OK. I live in California. I'm* allowed *to say things like that.*

This is not something a captioner can control — at least not in an analog broadcast environment. Fancy-edged characters can be accomplished by using a decoder that can produce them (SoftTouch and Ultech make them) or when the video is open-captioned rather than closed-captioned.

In digital television, there are options for edged and shadowed letters. This capability is, however, optional in the TV captioning specification, so not all digital TV sets will support it.

OTHER FONTS

I am also asked often about fonts. Mostly, people want a more readable font. Again, the closed-captioning data in the TV signal can only specify what letter is going to be placed where and a few attributes of the letter, such as its color, and whether it is underlined, italicized or (gasp!) flashing. The font is determined entirely by the decoder.

If you don't like the way the captions look on your television during the 6 p.m. news, you're not going to like them during the *I Dream of Jeannie* reruns, either.

Again, this changes in DTV, where the captioner can choose between a variety of font types, including serif, sans serif, script and so on. With open captioning using a character generator, you have many more choices, and in CART, as you'll see in the next chapter, your selection of fonts is virtually unlimited.

LINE LENGTHS

In captioning, a line is limited to 32 characters. This doesn't mean that you always want your line width set to the maximum. Many TV stations and networks now place a "bug" in the lower-right corner of the screen. No, in this context a bug is not a wayward insect, nor a programming error. It is a small logo, often translucent, that identifies the source of the video.

Check with your client before setting your line length. If the client wants the bug always visible, you'll need to chop a few characters off the end of the line to accommodate it.

Also, check the documentation on your captioning system for "soft" line lengths. This provides a place to put punctuation marks or word endings that would otherwise cause word wrapping.

For example, if your line length is 26 characters, and you write "THIS IS A MIGHTY FULL LINE" and then pause, the system will output all of the text. Now, what happens if you add a period or a comma? The system has to tell the caption encoder to backspace over the word LINE and move it down a row to make room for the punctuation mark. If you have soft line lengths on the system, one extra column is reserved for just this situation. That particular line will end up one character longer than the normal maximum, and there won't be any erasing and rewriting of text.

NUMBER OF ROWS

Captioning allows for a maximum of four visible rows of text at a time. With the screen only being 15 rows high, four caption rows would take up over one-quarter of the total screen area.[12] That's a lot of screen real estate, so four-row captions are rarely used. The majority of broadcast realtime captioning is three-row if it is all the way at the bottom of the screen, or two-row anywhere else, although there are plenty of exceptions.

When deciding how many rows to use, you have to balance two conflicting goals: keeping as much text on the screen as you can (to make it easier to read) and covering as little of the picture as possible. Often, your customer will dictate how it should look, absolving you of the responsibility for making this decision.

SPEAKER IDS

Each captioning company has its own style for denoting who is speaking. Sometimes, a single captioning company will use several styles, depending on the customer. There are only two absolutes:

---

[12] *Well, actually, there is a "safe area" of about 10 percent of the screen height reserved on the top and bottom of the screen. Depending on the TV set, your four-row caption could cover anywhere from about 21 to 27 percent of the height of the screen. Aren't you glad you read footnotes?*

>> indicates a new person speaking.

>>> indicates the start of a new story in a newscast.

These two markers are recognized by caption users and are also being used increasingly by automated programs that scan caption text looking for information.

Some companies like the speaker's name in lowercase after the > marker, some like it in all caps before, and I've seen some very strange ones on top of it. The most common are:

>> Bob: THAT WAS A GOOD ONE.

BOB>> THAT WAS A GOOD ONE.

>>BOB: THAT WAS A GOOD ONE.

In England, you'll often see a different color assigned to each of the people speaking. This is rarely (if ever) done in the United States, although there is no technical barrier preventing it. It is partially a holdover from the days before decoders were built into TV sets, when the external decoders couldn't display colored captions.

Non-English Captioning

Since Line 21 captioning was designed in the United States for the United States, the basic needs of Americans were quite well covered. In addition, the £ symbol (pounds sterling) was added for our friends across the Atlantic in the United Kingdom. Some specific concessions also were made for French and Spanish, so other languages certainly can be captioned using Line 21 technology.

French

With all of the accented letters added to the character set, the major holes in the character set for French are the lack of a dieresis (as in Noël) and the u with a grave accent (ù). The rest of the lowercase vowels with accents, including grave, aigu and circumflex, are present and accounted for, as is the c-cedilla (ç).

In the opinion of Valerie Waite, who owns a captioning firm in Canada, most consumers are happy to get captioning at all these days, and the lack of letters like the ö is just "an excuse for not captioning." She feels that professionals should do their best with the tools that are available — an opinion shared by many others.

Unfortunately, Line 21 captions have no accented capital letters. This leaves French captioners in Quebec with a dilemma: They can either caption in mixed case (unlike the United States) or lose the accent marks on their vowels.

Quite a few captioning companies are located in Quebec, creating both realtime and offline captions. Later in this book, we'll see a profile of a captioning company that's done realtime captioning simultaneously in French and English for the Canadian Parliament.

Spanish

Spanish is fairly well covered by the Line 21 captioning character set. Not only are there accented letters and both upper- and lowercase ñ, but the inverse (open) question mark was added as well,[13] so that captioners can write things like: ¿Qué pasa? The inverse (open) exclamation mark (¡) was omitted, but that is far less important to the language than the question mark, and you can always improvise by using a lowercase *I.*

Quite a bit of captioning has been done in Spanish. The majority of it has been offline (post-production) captioning, but there is realtime Spanish captioning happening as well. Professor Fernando Altamirano of Puerto Rico has developed a theory for writing realtime Spanish using a standard American steno machine. This required some modification to the basic structure and meaning of the keys, so that he could, for example, represent the ñ sound. You'll read more about Fernando in the case studies in Chapter 11.

---

[13] *Spanish has both an opening question mark (¿) and a closing question mark (?), which are used at the beginning and end of a question, respectively.*

German

The Line 21 character set was simply not designed for German. While German captioning is fairly readable, the legibility is affected by the loss of the umlaut (used in ä, ö and ü) and the letter β (estset, or "sharp S"). The β is used in certain circumstances to represent an "s" sound. Captioners can always write the word with a double s instead (rendering, for example, *schloβ* as *schloss*). Technically, this could modify the pronunciation of the word, because β in the middle of a word makes the preceding vowel long, and *ss* in the middle of a word makes the preceding vowel short. However, this is more of an annoyance than an impediment to understanding.

Non-Latin Alphabets

Since the character set resides in the TV set or decoder rather than in the encoder, there's no way to replace the alphabet. Rendering a language like Russian (which uses the Cyrillic alphabet), Arabic, Greek or Japanese (kanji or katakana) requires that the language be rendered using the Latin alphabet.

Summary of Alphabets

Here is a rough summary of the letters and accents required for most "Line 21-captionable" Latin-alphabet-based languages, showing what the Line 21 character set does, and doesn't, contain. Languages containing a large number of letters that can't be represented are not listed here.

The letters are broken into two sets: those that are required and those that are considered important but possibly optional when writing in that language. Obviously, there can be some disagreement over what is required and what is merely "important." In this table, I am merely attempting to show how close you can get to a proper representation of the language, given the limited tools available. In each case, the letters in the "available" column are in the Line 21 character set, and the letters in the "not available" column are not.

The base alphabet, as used in English (uppercase A-Z and lowercase a-z), is not included in the list of letters.

Language	Required		Important	
	Available	Not Available	Available	Not Available
Afrikaans	áé è âêîôû	ëïö ÁÉ È ÂÊÎÔÛ ËÏÖ		
Danish		æ åø ÆÅØ	áéíóú	ÁÉÍÓÚý´Y
Finnish		äö ÄÖ		
French [14]	àè é ç	ù Ç	âêîôû	œ ëïü
(Quebecois)	àè é ç	ù ÀÈ É Ù Ç	âêîôû	œ ëïü Œ ËÏÜ
Gaelic	áé àè	ìòù ÁÉ ÀÈÌÒÙ		
German		äöü ÄÖÜ β	àé	ÀÉ
Irish	áéíóú	ÁÉÍÓÚ		
Italian	éó àè	ìò ÉÓ ÀÈÌÒ	íú	ù ï ÍÚÙÏ
Portuguese	ç	ãõ ÃÕ Ç	áéíóú àò âêô	üÁÉÍÓÚ ÀÒ ÂÊÔÜ
Spanish[15]	ñÑ ¿	¡	áéíóú ç	ü ÁÉÍÓÚÜ Ç ° a
Swedish		äö å ÄÖÅ	áé	ëü ÁÉ ËÜ

Almost all of these letters and symbols are available in the EIA-708 standard for DTV.

Captioning Software

The most important thing to understand about online captioning software is that it is not CAT software. The only thing they have in common is realtime translation. You can find some combined or integrated CAT/captioning systems that share tools like a dictionary editor, but in general, you'll find that captioning software doesn't handle legal transcript formats, litigation-support interfaces, compressed printing, batch (nonrealtime) translation and so forth.

---

[14] *Old French also uses æ, Æ, ÿ and Ÿ, but they are very uncommon today.*

[15] *That's not a lowercase "i" under Spanish — it's an inverted (upside-down) exclamation mark. The ° and ª are masculine and feminine ordinal indicators.*

Picking a Product

There are a lot of factors to consider when purchasing a captioning software program. In preparing this book, I surveyed all captioning vendors that I knew of. Most vendors filled out the survey. Several did not, even after multiple e-mails and phone calls. Rather than compare the products directly and draw a conclusion, which would make this book obsolete by the time it was printed, I'll go through the criteria for selection and let you talk to the vendors yourself. There's a list of the vendors on page 271.

REALTIME CAPABILITIES

The majority of the time you spend captioning will be spent writing realtime. You *must* be comfortable with the translation. When you narrow your selection to the point where you'll be getting demonstrations of the programs, make sure you actually load your dictionary into each system and try it out. Virtually all programs can import an RTF/CRE dictionary now, so the conversion shouldn't be difficult.

- Check the speed. Is the translation smooth and steady, or does it lag behind and rush to catch up?

- Can you adjust the delay to allow time for correction?

- How does it handle word endings?

- If you have conflicts in your writing, does the program resolve them for you *correctly*?

- Can you create "macros" to do things like move the captions around on the screen, blank all captions on the screen, change the number of roll-up lines, feed scripts, call up stock captions and so on?

- Can you perform globals from the steno keyboard?

- If there are any commands that must be issued using the computer keyboard rather than the steno keyboard, can they be done easily one-handed, without using the control, shift or alt keys?

FORMAT CHANGES

Captioning requires more than just a stream of text. You must be sure that the text isn't covering anything crucial on the picture. Make sure that the captioning software supports moving the captions around on the screen *easily*, changing the row, column, line width and number of lines being displayed.

Within the text itself you should be able to use attributes like italics and underlining. While color isn't used much now, its importance will grow as time goes on. Make sure you can define steno strokes to turn on and off these attributes.

While flashing text is offered as one of the Line 21 formatting options, it is rarely used. Personally, I consider this a good thing, and I wouldn't worry if your software doesn't support flashing text.

Some captioning software allows you to write realtime pop-on captioning in addition to the traditional roll-up format. I'm not sure why.

THE LINE 21 CHARACTER SET

Make sure that your software supports the full Line 21 character set, including the music notes. What *is* the full character set, you ask? It consists of:

- Uppercase and lowercase letters: A-Z, a-z
- Acute (or "aigu") accents: á é í ó ú
- Grave accents: à è
- Circumflex accents: â ê î ô û
- N-tilde for Spanish and Portuguese: ñ Ñ
- C-cedilla for French and Portuguese: ç
- Numbers: 0–9
- Punctuation marks: , . ! ¿ ? - ; : ' " " ( ) [ ]

- Currency symbols: $ £ ¢
- Math symbols: + ÷ < = > %
- Other symbols: ½ ° ® ™ # & @

Notice that there are some characters you're used to having in standard ASCII that are missing in the Line 21 character set. The one you're most likely to miss is the asterisk (*). You can't "bleep" out a word by replacing it with asterisks, as there is no way for a decoder to display them. Other ASCII characters not present in Line 21 include the backslash (\), caret (^), curly braces ({ }) and tilde (~).

Older decoders had ¼ and ¾ symbols instead of the ® and ™ symbols. In fact, if you use the trademark symbols today, they'll show up as fractions on the old TeleCaption decoders. For this reason, they are still used sparingly.

STENO MACHINE COMPATIBILITY

Don't just look to see if the software supports the machine you're using at the moment. You never know when you might see a deal on a great used steno machine, or when you might want to sell your software to someone with a different model. If the software doesn't support that person's writer, she won't buy it from you.[16]

Look for support for the Stenograph machines (the Stentura and SmartWriter use the same interface, as did AssemblyFAB's Optimate and Legit'i'Mate machines), ProCAT's Flash Writer and ProWriter, Xscribe machines (again, all StenoRams, FirstCATs and Visions are compatible), the BaronData Transcriptor X, the Gemini, the MeritWriter (which was also marketed by Cheetah as the TurboWriter and by StenoCAT as the StenoWriter), and the various incarnations of Digitext machines (AccuWriter, Fon'iksWriter, Impression and ImpactWriter). Some systems also support older machines like the EZ-Writer and CatWriter.

---

[16] *As we'll discuss a little later, you also need to see whether you can sell the software in the first place!*

When you try out software, make sure you use your own writer. Don't forget to take along your realtime cable, as the software vendor is not likely to have all of the various types of realtime cable handy.

CAPTION ENCODER SUPPORT

While EEG certainly has the lion's share of the caption encoder market, it is not the only vendor. Make sure that the software works with EEG's latest encoders and character generators, as well as its older models (there are a *lot* of EN-270 Smart Encoders out there), and encoders from companies like Evertz, SoftTouch, Norpak and Ultech.

OTHER OUTPUT FORMATS AND CAPTION STANDARDS

Today it's easy to build a captioning business without thinking about anything except good old American Line 21 captioning. As your business grows and expands, however, you may need to handle Teletext (the European equivalent of our Line 21), DTV (using the new EIA-708 standards), and captioning of Internet streaming media using SAMI or SMIL. Talk to the software vendor and see if its product supports any of these standards or if it has plans to add them.

If you plan to do CART work, see if the captioning software supports any alternative output devices, like LED signs or video character generators such as the Chyron CODI.

MODEM HANDLING

The majority of broadcast captioning is done remotely, meaning that you'll be connecting to the caption encoder using a modem. Carefully check out the software's modem handling capability. It should be able to:

- Store a long list of phone numbers, with descriptions long enough to be meaningful (e.g., WXXX control room A);
- Add dialing codes and pauses, like using *70 to turn off call waiting or activate other phone line features;
- Alert you if the connection drops;
- Redial quickly and easily in the case of a dropped connection; and

- Save and load lists of phone numbers so you can transfer them to another computer or swap with a co-worker.

LIVE DISPLAY (SCRIPTING)

Script handling isn't only for newscasts. While you won't have any scripts to worry about in sports captioning, live display can be tremendously useful in many other situations, from public meetings (text of agenda items, proclamations and items to be voted on) to church services (Bible readings, hymns and upcoming events).

Look for these script-handling capabilities:

- Loading scripts from multiple files, and in multiple formats, such as plain ASCII text and transcript files from your CAT software;

- Holding multiple stories in a queue (called a "rundown" in the news business) and being able to shuffle the order of the stories *quickly* on-the-fly;

- Being able to jump around in the script easily, going from story to story, skipping lines, and searching forward and backward for text;

- Being able to feed scripts from the computer keyboard or the steno keyboard without having to switch in and out of realtime;

- Having at least rudimentary script editing capabilities, allowing you to swiftly clean up small problems in the scripts or insert speaker IDs;

- Making changes globally (search and replace) in the scripts, so that you can correct a spelling error that was made throughout an entire script file;

- Being able to import scripts directly from a newsroom computer system or TelePrompTer would be a wonderful feature, but none of the systems surveyed currently have this ability; and

- Being able to quickly reload the script file(s) that you're using to bring in updates or edits.

STOCK CAPTIONS

Stock captions are like text macros: They contain the text and formatting information for something that is repeated frequently. As an example, if you do a lot of live events, you'll probably have one that displays [APPLAUSE] or [LAUGHTER]. If you work in broadcast television, you'll have a pop-up stock caption for your credits.

DOCUMENTATION

Software documentation comes in many forms these days. It may be a printed manual, a hypertext manual on CD-ROM, a set of help files, a videotape, a CD-ROM training program or any combination of these. See what's available and how readable it is. Look for specific pieces of information and determine how easy they are to find. You'll be depending on the documentation once you commit to the software, so make sure it has all you need.

WIDESPREAD USE

Find out how many people use the software. While you shouldn't necessarily rule out a new program, it'll be a lot easier to get peer support if you find something used by many others. If you're new to the captioning business, you have enough to worry about without testing untried software — choose something that's been out for a while and is stable.

NONCAPTIONING CAPABILITIES

Remember the good old days when all a captioner had to worry about was putting words on the screen? Well, those days are drawing to a close. There's a lot of other information transmitted along with the caption data, and you need to make sure you can handle it when the need arises. All of these were discussed earlier in this chapter.

- **Alternate caption channels.** Captions can be transmitted on CC1, CC2, CC3 and CC4. While CC2 and CC4 are rarely used, you should make sure that your software can handle at least CC1 and CC3.

- **Text channels.** In addition to the four caption channels, there are four text channels. They are not used much in broadcast, but there are times when you might want to show a full screen of text in a live event.

- **XDS data.** Most of the time, you'll be captioning in field 1 (as you may recall, that's where CC1 is), and XDS data is placed in field 2. This allows TV stations to easily insert all of the XDS data, including V-Chip codes, without involving captioners at all. Still, there may be times when a TV station without its own XDS encoder may ask the captioner to do it. If you have the capability, you get the job.

- **ITV Links.** Unlike XDS data, the ITV Links are inserted in the same field of Line 21 as the primary caption data, so the easiest way to insert them is to have the captioner do it.

Choosing a Software Vendor

There's more to selecting a captioning program than the product itself. You need to take into consideration a variety of factors that relate directly to the company that created the software.

ONE VENDOR — TWO PROGRAMS?

If your CAT vendor also has captioning software, this could represent a major savings for you — possibly thousands of dollars. You should still evaluate all of the other products that are available, of course, but take the pricing into consideration.

TRAINING

Ask the vendor what training it offers. If you're new to captioning, see if the vendor can train you in captioning as well as in the operation of the software. This is one area that's lacking in the field now. Most of the software vendors selling captioning software know little about how the program is actually used, and they can provide little help. If the vendor can't provide what you need, see if it can steer you to independent seminars or user groups.

TECHNICAL SUPPORT

Check the hours of the technical support line. Will someone be there if you're setting up for an event at 7 a.m. on a Sunday morning? Will the support line be staffed when you're captioning a late-night news program?

Since most online captioning technical support is handled by the same staff that handles CAT support, it's important to verify that they actually know something about the captioning software. Ask the sales representative if you can try a test. Call the technical support line and ask a question about captioning. It doesn't have to be a complicated one. Asking something simple like "How do I define a dictionary entry to clear the captions from the screen?" or "How do I set the software to work with an Ultech encoder?" should tell you a lot.

See how you can contact tech support. Sometimes a phone call won't be convenient. Is there a message board on the Internet? Can you use e-mail? Can the vendor fax you answers to questions?

SERVICE CONTRACTS

Generally, a service contract gets you updates to the software and technical assistance when you need it. In most software industries, service contracts cost about one percent of the retail price of the program per month, so a $4,000 program would have a $480 per year support agreement. In CAT and captioning, the price may run a bit higher than that.

The price of the software should include support for some period of time. Some vendors offer 90 days, and some offer as much as a year. See if you can get a discount for buying extra support at the same time as you purchase the software.

Find out how updates are handled. Do they come with new documentation? Are they shipped to you automatically, or do you have to download them online? How are they tested before they are released? Does the company make its bug list public? Are the updates completely free, or is there a charge (these sometimes masquerade as "shipping and handling" charges)?

Is the technical support unlimited, or do they have a maximum number of instances or minutes? What happens if you exceed the maximum? Do you pay by the minute or by the problem?

Ask if the service contract is transferable. If you sell the program, a service agreement could add significantly to its value.

See what happens if the contract expires. Some companies allow you to just start paying fees again, but this is rare. If they let you stop and restart the contract at will, you would only pay it when you had a problem or needed a specific update, so most companies have a reinstatement fee. One company used to have a policy where you had to pay all of the missed time — if your contract expired three years ago, you'd have to pay three years' worth of fees to get back up-to-date. I don't know if the vendor still does this.

WHAT DO YOU OWN?

Carefully review the purchase agreement and the software license. In some cases, you are actually purchasing a copy of the software, and you may do as you please with it, including reselling it. In other cases, you are buying a severely restricted right to use the program. Some companies charge a "software license transfer fee" and require their written permission in advance before you can sell the program.

Credits and Logos

You've probably seen the "CC" symbol on your TV screen or on the box for a videotape and wondered how to view the captions. Typically, it will be a logo like one of these:

The one on the left is a generic logo for closed captioning. The one on the right is a trademark of the National Captioning Institute, and indicates that it captioned the program.

Chapter 3

CART

What Is CART?

CART is a profession halfway between court reporting and closed captioning.

Like court reporting, CART is usually done with traditional CAT software and takes place "on location."

Like captioning, the goal of CART is to help people who can't hear what's going on, so it often involves paraphrasing rather than verbatim reporting.

Depending on who you ask, CART stands for computer-aided realtime translation or communication access realtime translation. Either way, it refers to a court reporter using realtime technology to act as an interpreter for a deaf or hard-of-hearing person.

CART vs. Captioning: The Fuzzy Line

By the strictest of definitions, captioning is words *on a picture*, so if there's no TV picture involved, it's not captioning. If you set up your CAT system so that a deaf person can read the screen, it's CART. If your realtime is going through a caption encoder and being broadcast on television, it's captioning.

But what do you have when your text is all that appears on the TV screen? You could do this by using a captioning system with no picture,[1] or by using CAT software and showing the screen on a television rather than a computer monitor.[2]

There is a wide, fuzzy line between captioning and CART, and there are many tasks that can be accomplished either way. The sign of a professional is being able to determine your customers' needs and then figuring out the best way to serve them with the tools at your disposal. That means that you may have both CART and captioning tools and use them interchangeably.

What Your Customers Really Want

What the people want isn't always what they ask for. It's up to you to ask the right questions. You'll look better just for knowing what to ask, and the job will go smoother because you did.

How many people will actually be watching the realtime? This is a key question. There may be 1,000 people at the conference, but only 10 need to see the realtime. If you find that out in advance, it'll save you a bundle in presentation equipment.

Will you be working with a sign language interpreter? If so, coordinate with the interpreter in advance and work out placement. Later in the book, we'll go over some tips on working with interpreters.

Do they want CART or captioning? Unfortunately, many CART reporters present themselves as captioners, which confuses the people using the services. Make sure that your customers understand the difference and that you're providing what they want.

Will there be any breaks? If you're expected to write for 10 straight hours, you'll probably need a relief reporter. Make sure all of the realtime display equipment is compatible with both of your systems.

---

[1] *Actually, you would need a piece of equipment called a "black burst generator" to create a blank screen, as captions won't display on static.*

[2] *This is done using a scan converter, as we'll see later in the chapter.*

Whatever setup you use, test it *before* the job! If you haul in a bunch of gear on conference day and can't hook it up or make it work, your chances of getting called back are minimal. I was helping my wife, Kathy, with a CART job for a deaf group once. We had about 20 people reading her realtime. Setup took about five minutes. After the conference, the group leader told us that she had used four different reporters/captioners, and we were the first ones who hooked up the equipment without problems. The setup is so simple that I can only assume the others had never even tried it beforehand.

Making Your Text Look Good

Always remember that you have two objectives for a job, and keep them both in mind when you are prepping. It's obviously important to keep your audience happy, but don't neglect the folks who hired you. The one paying your bill is not always the one receiving the benefit of your services. They are, however, likely to be the ones who decide whether you get the next contract, so work hard to keep them happy.

Preparation Before the Job

Nothing you can do during a CART assignment can make up for poor preparation.

Practice the actual material. If you'll be working in school, tape some of the instructor's classes. Many churches have tapes of their services available. Ask what's on the agenda at meetings. Get comfortable with the flow of the material.

Build your dictionary. If you'll be doing a college chemistry course or a church service, be ready to add a lot to your dictionary. Focus on word parts, where you get more mileage from each dictionary entry. Don't be surprised if your first job in a given field adds hundreds of entries to your dictionary.

Get the names! Want to lower your chances at repeat business? Spell someone's name wrong. You should have the names of all organizations, sponsoring companies and individuals in your dictionary. Read over the agenda, announcement, class notes or whatever other material you can get and enter every single name you encounter.

Your dictionary should have plenty of name parts, too, so you have a good chance of building a name on the fly.

Plan and test your display. Whether someone will be reading your screen or your words will be on a 20-foot-tall sign, test everything beforehand. Do you have a table for the screen? Extension cords? Do you know how to set your notebook computer for external display? Is your text big enough? Answer all these questions before the meeting (or class or service, etc.) begins.

Hook everything up *before* you take it to the job site, and make sure it is all fully functional.

Your Computer Screen

There are a lot of different possible CART output devices, which we'll discuss later in this chapter. In most cases, you'll be using your computer screen, either directly or through some kind of projection system. Spend some time playing around with different looks, and come up with one that is clear and easy to read from a distance.

SCREEN LAYOUT

If people will be reading your computer screen, make it as clean and clutter-free as you possibly can. If your CAT software allows it, turn off line numbers, time stamps, paragraph markers, headers, footers, on-screen menus, toolbars, page numbers and all other extraneous information. Show only the text and speaker identifications. If your program leaves a mouse pointer (cursor) on the screen while you write, then tuck it unobtrusively away in a corner where it won't be seen.

If you are using Microsoft Windows, you can set your taskbar (the bar where the Start button is) to be invisible as well. You can do this either by shrinking it out of the way or using the Auto-Hide mode. To activate Auto-Hide, click on the Start button, select Settings and then Taskbar. Auto-Hide is one of the options you can check. When it is active, the taskbar only shows up when the mouse pointer is all the way at the bottom of the screen.

If you use Microsoft Office, make sure you turn off the Office toolbar as well. There are a few other programs that create menus or toolbars that eat up some of your screen space, and you want to get rid of them all.

The primary rule for a good CART screen is to eliminate all distractions so that your realtime is all people can see.

COLORS

Choose colors carefully. High-contrast colors are easiest to read, like black on white or white on black. If you want to soften the display a bit, go with a dark blue rather than black, or yellow rather than white, but keep the combination high-contrast.

To test the combination, view it with the screen intensity turned way down and with the ambient light level very high. Try putting your screen in direct sunlight or viewing it in a brightly lit room. Projection screens especially tend to wash out, and something that looks good under ideal lighting can be totally illegible in the real world.

Many projection systems limit the number of colors you can use, often to the basic set of 16. Your best bet, unless you know the projector you'll be using, is to stay with basic colors like blue, red, green and so forth.

If you will be using TV sets to show your text, stay away from red. The standard NTSC TV system in the United States is notorious for "red smear" problems, where anything colored bright red smears horizontally across the screen (S-Video helps with red smear). A dark red or maroon would work fine on a white background, but bright red on black is difficult to read on most televisions. Make sure you check out your color selections beforehand on the screen you'll be using.

If your system provides you with a way to use different colors as you write, you can consider doing this *if it adds to the presentation.* Don't use different colors just for the sake of doing it, or you'll just distract your audience. The most common use of color in CART work is for speaker identification. In a classroom, for example, you might designate one color for the teacher/professor and another for questions from the students.

Most CAT software does not allow you to define a stroke that says "make the text green from here on" or "change this paragraph to blue," but several systems allow you to designate different colors by paragraph type. As an example, you might define your question paragraph to be green and your colloquy and answer paragraphs to be blue. Then everything would be blue except for questions from the students.

FONTS

With DOS-based CAT/CART software, your choice of fonts was always limited, if you had a choice at all. With the advent of Windows, the choices became almost unlimited. The first rule of choosing a font is that the font itself should never be noticed. If people say, "Wow, what a cool font," then they have been distracted from the actual message in the realtime text.

Serif (Times New Roman)
Sans-Serif (Verdana)
Monospaced (Courier New)
Display (Broadway)
Script (Brush Script MT)

Serif fonts are used for large bodies of text in print form, such as books and magazines. A "serif" is a small line at the end of a main stroke of a letter. See, for example, the letter *i* in *Times* in the illustration above, or a lower-case *l* in the print of this book. Numerous studies have shown that serif fonts are easier to read than sans-serif fonts *in print*. This is not necessarily the case on a computer screen.

The most common serif font is Times (named for the *New York Times* newspaper) and all of its takeoffs.

Sans-Serif[3] fonts, also known as Gothic fonts, have only the main strokes of the letters — no flourishes or decorations. They are generally easier to read on a computer screen or in very small sizes. The Verdana

---

[3] *Sans-serif means "without a serif."*

font used in the illustration was designed specifically for readability on a computer screen and is distributed free of charge by Microsoft on its Web site and in Microsoft Internet Explorer. It is common in Web pages and makes an excellent choice for CART work.

Two other common sans-serif fonts are Helvetica (distributed on all Macintoshes) and Arial (included with Microsoft Windows).

Monospaced fonts, as the name implies, have the same spacing for all letters. Notice in the example above that the *i* in *Times* takes up much less space than the *m*, but in the monospaced font, the characters are equally spaced, just like with a typewriter. Courier is, in fact, derived from a standard typewriter font. Everything in the DOS world was monospaced. Monospaced fonts fit considerably less information on the screen at a time than proportionally spaced fonts and are not a good choice for CART.

Display fonts, sometimes known as headline fonts, are used for signs, headlines, billboards and ad copy. Avoid at all costs the temptation to pick a display font for your CART work. While they have a lot of visual impact, they tend to be quite fatiguing to read and will annoy audiences. Display fonts also often have some of the strokes very wide and others very thin, so that from a distance, the thin strokes can't be seen. Once again, this hinders readability, which is a cardinal sin in realtime.

Script fonts attempt to make computer-generated type look handwritten. We all know that one of the big advantages of typewriters and computers is increased readability over handwriting. While a script font may be appropriate for an invitation to your open house, it should not be used for a CART display, no matter how attractive it may look to you.

When selecting a font for your CART display, focus on readability. Enter a few paragraphs of text and select a font size that shows roughly 35 to 40 characters per line of text (this will vary from line to line, because you'll be using a proportionally spaced font), and space the lines to show about eight to 12 lines of text on the screen. With most fonts, 24-point text is a good starting size on a 640x480-pixel display and 36-point text on a 1024x768-pixel display. Make sure the lines are far enough apart to let your eyes scan across a line without losing your place and wandering to the line above or below.

Now stand back 10 feet or more. Can you read it? Adjust the size of the text up or down until you have a comfortable balance between readability and the amount of text shown on the screen. If there's too little text showing, it will scroll by too fast to read. If there's too much, it will tend to be too small to read comfortably.

For reference, the standard closed-captioning font is monospaced, with 32 characters per line, and shows 15 lines of text at a time. For CART work, something a bit larger is usually called for, as the audience tends to be farther away and the screens tend to be smaller.

ENLARGING TEXT ON DOS SYSTEMS

The most common question I get regarding display realtime is, "How do I enlarge my text?" In captioning, the text size relative to the screen is fixed (both by the decoder and by FCC regulations). If you want bigger text, you need a bigger screen. In CART, those restrictions are removed, because you're just showing people your computer screen.

If you have one of the DOS-based systems without font selections, you still have some alternatives. Most of the DOS systems offer a "big text" option, although this generally only enlarges the text by 40 percent or so. A product called LapZoom doubles the DOS text size on the screen by only showing a quarter of the screen at a time.

To use LapZoom or an equivalent product effectively, you must plan ahead. Set the width of your text-display to no more than 40 characters (37 or 38 is safer). Write enough text to fill an entire screen. Now enable your screen-enlarging software. It will be showing about one-quarter of the screen, but it is almost certainly not going to be the specific one-quarter that you want. Adjust the screen position until the bottom line of realtime (the one where the fresh realtime goes) is fully visible, and the text looks reasonably centered on the screen.

If your CAT software has a "big text" mode, it may or may not be compatible with LapZoom. Screen enlargers and large text modes tend to work better with the older, simpler computers and video cards.

Yet another option is to run your DOS software from within Microsoft Windows. Set the DOS program to be a window on the Windows screen. You can then set the text font used within the DOS window. The exact process varies depending on what version of Windows you're using (Windows 3.1, 95, 98, NT4, 2000), but you can generally get a more attractive display than straight DOS would offer. It is also possible in some cases to get a font so big that the whole DOS window won't fit on the screen. In this case, adjust the window as you would for LapZoom to be sure that the last line of realtime shows clearly on the screen.

Types of Video

If you're going to communicate with video people or purchase video equipment, you need to know just a little bit of terminology. There are five different video connections that you may encounter, and you need to understand which one(s) your equipment supports.

VGA and EGA connectors

VGA output is the standard for computer monitors. It stands for Virtual Graphics Array (not that you really care) and is a high-resolution digital format, usually supporting up to 800x600 pixel resolution. The expensive displays may go up to 1024x768, 1280x1024 or even 1600x1200 resolution. There are various extended formats like SVGA and XGA, but VGA is by far the most common standard interface. VGA uses DB-15 connectors, which are D-shaped with three rows of pins (it's the cable on the left in the photo on page 93).

EGA is an older color monitor standard, which is rarely found on notebook computers anymore, but is supported by quite a few display systems. It uses a DB-9 connector that is the same shape as the VGA connector, but has only two rows of pins (the one on the right in the photo on page 93). It is not compatible with VGA, and you can't just use an adapter cable to connect EGA equipment to VGA equipment. Most EGA equipment supports only 640x480 resolution.

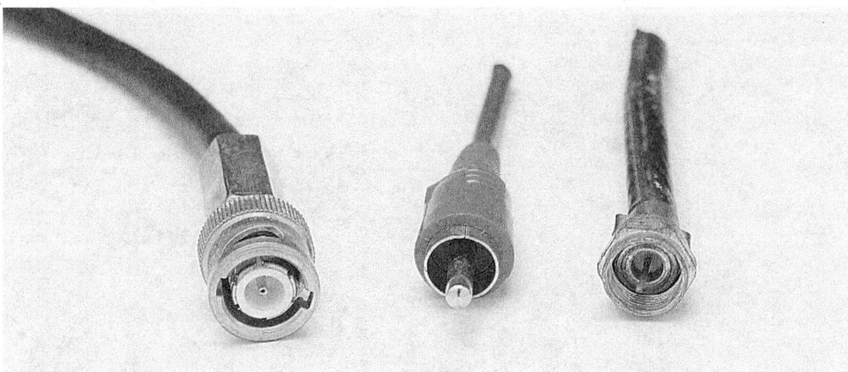

BNC, RCA and F connectors

Antenna video goes to that "Ant/Cable" jack on your television. It usually uses a coaxial cable that's fairly thick and has an F-type connector on the end, as shown on the right in the photo above. The connector is round with a piece of copper wire sticking out in the middle. The connector is usually threaded to screw onto the jack, but sometimes they just slip into place. Antenna or cable signals can carry many modulated channels on the same wire and are usually the lowest quality picture you can get.

NTSC video, also known as composite video, is a higher-quality signal that carries only one picture, rather than the multiple channels on the antenna wire. Home video equipment uses RCA connectors (the middle cable in the photo above) — the same plugs you use on your stereo equipment. The jack on the television or VCR is usually labeled "Video in." Professional video equipment uses the same signal, but with a locking connector called a BNC or bayonet connector (the left-hand cable in the photo above). The end of the cable slides over a post, and then twists to lock in place.

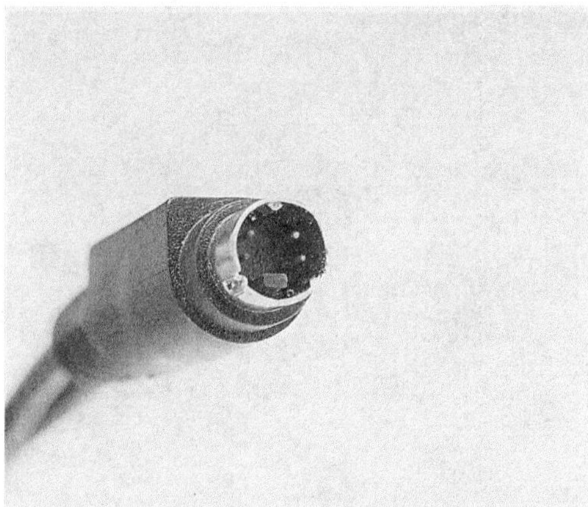

DIN connector

S-Video is a higher-quality signal than standard home NTSC. The name comes from "Super VHS," which is a type of videotape. While still not as high quality as computer video, S-Video is the best you'll find in consumer equipment without going digital. S-Video also eliminates or reduces the red smear that NTSC video is known for.

S-Video uses DIN connectors, which are round with the pins spaced in a circle (pictured above). Just as the BNC connector is used in professional equipment instead of an RCA connector, there is a professional S-Video connector, too. It, like the consumer connector, is a DIN, but it is larger. You are unlikely to encounter these in your everyday CART or captioning work.

Engineers may refer to S-Video as Y/C video. Don't ask why. You don't want to know.

Be Adaptable

If you'll be doing a lot of CART or captioning work, pick up a handful of various adapters, and keep them in your laptop case.

BNC to RCA adapters and RCA to BNC adapters will come in handy many times. Hotel AV departments and TV engineers may have BNC cables when your equipment has RCA connectors or vice versa. For under $20, you can get a set of adapters that will cover most contingencies.

BNC and RCA adapters

In this photo, there are three BNC to RCA (or vice versa) adapters in the upper-left corner, plus some other useful adapters as well.

In the bottom-left corner are two barrel connectors (BNC on the left, RCA on the right). These allow you to connect two short cables to form a single longer one.

The T-shaped device on the right is called (are you ready for this?) a T connector. You can plug the base of the "T" into your piece of equipment and then run two cables from it, using it as a splitter. Having one of these has saved my hide more than once.

Serial cable adapters

Normally, you will have your equipment set up and tested before you go, and you won't be renting computers and steno machines. Sometimes, however, you'll need to rent encoders or other serial-port devices, and it's very helpful to have a full set of serial cable adapters with you.

The three devices at the top of the photo convert from the 25-pin serial connector (called a DB-25) that used to be the industry standard to the 9-pin connector (DB-9) used by all laptops and most other equipment. Carry at least two of these, one going from male DB-9 to female DB-25, and the other going from male DB-25 to female DB-9.[4]

At the bottom of the photo, you see some block-type devices, one 9-pin and one 25-pin. There are generally two types of block adapters, known as gender changers and null modems. A gender changer allows you to connect two female cables or two male cables. The wires inside a gender changer connect straight through. A null modem adapter usually has a male connector on one end and female on the other and can be hooked up either way. Internally, the send and receive lines are swapped over, so it can be used to hook two computers together without using a modem (hence the other common name for this device: the modem eliminator).

---

[4] *The male connector is the one with the pins. The female is the one with the holes. Hey, I didn't make up this terminology, I'm just telling you what it is!*

CART Equipment

CAT/CART Software

Most court reporters have already invested in CAT software, so it makes sense to use what you already have. If you are in the market for something new, however, then you have some other alternatives available.

SHOPPING: CAT VS. TEXT ENTRY

Many CAT software companies, in addition to their main CAT product, offer a program designed specifically for high-speed text entry. Examples are RapidWrite, OpenWrite, RapidText and RiTE (see the Resources section on page 271 for manufacturers and contact information).

Usually, text-entry software costs quite a bit less than CAT software, which can lessen the pain of the initial investment.

A text-entry program does the realtime translation and then feeds the text into some other program running on your computer. Typically, this will be a word processor, like Microsoft Word or Corel WordPerfect.

When you're shopping, here are some of the things to keep in mind:

- **Look specifically at realtime.** Unless you'll be using this program for court reporting work as well, don't be distracted by editing features and special litigation-support capabilities.

- **Look carefully at delays (lag times).** In court reporting work, it doesn't make a big difference if it takes a few extra seconds for your words to appear on the attorney's litigation-support screen. In CART work, delays can lead to confusion. You want your text to go out as fast as possible.

- **Talk to others before you decide.** Knowing others on the same software can help build an informal peer-based support system. If there's a user group in your area, ask if you can attend a meeting.

- **Look at *all* of the costs.** Look past the initial purchase price and consider the cost of support, updates and upgrades, and hidden "gotchas" in the contract. For example, some vendors actually charge a fee when you sell their software, so if you get out of the business in a few years, you won't recover as much of the software cost as you think.[5] Service contracts can have hidden costs, too. For example, vendors may state that updates are free, but charge a $50 shipping and handling fee to send it to you. A disturbing trend in the software industry is the elimination of printed documentation. You get documentation on CD, and if you want a manual, you have to either print it yourself or buy a copy.

- **Check the hours for the support line.** CART work often happens outside normal business hours. If you have a problem when realtiming at night school, during a Sunday church service or in a Saturday seminar, you want to make sure help will be available if you need it.

- **Check copy-protection policies.** What happens if you run into a problem on the job and forget your dongle (software key)? Can the vendor activate the software over the phone? Is there a launch code of some kind? Can you get a spare key to keep in your steno case or notebook case?

A good realtime software package stands invisibly between your steno machine and the realtime text display. The audience won't notice it, and you won't have to think about it.

Setting Up Your Screen(s)

If you're doing CART, small groups are easy. If it's just a few people, then a large VGA monitor may be enough. Virtually all notebook computers have a port for connecting an external monitor, so you can just plug one in and go.

The methods for making your notebook use the external VGA connec-

---

5 *They call these "software license transfer fees." They can get away with this practice because the purchase agreement with these vendors says that you never actually* own *the software you're buying — you're just paying for the right to use it. You can't sell it to someone else unless they approve the purchaser and you pay them a fee.*

tion vary. Some use a DOS utility, some use a magic function key on the keyboard, and some use a special driver configured with the Display Properties setting in Windows.[6] Some detect an external VGA monitor when they boot up and switch to it automatically, which means you have to reboot to hook up a monitor. Figure out in advance which method yours uses and practice it.

I hired a CART reporter once for a meeting, and she arrived with notebook computer and steno machine, ready to go. We plugged the big screen into her VGA port and told her to switch to external display. She had no idea how to do it. We ended up delaying the meeting by almost half an hour while we called tech support for the company that made her notebook computer to find out how to switch it. Do you think that group ever called her back?

Some notebook computers allow you to use your internal LCD screen at the same time as an external VGA monitor. If you're buying a new computer, look for this feature. It allows you to see what you're doing while using a monitor that's aimed away from you (hopefully toward your audience).

If there are only a couple of people, and they will be sitting close, then a single standard monitor (14 or 15 inches) should be fine. You will probably want to enlarge the text, but you won't need a bigger screen. Even with a DOS screen, I've used 19-inch monitors (with large type) for people as far as 15 feet away with no complaints, which accommodates about a dozen people.

One alternative to using bigger screens is to use more of them. Black Box Corporation, for example, sells a line of VGA video splitters that allow you to connect multiple monitors, spacing them as far as 250 feet apart. Prices range from about $300 for the two-way splitter up to about $1,200 for the 10-way.

---

[6] *To do this, right-click on the Windows background or wallpaper and select Properties. One of the tabs in the window that pops up should let you switch between your internal LCD screen and the external monitor.*

TV Sets

Sometimes the best way to show your realtime text to the audience is the simplest solution: a TV set. Televisions are considerably less expensive than computer monitors, and large ones are easier to find.

Televisions in the 27- to 35-inch range work well for a medium-sized meeting, but they're bulky and difficult to carry around. You'll probably want to see if the facility can provide you with one rather than trying to drag your own out to the site. This is especially true if you have to travel. I've found that the typical consumer TV set doesn't survive long when you're shipping it from site to site, and the rental cost isn't much more than the shipping cost.

NTSC video resolution is not as good as even the cheapest of PC monitors. If you use small text, the picture that looks sharp and clear on your notebook screen will look fuzzy and illegible on the television, even at 640x480 resolution. Again, S-Video helps out here, because it increases the resolution, but most consumer video equipment doesn't support S-Video.

Make the text large, and if you have selectable fonts, pick one that's simple and easy to read. Making the font bold may help readability and contrast, but stay away from italics.

Keep your text away from the edges of the screen. Many of the scan converters (devices that convert computer video to NTSC video) clip off some of the video at the top, bottom and sides.

In the picture on the next page, you see a hybrid solution we used at a meeting of the California chapter of the Alexander Graham Bell Society (an association of educators and parents of deaf children).

The realtimer,[7] located under the far left television, is using captioning software in this example, but it could just as easily be CAT software for this application. This uses a daisy-chain approach for the video to save the trouble and expense of a video splitter.

---

[7] *Yes, that's my wife, Kathy.*

The realtime text goes from the realtimer's main computer using a serial cable to a second "display" computer, which in this case is a notebook visible in the picture on the table in front of the realtimer. If you're using CAT software on your main computer, you might choose to use realtime litigation-support software on this system, like CaseView, Total Access, Summation or LiveNote, if you can get a clean, uncluttered display that you like. At this meeting, we were using a program that I wrote called CARTscreen, which translates caption encoder data into a smooth-scrolling display with a highly readable font.[8]

Why use two computers? It's more trouble to set up and cart around (or CART around, as the case may be), but you'll be glad you did it. This way, when you want to add some dictionary entries, change setup or perform other editing tasks, the audience won't be watching what you're doing, since they can't see your main computer screen.

---

[8] *The font that I prefer for applications like this is Verdana, which was designed specifically for readability on computer screens, especially at small sizes and on low-resolution devices. If you wish to use it, you can download it from the microsoft.com Web site or get it from recent releases of Microsoft Internet Explorer, where it is bundled in for free.*

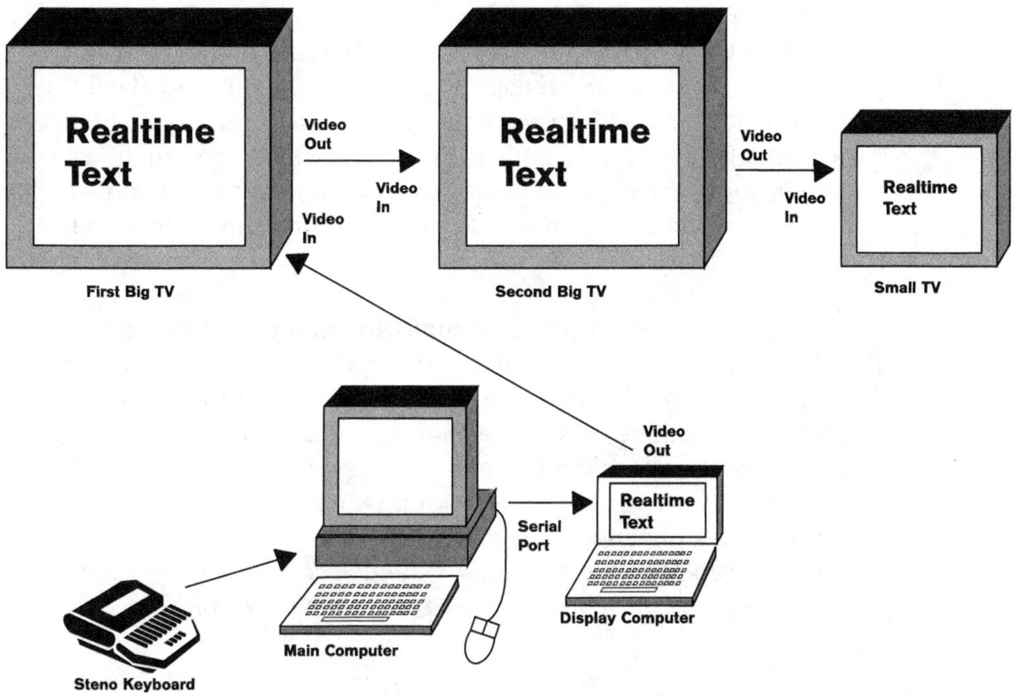

This particular notebook computer has an NTSC video output on the back, which can be run directly into the "video in" connector on a TV set. If your computer doesn't have such a connection, you can buy or rent a device called a "scan converter" or "VGA→NTSC converter." It allows your computer screen to be displayed on a TV set. Professional quality scan converters are quite expensive, but an acceptable unit for CART is much less. One popular device, the AVerKey, can be purchased for a couple hundred dollars.

The large television above the captioner's head in the picture is a 27-inch set. With text this size (seven lines of about 20 to 25 characters each), it is clearly readable from 45 feet, and people with good eyes can read it from even farther away. With one television in the front left side of the room and one in the front right, you can easily accommodate an audience of over 100 people. By using TV sets with "video out" connections, we could just run a video cable from the computer to the first television, and another cable to the second television.

A key word in the above paragraph is "audience." The two large televisions took care of the audience, but what about the people on the podium? In the photo on page 102, you see a panel of deaf college students who can't easily lipread questions from the audience. To accommodate their needs, we added a third television — the small white one sitting above the captioner's computer in the photo. Even a 13-inch set is clearly readable for the whole panel and from the lectern 10 feet away.

The best way to gauge the readability for your particular setup is to test it in advance. You don't need a lecture hall to do this — a little math takes care of everything. I can't give you a formula that says letters "X" inches high can be read "Y" feet away, because there are so many other factors, like the font family, color choices and letter spacing. What you should do is measure the size of your computer screen, and then stand back varying distances to see how well you can read the screen. If you have very good eyesight, enlist the help of someone who wears glasses so that you're able to accommodate everyone involved.

Let's say your text can be read from a distance of 15 feet, and you've measured your screen at 13.5 inches diagonally.[9] Divide the readability distance by the screen size to get a number we'll call the readability distance factor for your font and color choices. Just to make you feel like a geek insider, we'll acronymize (cool word, eh?) that and call it our RDF. Remember what units you used! In this case, we're using feet for the distance and inches for the screen size, so you'll need to stick with it. Our RDF is 15/13.5, or 1.11 feet per inch.

Next measure the TV sets you'll be using for the display, and multiply their size by your RDF to find their readability distance. Let's say you find that they have a 32.5-inch display (fairly typical for a 35-inch television). Our RDF of 1.11 times a TV size of 32.5 gives a readability distance of about 36 feet.

---

[9] *Don't just use the size the salespeople gave you for your screen. In the United States, manufacturers give the size of the picture tube, which is often quite different from the actual usable screen size. As I write this, I'm using a 17-inch screen, which has an actual usable display area of 15.5 inches from corner to corner.*

Your screens do not have to be visible all the way from the back of the room unless your entire audience will be using them. Ask the coordinator for the event how many people in the audience will require captions and whether it is OK to seat them all in one area. With typical theater-style seating and a display about six feet in front of the front row, our 36-foot example would cover a half-circle going back 10 rows in the middle and stretching about 20 rows to each side.

This same formula applies to everything from computer monitors to huge video projectors. When you've arrived at a display setup that you like, memorize (or write down) the RDF, including the units. Then, when people ask how far away they'll be able to read the text on a 20-foot diagonal projection screen, you'll be able to swiftly tell them it's about 266 feet (20 feet is 240 inches, multiplied by your RDF of 1.11 is 266 feet).

Any time you change display programs, fonts, text size, colors, line spacing, character spacing or even switch between all caps and upper/lowercase, you should recalculate your RDF.

Video Projectors

When you're dealing with a large group, nothing can substitute for a good video projector. They're quite expensive, so you'll probably want to rent one unless you'll be using it a lot. A projector that you'd pay $7,000 for would probably rent for $500 per day. Do your homework, do the math and make your own decision.

Prices have been coming down fast in recent years, and it's likely that LCD projectors will be available in the $1,000 range soon — maybe even by the time you read this. The LCD projectors are much easier to use than the traditional RGB projectors, as they don't have to be aligned. Unless you know how to do the alignment and convergence yourself, you'll need to make sure the hotel's AV person is there with you during setup. The adjustment process can take as long as half an hour.

A video projector is the only reasonable way to handle captioning for large groups. Make sure you work with the videographer beforehand, though, to ensure that the top or bottom of the screen is kept clear for your captions. Although the bottom of the screen is the typical position for broadcast captions, I like putting the captions at the top for meetings, so that people in the back of the room can see them better. This requires cooperation with the videographer, who usually positions people's heads near the top of the screen for the same reason.

I've used traditional Sony video projectors connected to a notebook computer screen for CART with groups as large as 650 people. In that case, it was projecting onto a screen almost 20 feet wide and could be clearly read from anywhere in the room. These projectors are incredibly bright, so you don't have to turn out the lights like you would with an LCD panel (see below), but they'll still work best if the lights in the room are dimmed.

Older video projectors often had only NTSC video inputs (or possibly S-Video), but you can count on most of the newer ones having VGA input as well. This produces much crisper, sharper output than going through a scan converter. Any time you have a choice between VGA and NTSC, always opt for VGA.

Overhead Projector Panels

The same VGA port you use for an external monitor can be used to plug your notebook computer into a device known as an LCD panel or overhead projector panel. These are flat screens about a foot square and an inch thick. They sit on top of an overhead projector and allow your computer screen to be projected on a wall.

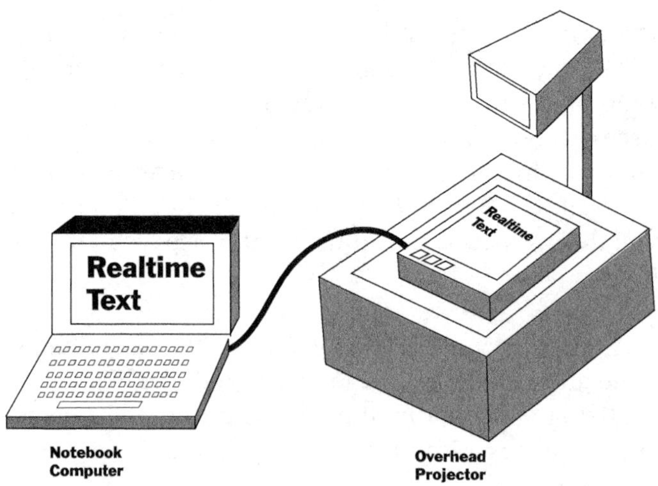

LCD panels can be rented from most hotel AV services and from video and equipment rental businesses in most major cities. You can purchase your own, but they are still fairly pricey. Expect to spend from $2,000 to $4,000, depending on features. LCD panels are also becoming less and less common with the advent of integrated low-cost portable LCD video projectors. InFocus, one of my favorite brands of LCD panel, now makes only projectors and has discontinued their line of LCD panels entirely.

I've used LCD panels for groups as large as 120 people, and the text is still readable in the back of the room, although it's marginal. That was in the days of DOS displays, and you could probably get away with even more if you used a good, clean Windows display with high contrast. Your biggest concern will be the light level. The room must be kept dim, if not dark, for the screen image to be readable. You'll get the best results using a very high contrast, like black text on white.

If you're renting the overhead projector, make sure it's the kind with the light source in the base as on the left, not the kind with the overhead light source and the reflector underneath.

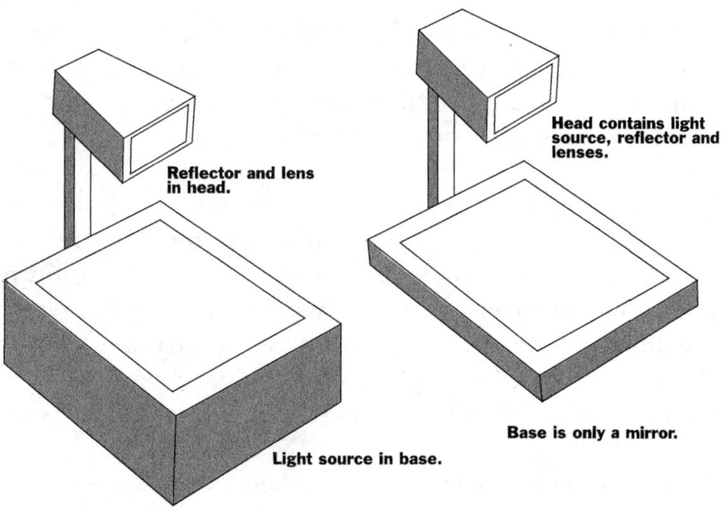

Since the light would have to pass through the LCD display twice to hit the reflector and come back up, using an overhead light source produces a display so dark it is completely illegible.

LED Signs

You see these signs all over the place, from train stations to the neighborhood deli. They range from about three feet long to gigantic, from a single line of text to four (some big custom signs have as many as eight). The letters are usually red, but some signs have yellow and green as well.

If you want to use an LED sign, talk to your software vendor to see what's supported. Some vendors support the signs only in their captioning software and others in their CAT software. Most support only one or two brands. Again, this is an important point — don't purchase or rent a sign until you've confirmed with your software vendor that it will work. Some of these signs can't do realtime at all. They are designed to have a fixed block of text loaded in, which they repeat over and over.

The Silent Radio sign is probably the most popular for CART reporters. An eight-foot-long sign with two lines of text is bright and readable from over 100 feet away, even in a well-lit room.

A Final Piece of CART Advice

If I were to sum up the whole subject of CART with a single piece of advice, it would have to be, "Test your setup before you use it." The better you prepare, the better your product will be, and the higher the likelihood that you'll be invited back.

Make sure you can recover from errors, too. See what happens if various cables come unplugged while you're working. Can you just plug them back in, or do you have to reset something? Do you know how? Shut everything down and start it up again from scratch. Do it again, until the process is smooth and easy. Carry a spare of every cable you use. Carry extra extension cords, power strips and power cords. Carry some duct tape to tape your cables down so that nobody trips over them.

If you go after the big jobs, you're likely to be competing with some extremely talented and knowledgeable captioners and CART reporters. In the big leagues, you have precisely one chance to prove that you know what you're doing, so put the equipment together beforehand, test it extensively and exude confidence when you walk in the door.

Chapter 4

Bloopers

Since realtime captioning involves real, live people writing as fast as they can, typos (or, as stenocaptioners call them, "misstrokes") are inevitable. Unlike typing, where an error results in one incorrect letter, a misstroke can change an entire word or phrase, often with amusing results.

Sometimes misstrokes lead to gibberish, and sometimes they make more sense than the original text. Oftentimes the results are racy or ribald. I've left the more offensive examples out, but this section includes a smattering of "dirty bloopers." If that might offend you, perhaps it's time for you to skip ahead to the next chapter.

OK, if you're still with me, you're ready to go. First, we'll take a look at how these malignant misfingerings metamorphose into magnificently merry malapropisms. Then, we can just sit back and enjoy the fun with a list of other great bloopers.

One other note: These bloopers are real, not urban legend. With each of them, I either saw it myself or got it from the stenocaptioner who blooped it. With one or two exceptions, I've omitted the captioner's name from the blooper in order to protect the innocent, as well as the guilty.

Anatomy of a Blooper

Martin Block, the father of realtime captioning, had begun his groundbreaking realtime captioning of the evening news for the National

Captioning Institute in 1982. He had worked as a court reporter for almost 20 years and had spent months honing his dictionary in preparation for taking realtime news captions on the air. One of the lead stories for the night was the death of Arthur Rubenstein, the world-famous pianist.

In all those years of working as a court reporter, Marty had never had to write the word *pianist.* It just doesn't come up in lawsuits very often. Marty, not realizing it wasn't in his dictionary, went ahead and wrote it. Have you figured out where this is going yet? Indeed, viewers with decoders that night saw:

"The world-famous *penis,* Arthur Rubenstein, died tonight."

Not having a word in the dictionary came back and bit a CART reporter with this one:

"I'd like to introduce the *bitch hop's* [Bishop's] regional director ..."

Homonyms

Another cause of bloopers is homonyms — words that sound alike, but are spelled differently. These cause serious headaches for court reporters and stenocaptioners who are used to writing phonetically. They take great care to write *to, two* and *too* differently, but every now and then something sneaks by:

"Up next, Joey Buttafuoco and his torrid *tail* [tale]."

"We can park the bikes and put the *lox* [locks] on them."

"Men with *sauce* [saws] climb the branches the kids once did."

Of course, sometimes this will happen even when the words aren't quite homonyms, but they are very close. That is what happened with these gems:

"Next up: Dining out with Pavarotti. What kind of a *male* [meal] does a large star consume?"

Female anchor: "What's that smell?"
Male anchor: "It's my *colon* [cologne]."

"I've been a *liar* [lawyer] all my life. It's what I do for a living, and I enjoy it."

I wonder if the stenocaptioner was making a subconscious statement of opinion about attorneys there? Hmmm.

Word-Boundary Problems

The homonym problem is exacerbated when you realize that *combinations* of words can form homonyms, depending on where you break the words apart. Court reporters and stenocaptioners call such combinations word-boundary problems, like when a courtroom reporter didn't have *acidic* in her dictionary, and the realtime transcript referred to an "*acid dick* solution." Ouch!

A perfect broadcast example of a word-boundary problem was when a sportscaster was interviewing San Francisco 49er football player Jerry Rice. When asked what kind of person quarterback Steve Young was, Rice responded by saying:

"He's a *fungi* [fun guy] to be around."

When former San Francisco Mayor Frank Jordan spoke, this was the result:

"I thank each and every one of you for allowing me to participate in the *grandpa raid* [grand parade] of San Francisco history."

Realtime translation of steno shorthand into English is complex. When a steno stroke, or strokes, appears that the computer doesn't recognize, it does its best to fit something to it. Sometimes the combination of strokes for a long, unrecognized word actually makes sense (to the computer, anyway) when split apart into several shorter words. That's what happened here:

"This whole situation is *lewd crows* [ludicrous]."

"Phoenix, bludgeoned by pigeon lovers, has decided not to *piss on* [poison] the pigeons."

And in this embarrassing exchange:

"Q. And they worked as —"

"A. *Asshole sale* [As wholesale] producers."

Misstrokes

Then you have just plain misstrokes. When deaf viewers see a single letter wrong, they understand that it's a typo. They often don't understand that missing just one of the keys that makes up a word ending can turn a word into something utterly different. Part of your mission is to educate everyone you talk to about how stenotype theory can produce these with just a single misfingering.

A misstroke doubling as a double entendre showed up on Kathy's first newscast. It was the night Audrey Hepburn died. What is it about death, first-time news captioners and sexual bloopers?

"Audrey Hepburn has *laid* [played] with some of Hollywood's greatest leading men."

Here are a few more:

"President Clinton addresses the *nag* [nation] at 6:00."

"George is *wilted* [wild] and crazy for one hour."

"... a *bowel* [bowl] of fruit."

"Sometimes you just have to tell the *prick* [public] to wait."

Fixing a Misstroke

Your options for backing up and correcting errors are limited in broadcast captioning. Once the caption decoder moves on to a new line, your blooper is there forever (or at least until you clear the screen). For that reason, many CART reporters and captioners will simply write a dash followed by the correct word. Most of the time, that's a good thing. Sometimes, it can make the blooper even funnier. How about this exchange from a British newscast where a news reporter was planted outside 10 Downing Street awaiting an important announcement:

Anchor: "So what's going on there now? Any sign yet?"

Reporter: "No, the sex-session has been going on for 15 minutes now and still no sign ..."

In another case, the realtimer knew that his CART session would include a doctor from the Department of Corrections. He loaded up his medical job dictionary in which some common medical words are defined several ways to avoid bloopers. In this case, he got a whopper of a double blooper out of it:

"I'm with the Maryland Department of *erections* [Corrections], and I'm here this evening to talk about services available in the *penile* [penal] system."[1]

Briefs

When a particular word or phrase comes up a lot, your instinct is to create a brief form for it. When you're writing realtime captioning or CART, watch out for your briefs! A brief for Nelson Mandela that was a tad too similar to a brief for a prominent (at the time) figure skater led to the captions in one newscast announcing that Nancy Kerrigan had just become president of South Africa!

One captioner told me that he was preparing for a newscast and came up with a new brief for a phrase that was to be used repeatedly. Unfortunately, he didn't define it properly. Thanks to the phonetic translator, it came out:

"Prince Andrew and the *dork* [Duchess of York] have now boarded the plane ..."

---

[1] *Hmmm. Maryland must be more progressive than I thought.*

Stacking

Our last category is stacking, where one stroke piles up on another one. In a live government meeting, Jack Boenau managed to stack a comma onto his stroke for *gentlemen,* and when a group of high-ranking officials were invited into the room, he wrote:

">> CHAIRMAN: *Jerks* please come in."

Ouch! That's also how this one came up during the Olympics. The announcer was talking about a member of the women's luge team and mentioned that her brother was also a luger. The next word, *who,* stacked up on the *er* in *luger* to produce:

"Her brother, also a *luge whore* ..."

That one actually resulted in complaints to the network.

More Bloopers, Just for Fun

Enough explanation? Let's just take a look at some more word-boundary and homonym problems and just plain boo-boos.

Sports

"The Giants say goodbye to exhibition baseball: *Spraining* [spring] training is over."

"Tom Watson, flirting with the leaderboard, nice *butt* [putt] at the 7th."

"And a great basketball player, out for two weeks with an *anal* [ankle] injury."

"We were able to sit down with members of the A's who *wormed* [worked] under Walter Haas Junior."

"A shot of Ken Harrelson, the former *White Sex* [White Sox] announcer."

"A 1:00 *sickoff* [kickoff] in San Diego, Sunday."

"The Braves won, too, so it comes down to a *thigh breaker* [tie-breaker] Monday night if necessary."

"And there's the *jello* [yellow] flag."

"I've been in New York before, but I've never *squatted* [skated] in this rink."

"Randall *uncan country ham* [Cunningham] is one of the best scramblers of all time."

And Now, on to the News

"... *fartly* [partly] cloudy skies."

"Now, John has the *nudes* [news] for us."

"*Erection* [election] night coverage ..."

"It turned out to be a *stink* [sting] operation by police."

"A large *shrimp* [shrimp boat] carrying a half ton of marijuana was seized earlier today."

"President Clinton hopes it will provide a basis for new *regular layings* [regulations] as well as voluntary standards."

"He had just exchanged rings and *vowels*[2] [vows] with his new bride."

"A low voter *tushout* [turnout] is expected."

"... Jordan becoming the *sexed* [sixth] nation to make formal peace with Israel."

"Now you can go to McDonald's and order *flies* [fries] and a Coke."

"His future is *sobriety* [so bright], he had to wear shades."

---

[2] *You don't suppose this fellow was marrying Vanna White, do you?*

"There was *areola salt* [a real assault]."

"The next step is culling out the *dumb cats* [duplicates]."

"I think *urine tract* [you're on track] with that one."

"This will be the best weekend for aspen *screwing* [viewing]."

"Good morning. I'm David *Heartburn* [Hartman]."

"That is unacceptable and stunning coming from a *syphilised* [civilized] democracy."

"The whole Mideast is such an incredible place. I like to think of it as a *hole* [home]."

"*Hell* [hello], David. Getting tired of seeing me this morning?"

"*Rot* [Rod] Stuart will be with us today."

"He denied the *wrong dong* [wrongdoing], but the question persisted."

And Some CART and Legal Miscellany

"Look at this *cross-sexual* [cross-sectional] diagram."

"That was the *sexy thought* [section I thought] I was referring to this morning."

"You have *aunts* [ants] in your pants?"

"*Icky lab rat* [I can elaborate]."

Chapter 5

Getting Started

Preparing for an Alternative Realtime Career

How you prepare for a job in CART or captioning depends largely on the skills and experience you already have. If, for example, you are a working official court reporter who writes in realtime every day, with output for your judge and the attorneys, you will require far less prep than a court reporting student getting ready to graduate.

"Far less prep," however, does not mean no preparation at all. If you've gotten this far in the book, you have already seen many differences between traditional court reporting and CART or captioning. No matter how much experience you have, read this section and look for steps you haven't yet taken.

Developing Your Skills

The first step is to develop your realtime skills. Equally important is to develop your *confidence* in your realtime skills. Realtime everything in sight. If you work as a court reporter, and you're not doing realtime every day, now is the time to start. Even if nobody in the room is interested in realtime, set up a notebook computer and watch what comes out when you write. Most reporters I've spoken to who have taken this step said that the number of untranslates in their writing went down by half in the first month.

Decide what you'd like to be captioning, and use it as practice material. Do you want to caption sports? Set up your system in front of the television and realtime every sporting event you watch. Would you like to do CART in college courses? See if you can get tapes of the kind of classes you are interested in. If you look just at those two examples, you'll see what a huge difference there can be in vocabulary.

Remember that you're likely to be tested when you look for a job. You and your dictionary must both be ready. If you intend to walk in the door at a captioning company and say, "Make me a sports captioner," you had better know the names of all the major league teams, their coaches and their star players. You had better know whether *touchdown* is one word or two. Make sure *Red Sox* doesn't translate as *red socks.*

Knowing what's current isn't enough. Winston Churchill is dead, but his name still comes up. A current football player may be compared to Joe Namath, or a current baseball player to Joe DiMaggio.

Certification

When your résumé or curriculum vitae joins a stream of dozens or even hundreds of others, you need to make sure it will stand out. The most prominent item on the page will be your name. Make sure there are some letters after it, like CSR, RPR, CRR and so forth. If you attended a school that offers a degree, see what it takes to get the degree. You may not think a two-year degree like an AS or AA is very impressive, but it shows you have the determination and persistence required to get it. Add those letters after your name as well.

Aren't those certifications just for the top people? Absolutely not. Many firms won't even consider your résumé unless you have at least a CSR or RPR certification. And if you're good enough to do captioning or CART professionally, you're good enough to pass the CRR. That doesn't mean you *will* pass it the first time. Test-taking nerves can cause even the most skilled people to freeze up and blow a test.

Believe me, though, it's worth it. The letters "CRR" after your name will move your résumé to the top of the pile and make it one of the first to be read.

Writing a Résumé or CV

A résumé is structured to show where you have worked and what your responsibilities were when you worked there. The curriculum vitae format, on the other hand, focuses on your accomplishments instead. You can choose either format, but a CV is usually more appropriate in captioning and CART, as a structured overview of your abilities and experience is more relevant than a list of where you've worked in the past. For simplicity, and to avoid saying "résumé or CV" throughout this section, we'll just call it a résumé.

Don't get overly fancy and artistic about the résumé. You're trying to get a job as a captioner, not an artist. Keep it simple, *readable*, professional, *readable*, concise and *readable*. And did I mention *readable?* Nothing's worse than a résumé prepared with eight-point script type. If the manager has to get out a magnifying glass and squint, the résumé is going in the trash.

Create your résumé with care. It may well be the most important document related to captioning or CART that you ever write. Let's go through some tips for creating a résumé, and then look at some good and bad examples.

Proofread, Proofread, Proofread

You are looking for a job that requires exacting and extensive knowledge of the English language. Perfectionism is not just prized, but expected. Tammie Shedd, who spent many years as the manager of realtime captioning at NCI, says that she looked for well-written résumés that demonstrate good grammar and punctuation skills. If your résumé had a spelling error, you *might* still get a chance to interview. If it had *two* spelling errors, it went straight into the garbage can.

This doesn't just apply to the résumé itself. Check over the cover letter and the envelope. If you aren't sure of the spelling of the firm name or the name of the individual you're sending the résumé to, call and verify it. If you misspell the name of the firm, your envelope may not even be opened.

A spelling checker isn't enough. It won't catch egregious errors in grammar, misuse of homonyms and capitalization or punctuation errors. All of these seriously damage your chances of getting the job.

The grammar checker in your word processor may help, but don't rely on it. Have someone else proofread your résumé for you.

Provide Complete Contact Information

You never know whether the company will want to contact you by phone, fax, regular mail or e-mail, so include everything. If you are using your home answering machine, make sure that the message is clear so that that person knows it's the right number.

Amy Bowlen, who hires the realtime captioners for VITAC, says that an e-mail address is important to her. "I've played phone tag with people for days," she told me, "when I could have taken care of everything with an e-mail message."

Include Information That Builds Your Credibility

The purpose of your résumé is to establish your credentials and show that you're the right person for the job. Anything that directly demonstrates useful skills or experience belongs on the résumé. Some of the things you should list on your résumé are:

- **Credentials.** All of them. Even if they've expired. This would include court reporting credentials (e.g., a CSR, RPR, RMR, RDR, CRR), college degrees, certificates of completion and teaching credentials. You never know which one might be the one that catches your future employer's attention. Even if you think that old associate degree in marine biology is totally irrelevant, it might be very important to a firm that's going to be captioning a nature show about ocean life or that needs someone to perform CART in a college biology department. Also, a college degree is a message to an employer that you are able to stick to something and finish it. Always include degrees.

- **Pro bono work.** This indicates to your potential employer that you're dedicated to your profession and you care about your customers. And, of course, experience is experience, whether you're paid for it or not.

- **Any relevant article or papers you've written.** Writing about your profession reinforces your reputation as an expert in your field and indicates your willingness to share what you know. Good writing is a further demonstration of your English skills, which are obviously crucial to a captioner or CART reporter.

- **All teaching or speaking experience.** Have you lectured at the local court reporting school? Did you put on a seminar for your state court reporting association? Have you spoken at high school career days about court reporting, captioning or CART? Again, activities like this build up your credibility as an expert.

- **Memberships.** A registered membership in NCRA requires continuing education, which is the mark of a dedicated professional. Memberships in other associations show how seriously you take your profession. If you've ever held office in any of those associations, list it. Firms take pride in the accomplishments of their people. Firm owners and their public relations, sales and marketing people love to be able to say, "We have a past president of our state association working here."

- **Related organizations.** Have you served on an advisory board for a court reporting school? For a deaf group? Have you worked on committees for community service organizations, such as chambers of commerce and clubs like the Elks, Lions or Rotary International? List them. Just one line each will do. Details are not required.

- **Foreign language skills.** There have been times when I've looked at two similar résumés and chosen the one with foreign language skills, because learning other languages increases your overall communications skill. It helps you deal with spelling foreign names and words that slip into our language. Having someone on staff who's fluent in another language may be the edge that gets the company a big contract. Make sure you specify how fluent you actually are, and be ready to back it up in the interview. If your language skills match a current requirement, the company may well have someone present in the interview who can test your fluency, or the potential employer may give you something to translate.

- **Sign language skills.** Captioners and CART reporters deal with deaf people. If you have any training or experience with ASL or SEE, by all means mention it. If you are fluent, highlight it. If you're actually a certified sign interpreter, make a big point of it. That's a huge selling point for you.

List the Types of Work You've Realtimed

Have you realtimed a wide variety of different work? Great! List the categories on your résumé. Some people actually make custom versions of their résumé for each firm they send it to, highlighting the types of work that firm does.

This can be a good thing. If, for example, you're applying for work at World's Biggest Sports Captioning Firm Inc., you'll want them to know you've captioned foosball tournaments and Saturday night bowling. Make a point of it.

This can also be a bad thing. You may play up your months of sports experience and downplay your years of realtiming corporate board meetings, only to discover that the company just landed a huge contract for board meetings. By downplaying it, you may have blown the job.

Just list the categories and give some indication of which ones you consider to be your specialties.

List the Most Important Information First

Unless the people doing the hiring are experiencing a serious dearth of résumés, in which case they'll read everything, you need to get their attention early. Show your strengths first. That will get the readers' attention and encourage them to read on.

Don't Clutter Up the Résumé With Irrelevancies

Do *not* include data like your marital status, number of children or age. That information may help or may hurt, but leaving it out is always safe. Keep in mind as well that the interviewer is prevented by law from asking these questions.

Also, do not include statements like "My father was a court reporter," or "I've always enjoyed watching television" or "My favorite hobby is mountain climbing." The résumé is a professional document intended to demonstrate your applicable work experience, not details of your private life. If you feel that any of those details are important, include them in the cover letter, not in the résumé itself.

Never Point Out the Negatives

Think of your résumé as your own personal sales brochure. Sell yourself! You never see a car brochure that says, "Really fast, but the trunk is incredibly tiny," do you? Once you've got them interested, they'll probe for weaknesses during the interview, and you should answer honestly. Listing your faults in the résumé may keep you from ever *getting* that interview in the first place, and it's a telltale sign of low self-esteem to the employer.

Keep it Totally Truthful

If you pad your résumé, you'll eventually get caught. This isn't a "good will triumph over evil" homily. It's close to a statistical certainty. I've read a lot of résumés over the years, and every time I've discovered something that wasn't true, that résumé has gone straight in the trash.

Keep it Short and Sweet

One or two pages is an ideal length. The people reading your résumé don't have a lot of time. A five-page résumé will not be read.

If your actual captioning and CART experience is limited, keep the résumé to a page. Don't fluff it out with extra material. If you have a lot of experience to list, focus on keeping it to two pages.

Keep References on a Separate List

This is mostly a matter of courtesy. If someone does you a favor by agreeing to act as a reference, you don't want them deluged by phone calls. You only want the firms that are *serious* about you to call.

Include the phrase "references available upon request" in your résumé, and have a printed sheet ready to send on a moment's notice.

Keeping the references separate also allows you to tweak the list depending on who you're sending it to, which is yet another part of the strategy of job-hunting.

Make sure you notify everyone on the list that you've included them and that they may be receiving calls about you. Not only is this the polite thing to do, but it gives your references a chance to think about what they're going to say.

Making Your Résumé Stand Out

When your résumé is sitting in a stack along with dozens of others, you want it to be easy to find and easy to remember. Avoid the temptation to do something really flashy, like write the résumé in a script font or print it on hot pink paper. This will make the résumé less readable and make you look less professional.

On the other hand, subtle ways of making the résumé stand out are good. Consider using a heavier paper, in a *delicate* color. Ivory, other off-whites or very pale blues and grays are good choices. If you have a color printer, use a dark color to highlight some important information, like the section headers and your name and contact information. Don't use something bright! Use a color that fits with the paper you picked. A dark navy blue, deep green or very dark burgundy works well. The use of color can be almost subliminal, and it will still make a surprisingly strong impact.

Simple graphics can help to make the résumé stand out as well. This does *not* mean color photos, clip-art cartoons or intricate borders. A simple dividing line or two makes a big difference.

You can be a bit more creative in your cover letter. Brighter colors, less formal fonts and a graphic image of some type on the stationery give the cover letter personality without detracting from the professionalism of the résumé.

E-mailing Résumés

E-mail can be a great way to send résumés, but you need to make sure the company is set up to accept them. Some companies have a single e-mail account that is only checked sporadically, and your résumé might not even get to the right person. Others have special e-mail addresses set up (resumes@company.com or jobs@company.com). Call the company's main number and ask. If you don't get some kind of acknowledgement in a week or two that your résumé has been received, it's OK to call and ask if the company got it, but don't call any sooner than that. You don't want to harass them.

When e-mailing your résumé, here are some important things to keep in mind:

- **Don't use attachments unless asked to.** Not everyone uses the same word processor you use. Most managers would rather get a 5K e-mail message that they can read in the e-mail program than a 40K attachment that they can't read, or that might potentially contain a virus. Some managers will specifically tell you to send your résumé as a Microsoft Word file or WordPerfect file. In that case, do as they asked.

- **Don't use formatted or HTML mail.** Yes, the fancy formatting looks great in your e-mail program, but what happens when it arrives at someone else's computer? When messages are going between different services and different programs, formatting can be mangled. Your beautiful green-on-beige résumé with the script text can come out as a string of meaningless gibberish, which doesn't make you look good.

- **Remember word wrapping.** Most e-mail programs wrap lines of incoming and/or outgoing text at somewhere between 72 and 80 characters. Send the résumé to yourself and to a few friends with different programs or services to ensure that it looks good *before* you start sending it out for real.

- **Don't just send a link.** Having your résumé on the Web is great. You can format it as you wish and provide links to relevant backup information. If you choose to do this, however, send the link *and* the text-only version of your résumé. That way, people without the time, access or inclination to visit your Web site can still read the résumé.

- **Don't attach pictures to the e-mail.** What you look like should make no difference to employers, and the picture files waste their time and disk space. Also, too much information can be a bad thing. Why send a picture if it might remind them of someone they don't like?

The Good, the Bad and the Ugly

Now that you've been deluged with tips on how to write a résumé, let's critique a few examples. This process can't be totally objective, as different managers react differently, but there are some things that are close to universal.

These résumés are fictitious, as are the names of all companies, courts and schools involved.

John Doe
101 Realtime Way • Reporterville, CO 94112
Home: 303/555-1212 • Email: jdoe@mail.com

Credentials

Degree:	AA in Court Reporting from Rocky Mt. Steno 1987
State:	State CSR License #9999 issued 1987
National:	RPR since 1987, RMR since 1991, CRR since 1994

Realtime Experience

Captioning:	Sat in on 2 newscasts Captioned one talk show on local cable TV
CART:	Public meeting for school board on deaf issues Volunteer at local SHHH meetings since 1999
Court:	Realtime for judge using CaseView since 1997

Business History

1994-present	Official Court Reporter Reporterville Municipal Court, Room 10
1991-1994	Official Court Reporter Mountain County Court, Room 22
1987-1991	Deposition Reporter Smith/Jones Reporting Service

Memberships and Volunteer Work

NCRA:	Member 1987-present Served on technology committee 1999
CCRA:	Member 1989-present
SHHH:	Volunteer CART reporter 1999-present
Other:	Guest lecturer at Rocky Mt. Steno once a year since 1993

References available upon request

The layout of John's résumé is clean and simple. It is all done with a single font family in only three different sizes, and bold and italics are used sparingly. It looks professional and readable. It would have been good to include a fax number on the contact information, but between snail mail, phone and e-mail address, there's probably enough.

Having dates on all of the credentials isn't really necessary, but the progression from RPR to RMR to CRR with a new credential every few years shows continuous self-improvement over an extended period of time, so in this case it is a good idea.

The realtime experience is good, as it shows both paid and volunteer work, and a relatively broad base for such limited experience. The categories should probably be listed in the reverse order, showing years of realtime experience in court before the skimpy captioning experience.

Most people include more business history information than this, showing actual responsibilities and accomplishments at each job. This résumé is short enough that there is plenty of room to add a few lines of accomplishments to each job and still fit comfortably on a single page.

The final section is good, although it might have been better to spell out what CCRA stands for when the résumé is being sent out-of-state. Managers *should* be able to figure out that it's the Colorado Court Reporter's Association, but there are other groups with the same acronym. The lectures at the court reporting school may sound insignificant, but including them sends some very good messages. First, it shows that John sticks with what he does, going back every year since 1993. Also, it shows that he's willing to volunteer time for his profession and that he's respected enough that the school asks him back every year to do it.

Jane's résumé (see next page) has problems. The overall look is fairly clean, but there are too many different fonts, and the main font (Comic Sans) is too playful for a professional résumé. Having the name and contact information in the upper-right corner is good. Since most papers are stapled at the upper-left, the upper-right corner is the one visible when flipping through a stack of papers.

The phone number on the résumé should be labeled as home or work (or daytime or evening), so that people know when they can call.

The résumé includes too much personal information. You shouldn't list your marital status, age and other information that doesn't apply to the

Jane Marissa Doe

101 Realtime Way, Reporterville, CO 94112
Phone: 303/555-1212
Fax: 303/555-1234
Email: jane@natureemail.com

EMPLOYMENT HISTORY

1989-present
Reporterville Deposition Service
While reporting for RDS, I covered all kinds of depositions, but specialized in environmental cases. My law firm customers won many major victories against polluters, mining companies, and logging companies.

1985-1988
Mike's Sporting Goods
I was the assistant store manager for the Reporterville store, handling purchasing, hiring of sales staff, and other duties.

1983-1985
Macy's
I was a sales clerk, responsible for a register in the sporting goods department, and became an expert in mountaineering and ski equipment.

EDUCATION

High School:
Reporterville High, 1980
College:
Reporterville Jr. College 1988 (court reporting certificate)

PERSONAL

I'm 37 years old and married with three children. My hobbies are skiing, mountaineering, and environmental activism. References available upon request

work you're looking for. It rarely accomplishes anything positive, and can be a negative.

A much larger problem is the information that *isn't* there.

The three lines of information describing her current job don't say a thing about her skills, only her personal interest in environmental issues. Nowhere on this résumé does it state whether Jane has done any realtime work in over a decade as a court reporter, nor does it state whether she is or has ever been certified. There are no professional associations listed, so the prospective employer must assume that she has little or no interest in the profession except as an 8-to-5 job.

To clean up this résumé, I'd dramatically expand on the experience at

RDS, showing skills and responsibilities. The sporting goods position could be kept or removed — it's a tossup because it's a management position — but I'd remove Macy's. There's no need to have so much non-reporting information, and it's a decade and a half old. By the same logic, the high school graduation date isn't needed. Replace it with information about certificates and professional memberships.

Most of all, though, get some mention of realtime experience in there. If Jane hasn't done any realtime, she should at least start dragging a notebook computer along on depositions and practicing.

CSR - 1990
RPR - 1990
RMR - 1993
CRR - 1998
RDR - 2000

Denise Stenoski

denise@stenoski.com

[illegible] Realtime Way
Reporterville, CO [illegible]
303.555.1212

REALTIME — *I have realtimed a wide variety of material, including over 100 depositions using LiveNote connections for attorneys. I have also provided realtime when working pro tem in court. I volunteer once a month to realtime for a public meeting at the local school for the deaf.*

WORK EXPERIENCE — ***1990-Present: Freelance court reporter***
The majority of my work has been for RVRT Depo, where I am currently assigned most of the high-profile realtime work.

1986-1989: Medical transcriptionist
While attending court reporting school, I sharpened my stenotype skills by doing medical transcription at Reporterville General Hospital

MEMBERSHIPS — ***National Court Reporters Association***
Member since 1990

Colorado Court Reporters Association
Member since 1990
Treasurer 1997
Vice President 1998
President 1999

Self-Help for Hard-of-Hearing People (SHHH)
Board member, Colorado chapter, 1999-2000

REFERENCES — *Available upon request*

Denise's résumé is something different entirely. The content is good. She brings up the realtime early in the résumé to get your attention. Her certifications (an impressive list) are right at the top. Including the years shows a steady progression of self-improvement which looks very good to someone doing the hiring.

The work experience is short and sweet and brings out the key points: realtime, dedication and self-improvement. Same thing with the memberships. It all looks good.

One problem, however: Denise is not applying for a job as a graphic designer. This résumé is too avant-garde for its own good. When the credentials are this strong, and the information is presented this clearly, she can get away with it, but a résumé design like this from an average reporter wouldn't be a good idea.

On the other hand, the fonts are kept simple and readable, and she only uses two font families — one display font for the name, and one easy-to-read sans-serif font for everything else. Normally, it isn't a good idea to present large blocks of information in italics, and it is only the high readability of the font that lets her get away with it here.

Cover Letters

Every résumé you send out should have a carefully customized cover letter. Amy Bowlen of VITAC likes to see a little bit of personality in the cover letters. She likes a cover letter to tell her what you're looking for. Do you want to work from home? Do you want to relocate and work at company headquarters? Can you start right away, or do you need to give your current employer a few weeks?

In the cover letter, you should state why you want to work for that particular company, and point out specific items of interest in the résumé. Here, also, is a place to fill in weaknesses. If your résumé shows no realtime experience, this would be the place to point out that you've been writing realtime on a notebook computer in the courtroom just for yourself. That's a very positive statement, because it shows initiative and that you care about your work.

Use cover letters in your e-mailed résumés, too. Write your personalized note first, then some kind of separator (a row of dashes works fine), and then include the résumé itself.

Making a Demo Tape

This is a tough one. If you're starting out and you don't have your own equipment, how are you supposed to prepare a demo tape? If you're serious about getting a good job, the demo tape can be a potent tool.

Demo tapes are mostly used by experienced captioners who can just pop a tape in the VCR and record their work as they do it. Very few companies expect someone with no captioning experience to have a demo tape, and if you're looking for CART work, virtually nobody has one.

This doesn't mean that a demo tape can't have a huge impact. In the case studies later in this book, you'll read about Kevin and Mary Daniel. When they prepared to pitch their first sports captioning contract, they took along a demo tape *prepared the night before the meeting*. Using such current material showed that this wasn't a heavily edited "highlights" tape, but an actual demonstration of their captioning abilities.

Applying for a Realtime Job

The arrangements vary from firm to firm. Some firms bring on all of their captioners as employees, supplying you with all of your equipment, fixed work hours, benefit plans and support staff. Others have you work from home, strictly as an independent contractor, providing your own equipment. Most firms operate somewhere between these two extremes.

If you're just starting out, you'll want to be prepared when you walk in the door. Successful captioning firms get a lot of inquiries from aspiring captioners, and you *will* want to stand out from the crowd. Here are some suggestions for accomplishing that:

1. **Get certified.** You won't make it past the front door at most captioning firms without at least a state CSR license. An RPR from the National Court Reporters Association helps. If you are a working court reporter, try for some of the advanced credentials before you apply, although opinions on the applicability of advanced certifica-

tions vary, as we'll discuss later in this chapter. A CRR or RMR is a great help, and you'll want such a designation to appear after your name on the very top line of your résumé. Speaking of which...

2. **Bring copies of your résumé or curriculum vitae to the interview.** It doesn't matter if you mailed one before. Bring it with you in case the interviewer requests another copy.

3. **Have the résumé ready *before* you start calling around.** If somebody says, "Yes, I'm interested. Please fax me your résumé," that's not the best time to start writing one.

4. **Do your homework.** Before applying to a company, check it out. See if it has a site on the World Wide Web. Talk to somebody who works there. Find out all you can, and *put it in your dictionary.* If you are asked to demonstrate your skills, it will certainly look good if the name of the company and the name of your interviewer come out spelled right.

5. **Dress professionally.** Even if you plan to wear a bathrobe and fuzzy pink bunny slippers while captioning from your home, wear professional business attire to the interview. Obviously, if you'll be working for a company in another state or country, and you never even have a face-to-face interview, you can go ahead and wear the bunny slippers.

6. **Be prepared to be tested.** Your résumé may show that you are the best in your profession, but the captioning company will still need to verify your skills. Don't be offended or get huffy when the interviewer asks to see you write. If you've gotten that far in the process, you're in the home stretch, so be relaxed and go for it.

   Captioning companies will often send you a test tape before you even have a chance to interview. VITAC and NCI both do this. VITAC's tapes check your writing theory. They'll want to look at your notes to see if your writing is consistent, accurate and clean. They aren't just looking for conflicts, says Amy Bowlen, "We look for patterns. If someone has a lot of briefs and phrases, and they misstroke a lot, we'll know that some of those misstrokes will come up as totally unrelated phrases." Word-boundary issues are another big issue for Amy.

7. **Brush up on your English skills.** Many firms will test your grammar, spelling and vocabulary before hiring you. It does no good to learn a theory that differentiates between word pairs like *principle* and *principal, levee* and *levy*, or *complement* and *compliment* if you don't know which one to write. Do not expect the so-called "artificial intelligence" of your software to handle this for you. They'll be testing you, not the program you use.

When you are hired, don't expect to start off with all of the plum assignments. A TV news reporter doesn't get assigned to a presidential press conference the first day on the job, so don't expect to caption one on your first day on the job.

Your first few months on the job could be rough. VITAC, for example, only hires people that it believes can be on the air in three months. Before you apply, make sure you are committed to making that happen.

ADVANCED CERTIFICATIONS

Certification is a thorny issue. On the one hand, well-respected captioners and owners of captioning firms tell me that court reporting certification is largely inapplicable to the captioning field. "The credentials that currently exist don't mean anything to me," says Valerie Waite of Waite & Associates, a well-known Canadian captioning firm. To secure an RPR or RMR requires passing written tests on American law, as well as verbatim writing skills with legal material. The certification does not test for even a rudimentary knowledge of captioning technology or skill.

On the other hand, Valerie goes on to say, "If someone can't pass the CRR, they're definitely not at a level where they're ready to go on the air." Most captioners I've spoken to agree with this. A captioner's daily work is more difficult and more demanding than the CRR exam. Whether the particular firm you approach believes a CRR is required, or not, having one will certainly give you a leg up over candidates who have not secured a CRR.

Tammie Shedd fine-tuned the hiring process as she hired over 50 captioners while at NCI. According to Tammie, she was most likely to call you if you have a CRR credential and computer experience, and if you learned the StenEd theory.

You'll find, over time, that there will be a particular field you like better than the others. You may like the variety and fast pace of a newscast, the intensity of professional sports or the personal feeling of one-on-one in a classroom. Whatever it is, if you develop your skills and become known as the best in your niche, you've got a career established.

This doesn't mean that's all you'll ever do. If you are a topnotch realtimer, you'll be called on to do the jobs that really matter. Assignments within a company aren't necessarily given based on seniority. They're based on skill. If your company lands a high-profile job, it'll assign the realtimer most likely to make the company look good.

Chapter 6

Captioning From Home

Your Home Office

If you've been working as a freelance court reporter, then you no doubt have a home office of some sort set up already, even if it's just a desk in the corner of the bedroom. To perform captioning work from home, you will probably need more.

You won't just be sitting at the computer now — you'll be writing real-time. You may be writing for long stretches at a time, depending on what kind of work you do. A good chair is critical. Don't scrimp on the chair!

You'll have more equipment, too, so you'll either need plenty of desk space or other places to put the equipment. I've become a big fan of articulating arms to hold computer monitors and small televisions. The arm clamps to the back of your desk (or to a shelf on the wall) and allows you to precisely adjust the height of the screen. You can still use the desk space under the screen and even swing it out of the way when you need extra work area.

Whether you use an articulating arm, a shelf or your desk surface, take the time to position your computer screen(s) and television(s) at the right height. It will pay off in reduced neck strain.

If it is impractical for you to position everything at eye level, figure out what you'll be looking at the most. If you have a second television, but only glance at it occasionally, it could be placed on top of a file cabinet or mounted to the wall up high in the corner. Your primary computer monitor is critical. Do whatever it takes to get it in the most comfortable position possible.

A Distraction-Free Environment

While we're on the subject of the family, if there's anyone else living in the house with you, make sure your office can be closed off. When you're on the air, you'll need quiet! It's very difficult to concentrate on your captioning with the television in the other room blaring, kids yelling, music playing, spouse talking on the phone, clothes dryer buzzing and dogs barking. Arrange your work space and train your family to achieve the distraction-free setting you need.

A very important part of this process is creating a "don't bother me" signal. The classic approach would be an "On Air" sign that you can turn on when you need to be left alone. Few people do this at home, because it's so easy to forget to turn the sign on and off.

An easy signal is your headphones. Explain to your family that when the headphones are on, you are not to be bothered.

Services to the House

When you set yourself up in your private retreat to caption from home, three things tie you to the outside world: power, phone lines and TV reception. All are critical.

Power

Power failures are a fact of life. No matter how rare they are in your area, you must be prepared. At the very least, you'll need a UPS, or uninterruptible power supply. A UPS can keep your computer running for 15 to 30 minutes when the power shuts down. It won't get you through a long power outage, but it'll handle short drops and brownouts and give you enough time to find someone else to take over for you.

When you go shopping for a UPS, be prepared for a lot of questions. There are many different sizes and configurations available, and the salesman has to understand your needs to help you choose the correct unit.

The storage capacity of a UPS is measured in volt-amps, or VA. There isn't a direct formula that will tell you how long a given size UPS will keep your system running, but a knowledgeable technical or sales representative should be able to give you a close estimate. Your needs aren't the same as a typical user, though, so make sure you explain the equipment setup to the rep. You'll want the UPS protecting at least your computer system, television and modem(s). If you keep the batteries charged in your steno machine, it shouldn't have to go through the UPS.

If you have commitments to your customers for emergency coverage, the UPS won't be enough. You'll need a generator. You can spend around $500 for an adequate gas-powered unit that'll keep your computer running for four hours or more on a tank of gas. The lower-priced units have a hand-starter like a lawn mower, and they're *loud!* Depending on what you want to spend, you can get generators powered by propane or natural gas, electric starters or even units that detect power outages, start themselves and switch the house power out of the circuit. Few captioners make that kind of investment, however.

TV Reception

Next is television. You can get your signal from an antenna, cable TV, a digital satellite dish (usually about a foot and a half across, and fixed in one position), or an analog satellite dish (up to nine feet across and steerable). Having more than one is good. Some broadcasters, in fact, require their captioners to have a second signal source as a backup.

The antenna will be your primary source of signal for local TV stations. If you have a roof-mounted antenna, make sure you fasten it firmly in position so that it can't pivot or fall in a strong wind. Even if you have cable, set up the antenna as well. You'll be glad of the backup, and it will allow the family to watch something different in the other room.

If you have a big steerable satellite dish, make sure you keep a satellite chart handy and preprogram every satellite you can. Many people feel that the big dishes are obsolete now that the digital dishes are available. That isn't true. They have their advantages, and my wife, Kathy, has had quite a bit of captioning work she wouldn't have been able to do without it.

The small DSS dishes are less expensive, easier to mount and have a plethora of channels. They don't, however, have everything. Special programming is available only on the big dish at times, and you have more flexibility in the service. The *big* disadvantage of the small dishes, however, is the delay. If you caption from DirecTV, you're getting the audio a couple of seconds later than someone captioning from a big dish, and that's a very noticeable delay in the captions.

Telephone Service

The final utility is telephone service. You may be able to get away with only two phone lines in the house, but three is better (we have four). You'll need one for your computer to connect to the caption encoder. Hook the other to a fax machine so that people can contact you for emergencies during a broadcast, and leave a phone on it so that you can call out. Keep the fax machine near your desk so that you can quickly grab incoming faxes during breaks and see if they're important. That's much easier than using an answering machine.

The third line allows your family to continue functioning while you're on the air and also serves as a backup audio source. If you need to caption something that you can't pick up on your antenna (or any of your other TV sources), that phone line may be the only way to do the job.

Most of today's cellular telephones can be connected to modems, but check carefully on how it is done with your particular phone. Some have an attachment that provides a standard telephone connection with tip and ring[1] connections. This allows any modem or other piece of phone equipment to be connected. Other cellular phones require you to use a special modem that the vendor supplies.

If you do a lot of work for a station outside your local calling area, look into a foreign exchange line. It was expensive for Kathy to install our San Francisco line (we're about an hour away from the city), but it cut our phone bill by $200 per month, so it paid off in well under a year.

---

[1] *These are the names used by telephone technicians and engineers for the two wires required to connect a standard telephone or other piece of equipment.*

At-Home Captioning Equipment

Your computer system will be the heart of your captioning equipment. As a big fan of redundancy, I recommend having two computers. If one breaks, you've always got the other one available so you can get back on the air fast. Make one of them a notebook computer, and you're ready to go on the road when you need to.

Many reporters let their computer function both as their CAT system and as a general household computer that they share with the family. That arrangement rarely works for captioners. If a family member accidentally changes something that keeps your captioning software from running properly, you don't have time to figure out what happened. You'll miss a broadcast, and that's something you simply can't do. Set up one computer for your captioning work and a different one for the family. These days, you can get a very nice computer for under $1,000.

Before plunking down the money for a new computer, check with your captioning software vendor to make sure it meets its minimum requirements regarding specifications like RAM and processor speed. At the very least, make sure you have:

- **A reasonably fast processor.** You won't need to spend the extra money to get the state-of-the-art, bleeding-edge, top-of-the-line, super-duper (insert other miscellaneous hyphenated adjective phrases here) processor, but don't go with last year's technology either.

- **At least double the RAM Windows requires.** Look at a copy of the variety of Windows you plan to use (Windows 95, 98, 2000, NT Workstation, NT Server), and see what it lists as a minimum. Consider the actual reasonable minimum to be double that amount.

- **Two available serial ports.** This gets harder and harder as manufacturers switch over to USB (Universal Serial Bus), but steno machines and caption encoders both require serial interfaces, so make sure you have two of them available. One possible approach is to get an adapter that connects to your USB port and allows you to connect serial devices.

• **A good monitor.** Don't scrimp here. You'll be spending many hours staring at the screen, so get one that has a sharp image. If you have any intention of doing CART work, pick a larger screen (17 or 19 inches). You may want to use it for presentations.

If you can set up both computers on the same desk, you'll gain some extra advantages. I know several captioners who keep their second computer dialed up to the Internet while they're captioning. That way during breaks they can research names and spellings. It also provides another point of emergency contact. Of course, leaving it online ties up another phone line!

Modems

Speaking of being online, you'll need a modem. I strongly recommend an external modem. It's convenient to have it inside the computer, and you can save a few bucks, too, but it just isn't the same. If there's a problem of any kind, you can look at the lights flashing on your external modem to see what's going on. After a while, you can tell at a glance whether everything's OK. Resetting an internal modem is difficult. You can reset an external modem with a quick flick of the power switch.

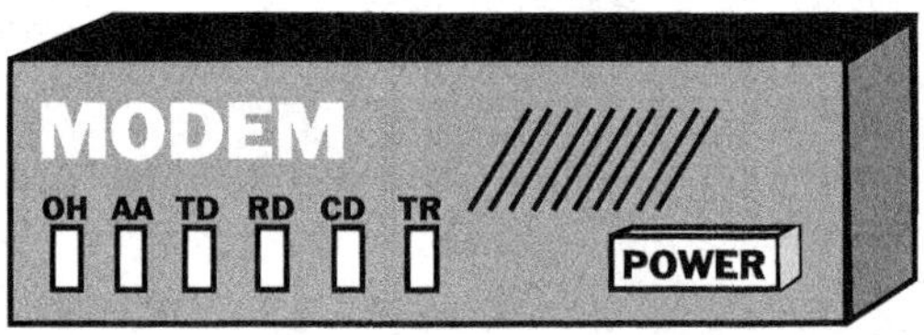

The lights on your modem may be labeled slightly differently from those in this diagram, but the meanings are the same. Here's what to look for:

OH (Off Hook) When this light is on, the phone is "off hook," meaning that the modem is using the telephone line. If this light goes out, your modem has hung up the phone.

AA (Auto Answer) When this light is on, your modem is set up to answer the phone whenever it rings. If you have a fax modem set up to receive faxes, this is what you want, otherwise look at your instructions for how to turn it off.

TD (Transmit Data — TX on some modems) TD shows information being sent out from your computer. When you are connected to a caption encoder, every stroke you write in realtime should cause this light to flicker.

RD (Receive Data — RX on some modems) This is the opposite of TD. It shows information being sent *to* your computer from the other end. Many encoders (notably the venerable EEG Smart Encoder) echo back everything sent to them.

CD (Carrier Detect) This light tells you whether the modem has established communications with a modem on the other end of the line. If this light goes out, you've lost your connection and you'll have to redial.

TR (Terminal Ready) This indicates that the modem is getting a "ready to go" signal from your computer.

When writing realtime captions to an encoder like the Smart Encoder, then, just confirm that CD and OH are both on, then send something to the encoder (a reset or a blank works fine if you don't want anything visible). If you see TD and RD both flicker, you are connected and all is well.

Modems for captioning don't need to be fast. You're unlikely to be writing faster than 300 wpm (600 wpm is the theoretical maximum speed for line 21 captions), so even a 1200 baud modem is plenty fast enough.[2]

---

[2] *You want the math? At low speeds,* baud *is the same as* bits per second *(take my word for that one, OK?). A word is usually defined as six characters (five letters plus a space). A character sent to an encoder is 10 bits (seven data bits, one parity bit, one start bit, one stop bit). Therefore, 600 words per minute is 10 words per second, which is 60 characters per second, which is 600 bits per second, ergo words per minute equals baud rate. There is a lot of formatting information not taken into account in this calculation, but it clearly shows that a 1200 baud modem is more than adequate for line 21 captioning.*

In fact, the slower modems are not nearly as sensitive to noise on the phone line or bad connections, so they are better for captioning in any case. Get a fast one for your Internet connection and an old slow one (even 2400 baud is fast enough) for your captioning.

SWITCHING MODEMS

Should you choose to have more than one modem (and, as I've said once or twice already, redundancy is a good thing), you want to be able to switch between them quickly and easily.

Most electronics stores carry various types of data switches. You want an RS-232 switch, probably with DB-9 connectors. You'll most likely set it up like this:

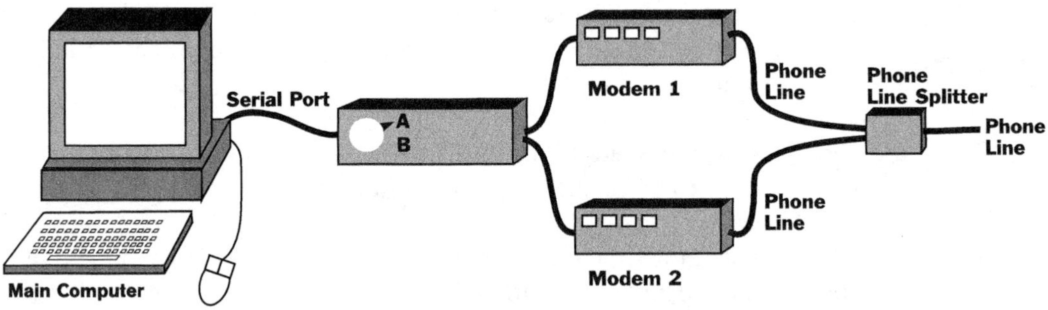

In the event of a problem with your modem, you can throw a switch and be using the second modem in just a second. It is generally a good idea to turn off the power switch on the modem you're switching away from *before* throwing the modem switch to make sure it releases the line.

The phone line splitter in the diagram is a small box that you can pick up from Radio Shack for a few dollars. It plugs into a modular telephone connection in the wall and gives you two outlets for the two modems.

The truly paranoid could add yet another level of backup by having the two modems use different telephone lines, making it quick and easy to deal with problems in your primary phone line.

TV Sets

You'll need a TV set (do you see this coming?) or two. The second one is useful as a backup and can also help you with caption placement. Set them up so that one has captioning turned on and the other has it off. Even if the second television (the one with the captions off) is just in your peripheral vision, that'll be enough to see whether a graphic is being covered by your captions.

Don't get large TV sets. You'll have them close, so you don't need them to be big. I recommend 13-inch sets. Place the main television right next to your computer monitor at the same height. The other one can go off to the side or above. You won't be staring at it for hours, so its position isn't as critical. Get televisions that have audio and video inputs, rather than just antenna input. Audio/video inputs will make your life easier if you connect decoders, encoders, amplifiers and other devices. A television that also has audio and video *output* is fantastic. It makes wiring the second television a snap, and you can send the audio output to an amplifier for headphones.

Audio Equipment

Get good headphones. Wireless headphones are nice because they let you move around during commercials. Even if your environment is quiet, headphones can make things much easier to understand.

You may be tempted to go with one of the lightweight headsets rather than headphones that have the full ear cup. Consider your environment before making that decision. Although the larger headphones with the ear cups are heavier and bulkier, they block out quite a bit of ambient noise, which is useful if you live in a noisy area.

If you ever anticipate having to take your audio from the phone, you'll need a device that can connect the phone line to an audio amplifier. Most captioners use a device from Gentner, which costs a few hundred dollars. An inexpensive amplifier from Radio Shack will let you connect your headphones and switch between the audio from your television and the audio from your Gentner.

If you use a stereo amplifier and stereo headphones, you'll be all set with the VCR, but there will be an issue with the Gentner device. It only

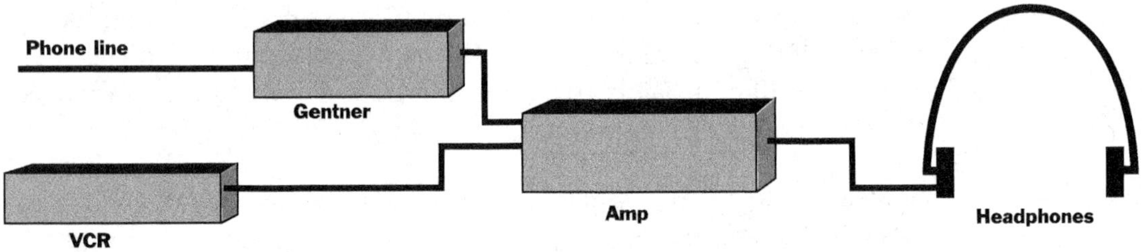

has a single output, and it will drive you crazy only having your sound in one ear. You can purchase a "Y" connector that will connect the Gentner's output to both the left and right channels on the amplifier. Most stereo companies and audio supply houses sell them for just a few dollars.

Make sure you run the outputs into tape, CD, aux or tuner inputs to the amp. The phono (record player) inputs are designed for significantly lower levels, and if you attempt to use them for line-level audio such as you get from a VCR or Gentner, you will have distortion problems.

Caption Decoders

If your TV set was manufactured after July 1, 1993, it has a caption decoder already built in.[3] If the television was made earlier than that, you have three choices:

1. Replace the television. We'll call this the "brute force" approach.

2. Buy an external decoder. If you're dealing with 13-inch televisions, this can cost you more than option 1. It can be handy to have an external decoder, but it's one more remote to deal with, one more piece of

---

[3] *Unless the television has a picture tube smaller than 13 inches, but I've yet to meet a captioner whose primary television was that small.*

equipment on the desk or shelf, and one more connection to wire up.

3. Get a VCR with a decoder in it. There aren't a lot of these around, but they are available. Using a VCR with a decoder allows you to connect any television or monitor, just like an external decoder, but you don't need that extra piece of equipment.

VCRs

You can get a decent VCR for under $100. It's a worthwhile investment. It allows you to make demo tapes of your work to show prospective employers and to tape your broadcasts for your own review later. The larger captioning companies will also ask you to make tapes of your broadcasts from time to time for quality-control purposes.

If you work for yourself, taping your broadcasts is a good idea for another reason: dispute resolution. The day may come when you get a call saying, "Why were there no captions during the last 10 minutes of the broadcast last Thursday?" If you don't have a tape of the broadcast, you have no backup data with which to defend yourself.

A VCR is also useful when you pick up new contracts. For example, if you get a news contract from a local station, tape all their newscasts for a few days and use the tapes as practice material.

As mentioned above, choosing a VCR with a built-in caption decoder adds another level of flexibility.

Caption Encoders

Most home captioners do not purchase encoders or character generators. While they are useful for making demo tapes, doing seminar work and other tasks, few captioners can justify $3,000 or more for a professional quality caption encoder. You may, however, wish to consider getting together with some other captioners and sharing one.

Captioning Software

Your big equipment expenditure will be the captioning software itself. There's a bit of a Catch-22 situation here, unfortunately. You have to know the software intimately and have a full captioning dictionary ready *before* you approach prospective employers or take pro bono jobs for the experience. On the other hand, some captioning companies provide the software when you become an employee, and others mandate which software you must use. Should you take the plunge and risk spending thousands of dollars on software you don't need, or should you put off the decision and possibly not get the job because you have no experience with captioning software? It's a tough call.

If you can afford the software, I'd recommend getting it. You'll be better prepared to look for work, you'll have more freedom in the freelance world and few companies provide the software for work-at-home captioners. As a point of disclosure, although I did own a CAT company and have developed captioning software, I no longer have a financial stake in any commercial captioning software.

Chapter 7

Going Solo

Starting Your Own Business

The ideal way to start a captioning company of your own is to have a customer or two the day you open the doors. If you are doing captioning work for someone else, this opens up a number of ethical issues that need to be addressed. Remember that your business may flourish and thrive, or it may die on the vine. If you start your business by stealing a client from your employer, and your business goes under, nobody will want to hire you again.

If you are determined to leave your current captioning employer and start your own business, the best way to do it is to start with a customer that your employer doesn't want. For example, most major broadcast captioning companies have no interest in captioning sales seminars, hospital conferences, corporate board meetings, city council meetings or church services. When in doubt, *ask*. Go to the owner and ask whether the company is interested in a specific type of business. If the answer is no, you're all set.

Many businesses require their employees to sign noncompete agreements, in which the employees agree not to work for a competitor (or become a competitor) for some fixed period of time after leaving the company. If you are working for a court reporting firm and you want to move into captioning, this isn't an issue. If you're working for a captioning or CART firm and you want to go solo, consult an attorney *first*. The best way to go is to pick a noncompeting field and explain what you're doing to your current employer. Leave with the firm's blessings and keep your options open for the future.

Marketing and Sales

No matter how good you are, if nobody knows about your services, your business is doomed to fail.

Court reporters are trained from the very beginning to be the quiet fixture in the corner of the room, hearing everything and saying nothing. To succeed as a freelance court reporter, you need only have a job with a good firm and do good work.

If you wish to set up your own shop, however, you must prepare yourself for a relentless program of self-promotion. You cannot be shy about getting the word out.

This doesn't mean you have to turn into a hard-core used car salesman. It does, however, mean that you should *always* have a stash of business cards with you. If you meet someone on a plane, in a restaurant or sitting in a doctor's office, start a conversation. If it sounds like that person may be a potential CART or captioning customer, offer a business card.

The Company Name and the Business Cards

Please note that all of the business names in this section are imaginary. Any resemblance to actual firms is coincidental and isn't intended to promote any particular business.

Business cards are a tough proposition in this business. A lawyer can simply write "Attorney at Law" on a card, and it's clear what she does. Everyone knows what an electrical engineer or plumber or auto mechanic or chiropractor does.

But if your card says CART reporter or realtime stenocaptioner, the majority of the world will have no idea what you do.

Avoid the temptation to make your company name too specific. When the local TV station wants someone to caption their news, they just might not call Educational Realtime Incorporated or Stockton Baseball Captioning, even though either company could have done a good job for them.

Names that are too regional can help you in your hometown, but hurt everywhere else. Although there are exceptions, a New Yorker is probably going to call Reliable Realtime before calling Philadelphia Realtime.

Look around at the names of other firms offering similar services. You don't want a name that is too similar and that is easily confused with the others.

For example, if you determine that you'll be competing with GlobalCART, NationalCART, AmeriCART and CART International, then a name like CART America or GlobalCaption would not be a good idea. It would sound too much like the other companies, and you would have a hard time making it stand out and building name recognition.

Choose a name that will be easy to remember. As you're thinking of names, play around with slogans, logos and ideas for making the name more recognizable and more memorable.

CREATE AND USE A TAG LINE

Once you've settled on a business name, come up with a slogan to use with it. Keep it short and sweet, so it fits on the business card without requiring tiny type. Choose the tag line carefully, because you'll want to use it everywhere. It should be on your business cards, letterhead, brochures and the sign on your door.

Tag lines are much easier to change than company names, so you can get more specific. The tag line should describe your specialty and stick in people's minds. If you're going after more than one market, it's even possible to use multiple slogans, but that's another topic.

Active words like *helping, providing* and *performing* are good. So are key words that people will recognize, like *deaf, ADA* or *captioning.*

Some possible tag lines for CART and captioning might be:

- Equal access for deaf and hard-of-hearing people
- Making meetings accessible

- Realtime interpreting for the deaf
- Providing TV captioning since 1993
- Helping doctors talk to deaf patients
- We can write as fast as you can talk
- A new way to communicate with your deaf clients
- Realtime for ADA compliance
- Our realtime helps you communicate
- Captioning and CART throughout New England
- The captioning experts

Note that some are general, and some are specific. Choose something that fits your personality. Don't use something like "We can write as fast as you can talk" unless you have the personality, talent and sense of humor to deal with someone who challenges you on it.

YOUR LOGO

Your logo does not need your company name in it. While many companies choose to use a logotype (their name rendered in a specific typeface and style), a simple logo is more recognizable at a glance or at a distance.

The logo can be a play on your name. Mountain Captioners? Try a "CC" symbol against a stylized mountain profile. Lyons Interpreters? Use a lion head. DesCARTes Realtime? A two-wheeled cart. St. Louis Captioning? Try a big arch with the company name in blocky white letters on black bars (like captions) beneath it. Some business owners arrive at a good logo and then pick a company name to go with it.

You can use thematic logos, incorporating items like the "CC" symbol, stylized images of captions, an ear, a television or a stenotype keyboard.

If you choose to use a logotype, make sure you do something distinctive with it. Hire a graphic artist or designer to give you ideas. Think of the blue lines of the IBM logo and the extended X in Exxon. People recognize the script Coca-Cola even if they can't read the words themselves.

The color is just as important as the rest of the imagery. Choose a good color combination, and *stick with it* (more about that later, when we discuss themes). Have a color version and a black-and-white version of your logo, but don't mess around with the colors!

Get a good, sharp contrast. Remember that when you're having things printed, colors can blur or drift. Don't use, for example, midnight blue and black next to each other. Your cards may come out with the blue so dark you can't tell it from the black.

Limit the number of colors. When printing business cards, letterhead and envelopes, the more colors you have, the more you pay. A four-color business card will cost dramatically more than a two-color business card. Most of the time, companies opt for black plus one other color, but don't feel obligated to do it that way. Remember that you can introduce color into your collateral materials in other ways, too, like with colored papers.

Keep your Web site in mind when designing the logo. Don't use something so intricate that it becomes an unrecognizable blob when reduced down to the corner of a Web page.

TITLES

While it is certainly gratifying to have President or CEO or Owner or Chairman on a business card, many times it is a liability. In a small business, you have to wear many hats, and the easiest way to do it is to have an extra set of cards printed that have your name, but no title.

When your card has no title, it's easy for you to be the sales representative, the accountant, the tech or one of the realtimers. When your card says President on it, you can't get away with statements like, "I'm sorry, but I can't authorize that" or "I'm going to have to get approval on that." Sometimes, you just need time to make a decision, and people will push much harder if they know you're the one in charge.

Press Releases

Press releases aren't completely free, but they're a whole lot cheaper than advertising. If you're not comfortable with your own ability to write a press release, consult a professional or look at examples of others and tweak them to fit. There's really no magic to a press release. It's an opportunity to get free publicity, so do all you can.

The sample "kickoff" press release shows how you might announce the opening of your new business.

Make sure that your press release has all of these required elements:

FOR IMMEDIATE RELEASE — *Release date*

For further information, contact
John Doe, RT Center
Voice/TTY: 929/555-1212
Fax: 929/555-1213
Email: john-doe@rtservices.com

Contact information for the editors

RT Center Launches Service for Communicating With Deaf and Hard-of-Hearing People

Headline

Merrytown, California, 1 January 2000 – RT Center announced today its new line of interpreting services for businesses that need to communicate with deaf and hard-of-hearing people.

Dateline and first paragraph

Many businesses now use sign language interpreters, but of the nation's estimated 20 million deaf and hard-of-hearing people, only two million are fluent in sign language. Communicating with the other 90% has been a problem for professionals and business owners – a problem that RT Center can now solve.

Body of press release

RT Center uses realtime stenocaptioning technology, similar to that used in courtrooms and on television news, to transcribe speech to text at speeds of over 200 words per minute. When communicating with deaf people, you can speak normally and the realtime professionals from RT Center turn your words into text on a computer screen in a large, easy-to-read font. Unlike speech-recognition systems, RT Center provides accuracy of 98% to 99% at high speeds, they can work with multiple speakers and multiple accents, and their realtime professionals have extensive medical and legal vocabularies.

"We're excited to bring this new service to Merrytown," said Jane Fingers, the President of RT Center. "We are dedicated to making all services in this town accessible to people with hearing impairments."

RT Center is located in the foothills of Merrytown, and offers a wide variety of realtime services, including closed captioning for the farm reports on channel 33. The company was formed in 1996. For more information about RT Center, visit their Web site at www.rtservices.com, email info@rtservices.com, phone 800/RT-SERVICES (voice/TTY), or fax 929/555-1213.

Closing "about the company" paragraph

-30-

End-of-story indicator

RELEASE DATE

Almost all of your press releases will have "For immediate release" as their release date. The only reason to use a different date is when you're working on a major announcement, and you're giving the press a little extra time to prepare their stories so that everything will hit at once. This is a strategy rarely used by smaller companies.

CONTACT INFORMATION FOR THE PRESS

You should list here the person that reporters and editors should contact with questions about the press release. This is likely to be different from the contact information in the closing paragraph of the body of the press release, which will (hopefully) be published along with the story.

HEADLINE

Don't worry about making the headline too concise. It's better to come up with a longer headline that says everything you need to say, as any editor who runs the story will write a new headline anyway. If the headline gets really ungainly, consider shortening the main headline and creating a subhead.

Make sure that the headline features your company name prominently. You have a much better chance of good placement with search programs and clipping services if the company name is in the headline.

Make sure the headline sounds like news. Write it in the present tense, and use action words like *announces, launches, releases* and *opens.* When you draft a headline, imagine a newspaper printing it or a news anchor reading it on the air.

DATELINE

The very first words in the body of the story should be your location (city and state) and the issue date of the release. These are typically set apart with bold type.

BODY

The first sentence of the press release should summarize what the story is about. Repeat what the headline says. Remember that the editors will write their own headlines anyway, so write a first paragraph that can stand alone.

Once you've established the story, use the second paragraph to set the context. Define a problem, and then solve it.

In our sample press release, the problem is that professionals and business owners have trouble communicating with 90 percent of the deaf and hard-of-hearing population. The solution is the new service from RT Center.

Use statistics, but *be ready to back them up*. Newspaper and magazine editors like to verify their facts. They may call around and check your numbers with someone else, or they may call you and ask for your source. When they ask you how you know there are 20,000,000 deaf people, have an answer like, "When the FCC implemented the closed-captioning portion of the Telecommunications Act of 1996, FCC Chairman Reed Hundt used that number in his statement." If you just say, "That's the number everyone uses," you lose your credibility.

Write the press release in the third person. It's a news story. You shouldn't say *I* or *we* or *us* except in direct quotes. Use the company name once in every paragraph. After the first use, you can say *they* or *them* or *it* if there is no ambiguity.

Be proactive about potential competition, so that reporters don't make unwarranted assumptions. If you simply announce that you can interpret for deaf people, there's no sizzle. Everyone knows sign language interpreters can do that already. If you explain that you turn speech into text, people assume you're using a speech-recognition computer system. By specifically addressing both alternatives and explaining why your service is better, those objections never have a chance to come out.

Somewhere in the body of the press release, include a quote. This is usually a principal in your company, although it could also be a prominent community member with something specific to say about your business. If you use someone outside the company, make it a well-known and well-respected person. In that quote, you can make statements that are "salesier" and more direct than in the main body of the press release, which should sound "newsy."

CLOSING PARAGRAPH

The closing paragraph in a press release should describe your company. It should be able to stand alone, without relying on the rest of the press release, and should define what the company does, where it is and how to contact the company.

The contact information in this paragraph is for your prospective customers, unlike the contact information at the top of the press release. Make sure you include telephone, fax and e-mail, and list your Web site. Since you're in a business that serves deaf and hard-of-hearing people, make sure you list a TTY number here as well. If you don't have a TTY, get one, and learn to use it.

END MARKER

If your press release is longer than a page, include a page number at the bottom of the page, and make sure it shows the total length of the release (e.g., "page 1 of 2"). If there is only one page, end it with ### or -30- to show that there isn't a second page.

Keep the press release to one page if you can. Short press releases are more likely to be read than long ones.

WHAT TO INCLUDE

Press releases are a gamble. Editors get hundreds of them. If yours comes in on a busy day, you'll take a back seat to the big news. If yours comes in on a slow day, it may turn into a feature article or live interview on the radio or television.

For this reason, it is better to send several short press releases rather than one long one. If you have a lot to say, send out a press release every week for a month rather than sending out a single long one. Each one can reference the prior ones with statements like, "RT Center, which just launched its realtime interpreting service in January, has now added a closed captioning department."

The more news you send out, the better your chances of getting it in print or on the air.

One major rule is to *never* announce early. If you put out a press release announcing your captioning contract with channel 33 before that contract is signed, you're giving your competition a chance to get in there and try to take the deal away. Don't announce anything until it is rock solid. Don't announce that a service will start on a certain day unless you're absolutely certain that you can make that date.

WHERE TO SEND PRESS RELEASES

Like many other business decisions, this one boils down to time and money. If you have just launched a new company, and you don't have much business yet, then you probably have plenty of time and not much money. In that case, send the press releases out yourself.

If you're buried with work, sign up with a service that can send them out for you. You can either use a public relations firm or a service like BusinessWire that specifically handles press releases. It costs money, but they do all the work for you, and they know how to reach people you may not know about.

If you're sending out the press releases yourself, make a list before you start, and add to it as you think of people who might be interested. Here's a starting point for you:

- **Local newspapers.** Get them all, including the free weekly paper and any community business journals. Ask around at professional offices and see what specialty publications they read. You may be surprised to find something highly specialized and regional, like the *North Pueblo Chiropractic News.* If you do, add it to your list.

- **Magazines.** Check with your local library to see what might be applicable. Talk to the librarian. Look at *Writer's Market, Bacon's Newspaper & Magazine Directories* and *Editor & Publisher.* Search the Web.

- **Local radio and TV stations.** Your chances of being interviewed on the 6 p.m. news on your local NBC station are slim, but you never know what might catch someone's attention or whether you might be mentioned in another story.

- **Associations.** Make sure your press release goes to all local chambers of commerce, deaf organizations and any other related group. If you do broadcasting, send it to the local chapters of RTNDA (the Radio/Television News Directors Association) and other broadcast groups. If you provide CART services to doctors, send it to the local AMA chapter and any specialty groups that have newsletters, including hospitals and HMOs.

- **Similar firms in the area.** Later in this chapter we'll be discussing businesses that might be considered competitors. Many of them are prime targets for your press releases.

When you send a press release, try your best to put a name on it. An envelope addressed to "Editor" isn't as likely to get where you want it as one addressed to "Benjamin Franklin, Editor-in-Chief" (assuming, of course, that the editor's name is Benjamin Franklin). With large newspapers, you may want to send more than one. Send a copy to the business editor and one to any reporters who have written stories on subjects related to disabilities, deafness or communications. Sending an extra copy costs next to nothing, and it may pay off handsomely in free publicity.

FOLLOW UP

Few people can afford to send out 100 press releases and then make phone calls to follow up on all 100. On the other hand, you should hand-pick the most important targets and follow through carefully.

For example, let's say you're targeting city government, and you intend to do CART work for any department that holds public meetings. The main local newspaper in your city and any other nearby municipalities that you'll be serving is key. It's probably the only publication read by people at all levels of local government. A magazine like *City & County* is probably too geographically widespread to give a major focus to, so it would go in your second tier list.

Your job would begin with a trip to the library. Scan recent issues of the target newspapers and gather names, addresses, phone numbers and titles of editors and reporters. You might consider actually making custom versions of the press release for top targets. For example, if you're really interested in working with the government of a particular small town, send a copy of the press release that focuses on doing business in the town. Change the headline to something like "RT Center offers new services in Smalltown," and mention the name of the town once or twice in the body of the press release. The publication is more likely to print it.

Similarly, if you're targeting a specific professional association, tailor a copy of the press release to the organization. The copy that goes to the local chapter of the AMA could read "RT Center offers doctors a new way to communicate with deaf patients."

The day after the press release arrives, contact each one on the top five list. Tell them you're following up on the press release and you wanted to see if they had any questions. Don't be pushy, but try to verify that they actually received it.

Creating Brochures and Promotional Materials

Unless you have a background in marketing materials along with both graphic arts and copywriting skills, you'll be better off hiring some professionals to create your brochures.

In the beginning, it probably won't be worth the money to create glossy four-color brochures. You can purchase specialty brochure blanks from companies like Paper Direct and have someone set up the appropriate pictures and text for you. Then, when you need more brochures, you just load the special paper in your laser or inkjet printer and print them yourself.

Have your promotional materials list all of your services and explain how to contact you. When writing them, keep in mind that they may sit around in someone's drawer for years. If there is any timely information, make sure that there's a prominent date on the piece. You should generally avoid putting information like pricing that's subject to change or fluctuation on brochures. Even if you print them on demand, you still have a problem with obsolete materials floating about.

Where to Promote Your Business

THE USUAL SPOTS

Starting a CART or a captioning business is like starting any other business. There are certain steps that should be taken right away to get the word out. If you will be dealing mostly with people outside of your geographic area, some of these aren't as important, but if you're offering CART services locally, don't miss a step.

When you get your office phone number assigned, get into the Yellow Pages. There's no standard category for CART services or captioning, so look carefully *before* you call to see where competitors and complementary businesses are listed. Check services for deaf people (also look under hearing-impaired or hard-of-hearing). Check interpreters. If you're doing broadcast work, look for other services TV stations use.

Once you've decided where you'd like to be listed, ask the phone company what it takes to be listed in more than one category. Rules (and prices) vary by region.

Next, talk to your local chamber of commerce. Most chambers base membership costs on the size of the business, and the price for a small startup isn't too onerous. The chamber will be a great place for meeting people (more on that when we discuss "Pounding the Pavement"), but that's not all you get.

A chamber of commerce exists to help small businesses. Depending on the size of your community, you'll see city directories and maps where you can get listed, business fairs, business-to-business networking clubs, governmental affairs people who can help you connect to the right people in local government, and chambers usually sponsor business seminars as well.

If you'll be offering CART interpreting services for businesses, consider joining a service club like Rotary International. When you're first introduced as a member, you'll have a minute to explain what you do, and you'll have an opportunity to meet a lot more people as you go. Many of those people will be service professionals who have to deal with deaf and hard-of-hearing people from time to time. Lawyers, insurance salespeople, members of the clergy, chiropractors, real estate agents, police officers and retailers are all potential customers.

SIGNAGE

Don't think of signs as just something to put on your office door. You want people to see and remember your business name and logo. Consider carrying a portfolio or notebook with your logo stenciled on the front. Put your logo on your briefcase and on the carrying cases for your CART and captioning equipment. If you have a van, consider a magnetic sign that you can put on the side when you're parked in a public space.

When you speak in public or exhibit at a business fair, you'll want a sign that can hang on a table or lectern or on the wall behind you.

This concept even extends to giveaways. Logo pens, notepads and coffee cups are all cheap advertising when handed out to the right people.

PROMOTING TO DEAF PEOPLE

The majority of CART reporters doing work for deaf people are not paid by the deaf people they work for. Their money comes from the business, school or government entity that is working with the deaf person.

This can lead to the erroneous assumption that you shouldn't market to deaf people. On the contrary, there are two *very* good reasons to market yourself to the deaf and hard-of-hearing communities!

First, many deaf and hard-of-hearing people don't even know that realtime CART and captioning services are available. They'll never think to ask for it unless someone explains it to them. Talk to deaf groups and do your best to get the word out. Hand out a lot of business cards.

Second, when a deaf person requests CART, the business or organization often has no idea where to procure CART services. If you've done your job, the deaf person will say, "I need realtime interpreting services, and here's the business card of someone who can do it."

Certainly, the deaf and hard-of-hearing communities shouldn't be the *only* place that you promote your services, but it should be high on your list of priorities.

Competitors? Maybe Not!

People have a natural (and understandable) tendency to avoid direct contact with their competitors. While such head-to-head confrontations are rarely productive, you must develop a clear picture of who your competitors actually are.

Later in this book, in the chapter "Threats, Real and Perceived," we'll take a look at sign-language interpreters. Do *not* treat them as competitors! You provide complementary services. Contact every interpreter in your area and exchange cards and brochures with them. Tell them that whenever someone contacts you, you'll be happy to ask whether they're also using sign interpreters and ask them to do the same for your CART services.

Most established firms develop specialties, and there are types of business they aren't interested in. If you are planning to do educational CART work, call all of the captioning firms in your area and ask if they also do educational CART. If not, offer to swap referrals. If someone calls you looking for broadcast captioning, pass the lead on to the captioning firm and ask them to do the same for you on educational CART.

The *best* way to make such calls is with a lead in-hand. If you get out and talk to people, you're sure to find someone looking for a service you don't provide. Offer to track down someone for them. That way, when you call your "competitor," you have something to offer *immediately*, which reduces suspicion. Also, the customer will remember that you were willing to help him even though you got nothing for it. When he *does* need your services, or when he finds someone who does, he'll call you first.

These relationships develop all the time. Keep in mind, though, that things change. At some point in the future, you may decide to expand your offerings, and your "competitor" may as well. That would turn you into actual competitors. Don't give away too much information. You shouldn't, for example, share your client lists and business strategies with someone who may end up going into the same business some day.

Advertising

PERIODICALS

In a niche market like CART or captioning, you will probably do very little paid print advertising. An ad in a broadcast magazine like *Broadcast & Cable* or *Broadcast Engineering* costs thousands of dollars per month, and most of the people reading it won't be interested in your services anyway. You can go with a less expensive showcase ad in a publication like *TV Technology*, but the techies reading that magazine rarely have anything to do with selecting captioning vendors.

If you want to advertise a CART business, things are a bit easier because your customers are localized. You can run fairly inexpensive ads in the Yellow Pages and local newsletters. When you visit a prospective customer, don't be shy about asking for tips. If you're pitching CART services to a doctor, ask what local doctors read and if there are any local associations with newsletters.

DIRECTORIES

Whether you advertise in periodicals or not, try to get listed in as many directories as possible. Many offer a basic listing for free, and then make expanded listings and ads available for a fee. Watch your budget and experiment. See which ones bring you the most business and concentrate your resources there.

Don't forget Web-based directories! There are directories of many different types of services available, ranging from searchable lists like the one on the NCRA Web site (www.ncraonline.org) to member lists for professional associations like CARTWheel.

BROADCAST MEDIA

Advertising on radio and local television is often less expensive than you expect. Taking our prior example, look over the listings on your local TV stations and community access cable TV. There might be a show hosted by a local doctor. See what it would cost to advertise on it.

Radio spots are relatively inexpensive to produce, because all you need is a sound studio. You can even get production costs down to zero by writing some good copy and having the host just read it. This is common during news and talk shows, and you'll even hear deejays reading ad copy sometimes.

TV spots are more expensive. Talk to the TV station and get its recommendations for someone who can produce the spot inexpensively. Many stations offer these services in-house.

INTERNET AND WEB

Banner advertising on the Web can cost just as much as buying ad space in magazines or ad times on broadcast media. Look for free listings first, and then consider buying ad banners. Also, see the recommendations later in this chapter for creating and promoting your own Web site.

Read the pricing carefully. Some sites charge by the impression (the number of times the banner is actually displayed) and some charge by the number of click-throughs (people actually clicking on your banner to go to your site). The rates are usually quoted in dollars per thousand impressions.

Make sure your contract has a maximum in it, or you can find yourself with unexpected bills. You could sign up for a banner, expecting to pay $100 for the month, and find that the site becomes suddenly very popular, and your ad is displayed to 10 times the expected number of people. This multiplies your ad cost by 10 as well.

If you choose to purchase banner advertising on the Web, consider having the banner designed professionally. There are people who do banner designs for a living, and they know how to increase the number of people who click on your ad.

TIPS AND TRICKS

If you're advertising in a periodical, use the advertising "rule of three," which states that your ad doesn't really "click" with people until the third time they see it. Don't just run an ad once and give up if you get no results. Plan in your budget to run it three times. Again, this is for periodicals that run weekly, monthly or even quarterly. It doesn't apply to things like directories and phone books that are only updated once per year but are referenced all year long.

Develop a consistent "look and feel" for your advertising, whether it is magazine, newspaper, billboards, bus stops, Web sites or TV commercials. Try to stick with a consistent color scheme. Always put your logo in the same place. Use the same fonts every time. Make the ads "feel" like they all come from the same company.

The single most important rule of advertising is to track your responses. Ask *every single person* who calls where he or she heard about you, and write it down. Every few months, compare the cost of each advertising campaign with the amount of business it brought you. Drop the ones that don't work, and keep up the ones that do.

Your Prospective Clients

When building your prospect list, it's important to think outside the box. I guarantee that every single captioning firm interested in broadcast work has called the news producer of your local NBC station. That doesn't mean you shouldn't try, but don't have high expectations. Instead, try calling the places they might *not* have called. Choosing small local customers and customers that require work to be performed on-site locks out all competitors outside your geographic area. Also, the bigger firms won't be interested in little local contracts that could be the bread-and-butter work for a small startup.

BROADCAST CAPTIONING

The TV listings in your local newspaper usually provide a list of TV stations in your area, often with contact information. There are also directories available on the Web. Scan the TV listings for locally produced live programs. If the programs aren't live, they can do their captioning offline, and if they're not locally produced, then someone else will be responsible for captioning anyway.

Also look at the community access channels on all cable systems in your area. Often, you can find a lot of specialized talk shows. They are usually produced on a small budget, so be prepared to hear their financial concerns.

NONBROADCAST CAPTIONING

Even events not out on the airwaves or available on cable can use captioning. Look for anywhere that live video production is done. Sports facilities often have in-house closed-circuit television which shows in the luxury boxes and concession areas.

CART

CART services have a place everywhere that there are deaf and hard-of-hearing people. When you're selling CART, you are selling the *concept* more than you are selling yourself. Your job is to educate people about CART and how it works. When and if they need the service, you'll be the one they call.

Here are a few starting points for your sales efforts:

- **Corporate human resources departments.** Tell them that you're prepared to realtime employee orientations, public meetings and other events. Explain that you're willing to sign nondisclosure agreements to do private meetings as well.

- **Schools.** Talk to universities, community colleges, college extensions, adult schools, public school boards, private high schools and prep schools, vocational training centers and private training centers.

- **Medical work.** Doctors have to do one-on-one consultations with deaf and hard-of-hearing people, *especially* doctors who handle hearing problems. CART can shorten these consultations dramatically. Talk to individual audiologists, ear-nose-throat (ENT) doctors and other specialists directly. Talk to the appropriate staff member at hospitals, private medical groups and HMO facilities.

- **Other medical practitioners.** Don't stop calling when you've gone through the local list of traditional medical doctors. Call the dentists, chiropractors, psychologists, psychiatrists, acupuncturists, acupressurists, councilors and therapists.

- **Government.** All levels of government exist to serve the public. If a member of the public is deaf or hard-of-hearing, the ADA mandates that the government agency accommodate that disability. Talk to city and county governments, police departments, fire departments, unemployment offices, vocational rehabilitation offices and any other department that holds public meetings. Look for PR offices. Many departments have a person or department dedicated to community outreach. Larger cities and counties have a PIO (Public Information Officer) dedicated to communicating with the public.

- **Courthouses.** Where better to use the court reporting skills you've developed than in a courthouse? Interpreting in court for deaf and hard-of-hearing people is *not* the same job the reporter is doing, and there are still official reporters who don't do realtime. For that matter, there are small courthouses (traffic court, for example) that don't have court reporters at all, but *do* have deaf people to work with.

- **Service clubs.** Organizations like Rotary International and the Elks do a lot of community work. You can generally contact your local Chamber of Commerce for a list of service clubs in your city or town. You *did* join the Chamber of Commerce, didn't you? If not, go back to the beginning of this chapter and start again! In addition to checking to see if a service club needs your skills, offer to be a guest speaker at one of their meetings.

- **Churches.** Start with your own faith, but don't forget that the others exist! If you're comfortable doing it, go through the whole list of churches, synagogues and temples in your area. Usually, you can get the list from the local Chamber of Commerce, city offices or newspaper.

- **Hotels and convention centers.** Larger facilities have their own AV (audiovisual) department, and smaller ones contract with an outside firm. Make sure the AV people know about you and your service, and make sure the hotel manager in charge of convention services has a stack of your cards.

- **Entertainment.** Talk to any group that puts on live stage productions of any kind.

All of these suggestions are only a starting point. The more you promote your services in your community, the more ideas you'll come up with.

Telephone Cold-Calling

No amount of advertising and public relations can replace good old-fashioned sales calls. Cold-calling on the phone is tough to do. You have to prepare yourself for rejection. There will be calls where nobody will talk to you, where you'll be hung up on, and where they don't understand what you offer and don't want to hear about it. There will also be calls that get you results.

Don't spend entire days calling, unless you really start to find yourself enjoying making cold calls. Instead, build up your list of leads, set a realistic quota on a daily basis and stick to it. Your quota might be five calls per day. It might be to keep calling each day until you actually get through to a human being who might be interested in your services. It doesn't matter how many calls you make, just make sure you do it every day.

The thought of making 500 sales calls on the phone is daunting, but that's just two calls per business day for a year.

Here are some tips for successful cold-calling:

- **Be polite.** Even when someone says "no" or gets abusive, you want to leave as good an impression as you can. Get off the phone as courteously as possible.
- **Prepare an outline of what you want to say so you don't leave anything out.**
- **Don't read from a prepared script when you call.** Outlines are great, but people can tell when you're reading to them, and they won't respond well to it.
- **Think through your calls before you start.** Try practicing on a friend or co-worker. Prepare a FAQ (frequently asked question) sheet so that you'll have answers at your fingertips.
- **Calling at the office is different from calling at home.** When dealing with professionals who have both home and office numbers, always try to catch them at the office.

- **Ask *every single person* that you talk to for recommendations of anyone else who might be interested in your services.** You'll be surprised how many people give you names. If you can get the phone number from them, too, that's great, but don't be pushy about it. Remember that they're doing you a favor when they give you a referral.

- **Get people's names before you call.** You have a much greater chance of success if you ask for Ann Smith rather than asking for the person who would handle disabilities access issues.

- **Use professional titles.** You don't know these people, so address them as "Dr. Jones" or "Ms. Smith" or "Professor Jacobson." If they want you to use their first names, they'll tell you so.

- **Don't be afraid to ask for the order.** When people are interested in what you're offering, ask if they have a particular event or meeting coming up where they could try out your service. If they don't, ask what would be a good time to stop by and deliver a brochure or rate sheet. Hand-delivery is always better than mailing such items. It gives you a chance to chat with them and lets them put a face to the name.

- **When you do get the order, *stop selling.*** Once they've invited you to come over and demonstrate your services, or booked you for a job, the pitch is over. Thank them politely, get the details you need for your records, and ask if they can recommend anyone else for you to talk to. If you keep selling after you've got the order, you just might lose it.

Pounding the Pavement

Sometimes a face-to-face sales call can get you into places that a phone call can't. Once you are in front of prospective clients, they're more likely to do business with you face-to-face than on the phone, and you can leave them with business cards and brochures.

For the most part, the same rules apply as were listed above for cold-calling on the phone. There are also a few more to keep in mind for face-to-face meetings.

- **Dress professionally.** Even if the people you're meeting with wear jeans to work, you should dress like a professional. This means a tie for men and appropriate business attire for women.

- **Always carry lots of business cards.** Even if you're just planning one sales call, you never know when someone will ask for some of your cards to hand around, or when that person will introduce you to other co-workers. Business cards are *cheap!* Don't be stingy with them.

- **Carry brochures and rate sheets.** It does no good to print them if you don't have them with you to hand out to prospects.

- **Smile.** It will help you get along with people, and it will also help you to relax. It may feel phony at first, but if you can relax and get a genuine smile on your face, people will see it and hear it in your voice. Make sure they know you *enjoy* what you do. People have more confidence in you when they feel that you're passionate about what you do.

- **Be prepared to show your stuff.** Have your steno keyboard and a notebook computer in your car at all times. Before each sales call, take a minute with your dictionary to be prepared. Add the name of the person you're meeting and the name of the company and any other words that jump to mind. Realtime is a unique and fascinating skill. Don't be afraid to show it off.

If you're not used to sales, you're going to be very tense and uncertain during your first few visits. As with the phone calls, it pays to practice. Make your pitch to the mirror, to a friend, to a co-worker. You know you're good at what you do, so pretend you're just explaining how it works to a friend. Let your enthusiasm for your profession show.

Follow Up

One contact isn't enough. If someone is interested, you need to follow up. Get a stack of thank-you cards printed with your company name and logo on them, and *hand write* a card to each person you visit, thanking that individual for his or her time. Preprinted thank-you cards don't make nearly the same impact. I once visited a customer at his office and saw a hand-written thank-you card on his bulletin board that I had sent him two years earlier.

Watch for interesting news stories that might give you an excuse to call again. Offer to send them something and then phone to see if they got it. Send a card during the holiday season.

If people haven't used CART before, and they find a sudden need for it, their tendency will be to call the last person they spoke to about it. Make sure that last person is you.

What to Charge

There are two pricing models to choose from: cost-based and market-based. Determine your rates both ways, compare the results, and decide from there what you want to charge.

Let's take care of a little marketing and business terminology before going any farther. The *price* of a service is what you charge somebody else. The *cost* is the expense you have to bear. The *profit* is the difference between the price and the cost.

COST-BASED PRICING

In a cost-based pricing scheme, you calculate *all* of your operating expenses, including the amount of money you intend to pay yourself, add in the appropriate amount to cover your overhead, and that sets the price.

You may choose to break out pricing or lump everything together. For example, you can charge separately for travel time or factor it into your overhead. You can charge rental fees for specific equipment, like video projectors, or factor them in your overall calculations.

Either way is fine, but make sure that your rate sheet isn't so complex that it becomes unreadable. Often, equipment is kept separate because you'll need to rent it yourself. It's tough for a small business to justify purchasing expensive items like video projectors unless you'll be using them a lot, so you need to factor in what it will cost you to rent one on a daily basis.

Calculating costs for overhead requires a little bit of guesswork on the number of hours you'll work. Let's say you add up your rent, telephone bills, power, stationery costs, lease payments on that Jaguar you just bought as your official company car and all the other incidentals. Your total: $1,200 per month.

The average month has $21\frac{2}{3}$ work days (52 weeks per year, multiplied by work days, divided by 12 months). We'll call it 20 for our purposes here, because it makes the calculations easier *and* more conservative. That makes the overhead $60 per day.

If you're going to be working an average of six billable hours per day, then you need to have $10 per hour in your prices set aside to cover the overhead. But what if you can't *find* that much work in the beginning? What if you're only averaging three billable hours per day? That means your prices need to include twice as much profit ($60/day divided by three hours), or $20 per hour for overhead.

Have you done this type of calculation before in a court reporting business? Then remember that it's different in CART or captioning, because there are usually no transcripts and you charge by the hour. Throw out your old cost models and create new ones.

MARKET-BASED PRICING

The other pricing model ignores your cost of doing business completely and sets your price based on what the market will bear.

The easy way to do this calculation is to determine what all of your competitors charge, average them all and that's your price. While that would work for court reporting, where all firms offer basically the same services, it's dangerous in CART and captioning.

Here's an example of why:

Company "A" provides CART for students at the local community college. Despite its grandiose name and fancy literature, it's really just one person working from home with little overhead. The only equipment the person has is a notebook computer, CAT software and a steno keyboard. Company A's rate: $20/hour.

Company "B" provides full-service closed captioning for the sports stadium in town. It has a moveable ("steerable") satellite dish, captioning software, a big LED sign that the company provides to the stadium, and two captioners writing realtime at each game, one on-site writing to the JumboTron on the scoreboard and the other off-site writing to the satellite uplink for broadcast television.[1] The company has created custom software to insert Interactive TV Links into the broadcast captions that point to online player statistics. Company B's rate: $320/hour.

Can you average these two, come up with $170/hour, and quote that to the otolaryngologist who needs CART for a deaf patient? Of course not.

Market-based pricing is called "what the market will bear" because it factors in what people are willing to pay for a service. What your competitors charge is only one handy yardstick for measuring customers' thresholds of pain.

Part of setting up a market-based pricing system is gut instinct. Find out how much your potential clients charge per hour for *their* time, and that will give you an idea of what they can afford to pay. Nothing says your rates for government work have to be the same as your rates for corporate work, or that you have to charge a school the same as you'd charge a doctor, as long as you have a way to justify the differences.

Your Web Site

The Internet is the first stop for many people shopping for services, and this trend is bound to continue. People will find your Web site in many ways: search engines, directories, your business card, links on other Web pages. For many of them, the front page of your Web site (known as the "home page") will be their first impression of your business. Take it seriously, and make it count.

---

[1] *The reason for two captioners is that the TV broadcast doesn't use the same announcer(s) as the in-stadium loudspeaker system uses.*

Setting Up the Web Site

Are you a graphic artist? Do you write your own ad copy? Do you have experience designing brochures and other marketing literature? Do you understand how Web search engines work? Do you know the differences between Netscape, Microsoft Internet Explorer, AOL's Web browser and WebTV, and what would make a Web page work on one without working on another?

If you answered "yes" to all of the above, then you should design and build your own Web site. If you answered "no" to any of them, it would make sense to get some assistance from a professional.

Whether you're building the site yourself, or having someone else build it, you'll still need to come up with an overall design, and you'll have to instruct the designers. Here are some overall tips for making the site a success:

- **Keep the front page simple, and make it easy to find the content within the site.** All critical information should be just a click away, and it should be obvious where to click.

- **Make the front page load fast.** This means keeping the graphics small and not loading it up with text. People are impatient. If your first page takes longer than 15 seconds to load (some say even less), you'll start to lose visitors.

- **Put navigation links on the front page.** A fancy "splash screen" with nothing on it but "click here to enter site" is useless and annoying.

- **Keep in mind that search engines may plop someone unceremoniously into the middle of your site.** Make sure you have a good navigation system that tells them where they are and how to get to the front page.

- **Put your firm name, location and phone number on *every page* of the site.** Your site should have a "contact us" page with full contact information, but potential customers shouldn't have to go looking for it if they want to call you.

- **Keep it strictly professional.** You're selling a service here. If you have a personal site for your hobbies, keep it separated from the business site.

- **Use the same overall theme you use for your printed materials.** Keep the color scheme, the logo and so forth, so that it looks like it came from the same company.

- **Include some pictures, but keep them small and don't use too many.** They slow down the site too much. A good approach for large pictures is to include a smaller "thumbnail" of the picture on your page with instructions to click on the thumbnail to see the full-size picture.

YOUR OWN DOMAIN NAME?

Everyone expects that Rosehips Realtime's site will be found at www.rosehipsrealtime.com. If your exact firm name is available, or some obvious portion of the name, then it makes sense to spend a few bucks (well under $100 at this writing) to grab the name.

If you have to distort your name horribly to find something that's available, then consider whether www.roseyreal.com is really worth it. Nobody will remember it anyway, so why not use the name you get free from your Internet service provider, which would be something like www.isp.com/rosehipsrealtime?

You should avoid the companies that provide free Web space in return for banner ads and pop-ups. It doesn't look good for someone visiting your site to be assaulted with advertising promoting a Web company, especially the obtrusive pop-ups favored by companies like GeoCities.

What to Include

Design of a Web site is a very personal matter. Web sites are as individual as marketing brochures. In fact, you could say that they are marketing brochures. Individuality aside, there are some "must-haves" for your captioning/CART Web site:

- **A "contact us" page.** It should include street address, phone (voice *and* TTY) and fax numbers, e-mail address and a simple fill-in-the-blanks form that visitors can fill out with comments or questions.

- **A detailed description of the services you provide.** Don't just say "captioning" and leave it at that. Explain what you can do and include pictures.

- **If clients will ever be coming to your office, include maps and driving directions.** There are several online services that offer maps, or you can draw your own.

- **Do you have some really good information in your brochure?** Put it on your Web site, too.

In addition to the must-have items above, there are some things that will definitely benefit your Web site and your business. Don't knock yourself out to get them into that first cut of the Web site, but consider developing them as soon as you can.

- **Short informative essays.** If you have had anything about captioning, CART or realtime published, put it on the Web site to build your credibility. If not, write something and get it published.

- **Information about technologies that compete with yours (or are perceived as competitors).** Add links on your front page for speech recognition, sign language and so forth. For sign language, you can explain that you're happy to work with sign interpreters and why your services are complementary. For speech recognition, explain why you can't simply buy a $99 speech program and replace a realtime provider with it.

- **A "for more information" page with carefully selected outgoing links.** Later in the chapter, we'll talk about link exchanges.

What *Not* to Include

Just as there are things every captioning/CART site should have, there are also things it should *not* have. That list includes:

- **Prices.** You don't want someone comparison-shopping on your Web site. You want to *talk* to them. Maybe your rates are negotiable, or you charge differently in different businesses. Either way, including the prices online doesn't help you.

- **Employee directories.** It may sound like a great service to list the names of each of your realtimers and all of your office staff with their direct e-mail addresses and/or phone numbers, but it's generally a bad idea. Why? It gives recruiters or competitors a list of everyone in your firm that they can try to hire away.

- **Client lists.** The same logic applies here. If someone wants to start a new CART business, your Web site would provide that person with a list of people already using CART, and he or she can go right to work at taking away your customers.

- **Anything that changes rapidly.** When the pace of business gets hectic, you may go for a month or two without updating your Web site. Some firms go *years* without updating them. Don't put anything up that will be swiftly dated unless you're sure you will be able to update it. This includes holiday greetings. Nobody wants to read your Christmas greeting message in June.

- **Wild backgrounds.** Don't put in an iridescent background image behind the text of your page just because you can. Keep the background either white, a light pastel or a very subtle repeating pattern. You want to keep the page both elegant and easy to read.

Examples

Let's take a look at a few site designs and see what works. Obviously, the impact of color is lost when the page is printed in this book in black and white, but this gives me an opportunity to make another point: When you are selecting your colors and designing the site, print it every so often on a black and white laser printer. Make sure that it is clean and legible. People *do* print Web pages for reference and to show friends and business associates.

First, let's take a peek at a page with some content mistakes:

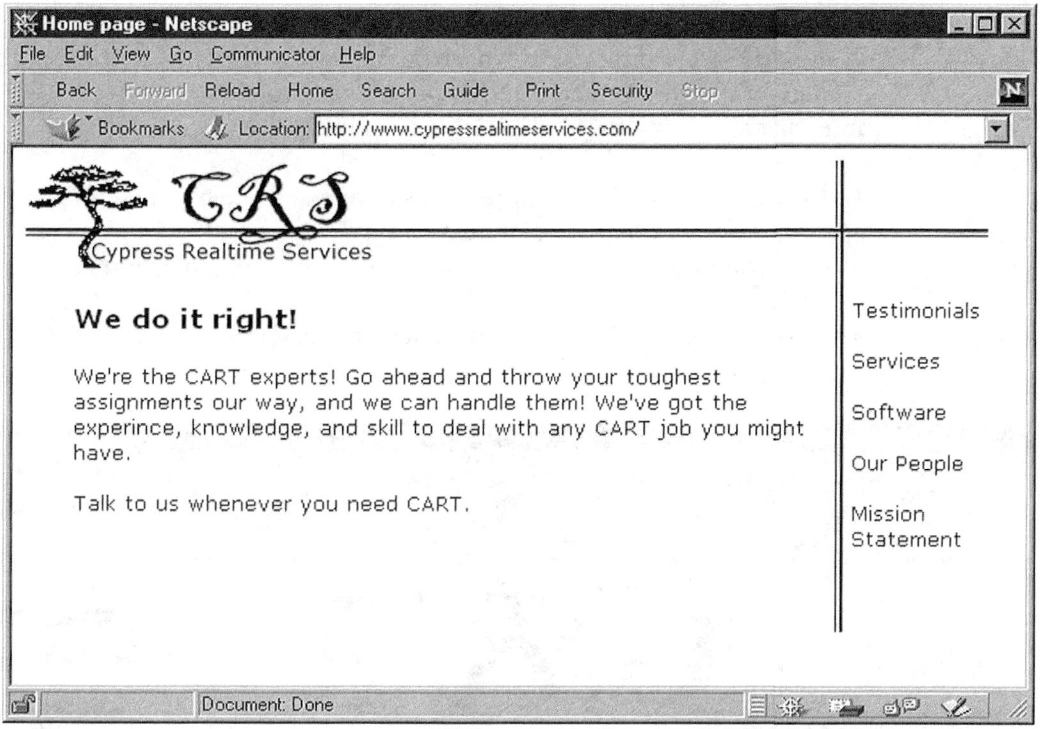

Let's start with the most serious mistake: This page doesn't tell your potential clients how to get hold of you. No phone number, no address and no obvious button that would have the information.

Another very serious problem is the description of what your firm does. If you don't know what CART is, you could read this page three times and still have no clue whatsoever what Cypress Realtime Services does.

A good description is important for another reason. Search engines on the Web index a page by the words it uses. Since words like realtime, closed captioning and deaf don't show up, your page wouldn't be found when people searched for those terms.[2]

---

[2] *The word* realtime *does appear in the logo, but search engines can't read graphic images, only text, so this page wouldn't be found in a search for* realtime.

The title in the Web browser's title bar (at the very top, where it says "Netscape") is "Home page." This imparts no useful information, and if someone sets a bookmark for this page, it will appear on their bookmark list as "Home page." This is no help in finding your firm!

As I stressed a couple of chapters ago when we discussed résumés, spelling errors are deadly. Nobody wants to hire a realtimer who can't spell. If you don't see the spelling error on this home page, look again.[3]

The overall design of this page from a graphical point of view isn't bad. There are much worse design examples, like this one:

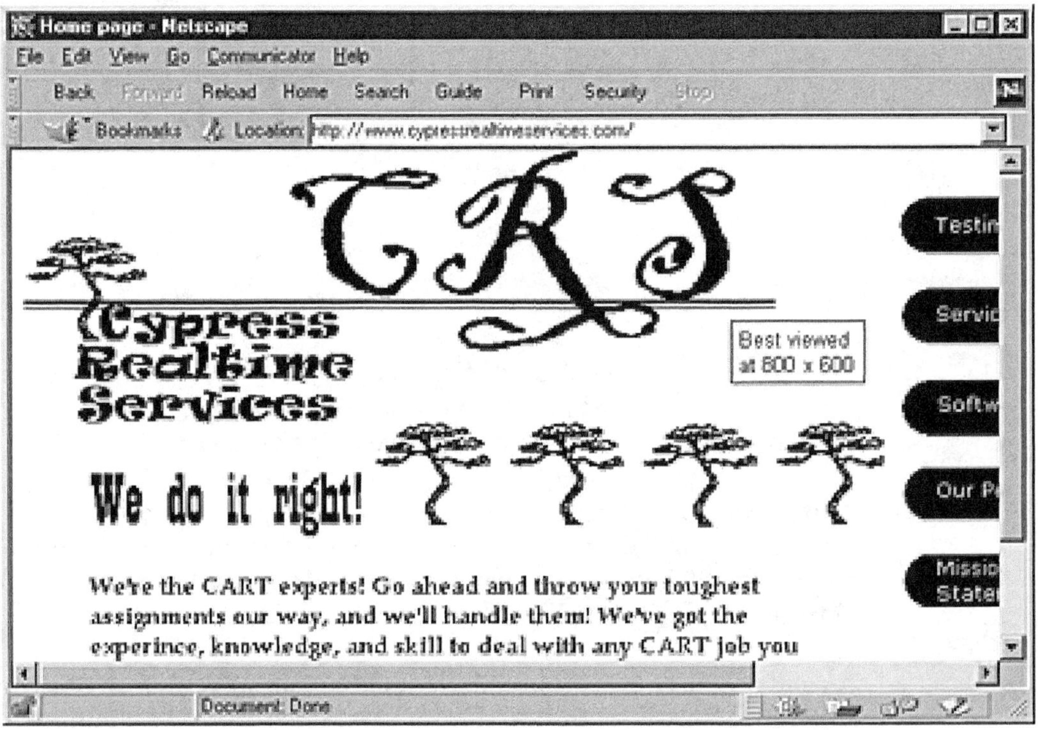

This is a graphical design nightmare. The huge CRS logo overpowers the rest of the page, and the cacophony of different fonts detracts seriously from the message. It's fine to use one font for the logo and then

3 Experience *is misspelled on the third line of the first main text paragraph.*

something different for the rest of the page, but using a half-dozen fonts without a common design base is a major no-no.

The "Best viewed at 800x600" is another big mistake. There are still a lot of people who use 640x480 resolution on their computers, and WebTV users have even less than that. Having to scroll sideways to see the navigation bar (or even read the body text) as in this example annoys your visitors for no reason.

There are also too many graphics, which clutters the page and slows down the load time. The steno-key menu buttons are nice, although few non-court reporters will get the connection. The row of cypress trees contributes nothing whatsoever, and the horizontal line through the logo doesn't tie in to anything else on the page.

How can we clean up this page?

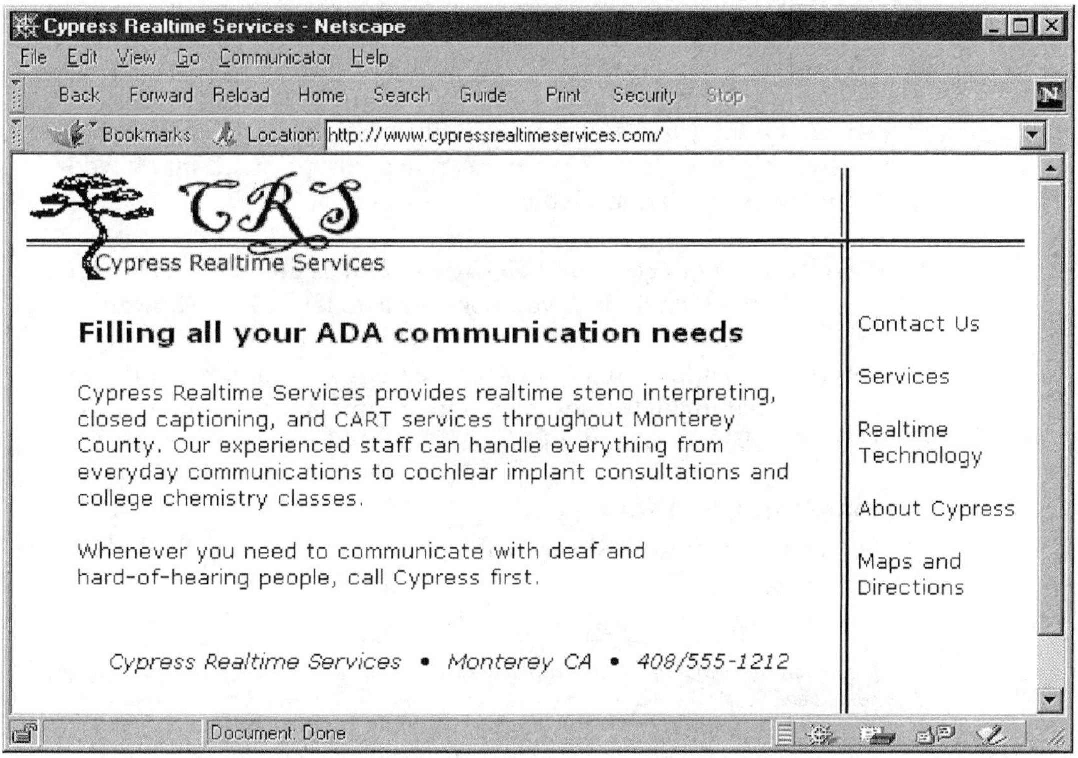

This page uses a logo that's large enough to catch the eye, but not so big that it overpowers the page. The design of the page is simple, and the key information is easy to find. The navigation bar on the right side is clear and short. The company phone number and location is right on the front page, and if you want more information, the very top button says "contact us."

The company name is in the title bar, in the logo, in the body of the text, at the bottom of the page by the page number and in the menu ("About Cypress"). It's not overdone, but it's clear whose page this is.

This page wouldn't win any graphic design awards. It doesn't use any clever layout techniques, but it does the job. The minimal use of graphics assures that it will load fast and tell visitors what they want to know.

Promoting the Site

The site is built. You have a URL (Uniform Resource Locator), also known as a Web address (www.hotfingerscart.com, for example).

The first thing you want to do is notify everyone. Put that Web address on your business cards, brochures, rate cards, print ads and in your standard e-mail signature block.[4]

Next, you want to get your Web site listed in as many related directories and search engines as you possibly can. If you know how to do this and you have the time, do it yourself. Otherwise, consider hiring a service to do it for you. Finding all the right specialty directories and getting meaningful listings takes a lot of time. If you're going to do it yourself, plan on days, not hours.

TARGETED LINK EXCHANGES

Set up a page on your site specifically for outgoing links. Include inter-

---

[4] *You don't have an e-mail signature block? Make one. Now. Set up your e-mail program so that every message you send out ends with your name followed by the name of your company and its Web site address. If you use the same address for personal and business e-mail, use common sense. You don't want your company name on your e-mails to off-color discussion lists or anything else that doesn't look good for the company.*

preters and other deaf services. Now contact everyone you might want to list there and offer to swap. You'll put their link on your page if they'll put your link on theirs.

You don't want to include too many links off of your site. After all, each one gives visitors an opportunity to leave. In fact, presenting a link *invites* them to leave!

Generally, though, by the time someone visits a "more information" page, they are on their way out of your site anyway. Keep the outgoing links localized there. Don't sprinkle them all over your site.

Chapter 8

Calling Deaf People on the Phone

These are the people you are going to serve. How do you communicate with them? What do they expect of you? How can they help you in your career?

If you are involved in the captioning industry, the time will certainly come when you need to communicate with deaf people. If the particular person you want to reach has e-mail capability or a fax machine, it will be just like communicating with a hearing person. If not, it's time to get acquainted with the TTY.

The name "TTY" comes from the computer industry's standard abbreviation for "Teletype," an early supplier of computer terminals with telephone modems. The TTY of today is based on that same technology, but has no relationship to Teletype Corporation. Other abbreviations have been tried and rejected. For example, Text Telephone abbreviated to "TT" is the sign a deaf child uses to indicate the need for a trip to the bathroom. Telecommunication Device for the Deaf enjoyed popularity for a while, but the deaf and hard-of-hearing population protested that they already had a perfectly good name for the device, so TTY has stuck.

The simplest TTY is a keyboard, a small display and an acoustic coupler. The telephone handset is placed in the coupler and the phone is dialed. Someone on the other end picks up the phone and places it in the acoustic coupler for their own TTY, and the conversation can begin. Anything typed on one keyboard appears on both displays. TTYs can also have printers, which typically use rolls of paper like adding machines use.

In this picture, you see my portable TTY. The phone handset is settled into the acoustic coupler. With this model you can charge up the batteries and then carry it around to any telephone.

The price of a TTY can be anywhere from around $200 for a basic unit up to $600 or more for the top-of-the-line machines with printers, answering machines, ring indicator lights and other fancy features.

Keeping it All Straight

This whole TTY concept has two holes in it. First, typing is much slower than speech or ASL signing. Second, there is nothing to prevent both people from typing at the same time, producing two screens full of gibberish. To address both problems, a shorthand has been developed.

The single most important abbreviation to know when communicating with a TTY is "GA," which stands for "go ahead." Protocol says that you always type "GA" when you're done talking, and don't start typing again until the other person types "GA."

At the end of the conversation, the abbreviation "SK" ("stop keying") means, "I'm done now and I want to hang up." This can also be written as "GA to SK," when conveying that you are done but the other person might not be. If the other person is done also, he or she will respond with "SK" (or sometimes "SKSK"), and the conversation is over.

A sample conversation might look something like the example below. Remember, too, that typing is much faster without worrying about shift keys, so much TTY conversation happens in uppercase.

```
HELLO THIS IS JOHN DOE. GA

HI JOHN. THIS IS MARY SMITH. IM CALLING TO FOLLOW UP
ON OUR MEETING FROM LAST WEEK ABOUT CAPTIONING YOUR
SHOW.   GA

IVE GOT SOME GOOD NEWS FOR YOU, MARY. WE START CAP-
TIONING EVERY SHOW AS OF NEXT WEEK. GA

FANTASTIC!  THANK YOU JOHN. THATS ALL I NEEDED.   GA

YOURE WELCOME AND ILL TALK TO YOU SOON. GA TO SK

BYE.  SKSK
```

At first, the whole thing looks a little odd, but you get used to it very fast. Something that may take a wee bit longer to get used to is the abbreviations. Apostrophes are difficult to type on many TTYs, so they are often omitted, leading to things like the "IM" for "I'm" and "IVE" for "I've" in the example above. Similarly, the question mark often requires shifting, so many people will press the Q twice instead, leading to exchanges like this:

```
DID YOU GET MY LETTER QQ GA

YES I DID. THANKS. GA
```

More importantly, there is a set of acronyms and abbreviations commonly used on the TTY, many of which have carried over into e-mail. These include:

R . . . . Are
U . . . . You (as in "R U GOING TONITE?")
UR . . . . Your
PLS . . . . Please

HD .... Hold (as in "PLS HD" when transferring)
BCNU .... Be Seeing You
CD or CLD ..... Could
CUL .... See You Later
HOH .... Hard Of Hearing
ILY .... I Love You
MTG .... Meeting
OFC .... Office
OIC .... Oh, I See
PPL .... People
THKS or THX ... Thanks
TMW .... Tomorrow
TTFN .... Ta-Ta For Now
TTYS .... Talk To You Soon

Of course, there are many more such abbreviations and acronyms; this is not intended to be a comprehensive list.

Other Conventions

Remember to always identify yourself when answering a TTY call. The other party can't identify your voice from your typing, so there's no way the person can be sure he or she reached the right number unless you state who you are.

Although many TTY machines have backspace keys, they are not always used or even useful. For example, once the paper has advanced in a TTY, it will not crank back (even if it could erase the burned-in text). For this reason, most deaf people use "XXX" to erase an error, as in "R U MWWT XXX MEETING US TONITE?" The "XXX" erases the typo "MWWT" to produce "R U MEETING US TONITE?"

When deaf people place TTY calls, they can never be sure whether the phone will be answered by a hearing person or by someone with a TTY. It is common practice to tap the space bar a few times if the indicator on your TTY shows that the phone has been answered but nobody has typed anything. This produces a warble that should signal the person on the other end to put the telephone handset into the TTY.

Many older TTYs don't have a set of number keys. There is a key much like the shift on a typewriter that switches to "number mode" and turns some of the letter keys into numbers. If someone should accidentally turn on number mode and leave it on, you will see gibberish on your screen. If this happens, tap the space or "X" key a few times until you've got the person's attention and she stops typing. Then type something like "IS YOUR NUMBER LOCK ON?"

Just a Modem, Right?

Many people have attempted to get their computer modem to communicate with their TTY and given up in frustration. Why? Because the TTY doesn't use the same communication protocols as today's modems.

Rather than the ASCII (American Standard Code for Information Interchange) format used by computer modems, TTYs use an older protocol called Baudot, named for J.M.E. Baudot, the French inventor. Baudot does not include all of the characters that ASCII has and uses a different encoding scheme for them.

There are some modems available that can communicate in both ASCII and Baudot, such as the NexCom 300vi (a combination standard modem/TTY modem/answering machine), which sells for about $300, and the AudiTech Intele-Modem, which is roughly the same price.

There is even a modem standard defined by the International Telecommunication Union, called V.18, which defines a specification for modems that can communicate with U.S. TTYs (45.45-baud Baudot), English and Australian TTYs (50-baud Baudot), EDTs (European Deaf Telephones) and others.

You can also purchase TTYs that can communicate in both Baudot and ASCII. When using these devices, you must make sure that the TTY on the other end is using the same protocol that you are.

Chapter 9

Threats, Real and Perceived

Speech Recognition

The popular media often picks up tales from speech-recognition technology firms about how court reporting and stenocaptioning will be an obsolete profession any day now. To court reporters and stenocaptioners not up to speed on the technology, this is a frightening prospect.

Prospective court reporting students are worried about whether starting court reporting school is a good idea. Existing students are wondering whether to stay, especially now that stenomask reporters using speech-recognition systems (they call themselves "voice writers") are getting certified in realtime.

So just how good *is* speech recognition these days?

I have attended a number of trade shows and seminars about speech technology (both recognition and synthesis). I visited every booth they had and really checked out the state-of-the-art from some of the companies developing the underlying technologies for tomorrow's speech-recognition systems — folks like Philips and AT&T.

PRODUCT AND TECHNOLOGY CATEGORIES

Speech synthesis is the electronic creation of speech. In other words, making a computer talk. This isn't of much interest to the captioning profession, where the objective is to turn speech to print rather than vice versa.

Speech recognition is computer comprehension of speech. There are several broad classifications of speech recognition, including discrete speech vs. continuous speech, speaker-dependent vs. speaker-independent, and context-sensitive vs. context-insensitive.

Discrete speech recognition requires that each word be an individually identifiable unit. Obviously, this isn't the way we talk. During normal speech, words are run together and even slurred (as in "gonna" for "going to"). To make speech recognition easier, many systems require a pause between words. A typical requirement is 100 milliseconds (one-tenth of a second). Given that it takes about two-tenths of a second to say a typical word, that puts a theoretical maximum of 200 words per minute on discrete speech recognition. Needless to say, that will never work in a sportscast.

Continuous speech recognition, the ability to recognize words exactly as they're spoken, slurs and all, is the hook everyone's hanging their hat on. The system uses a technology known as the "Hidden Markov Model" to separate the words into phonemes (individual sounds) and then reassembles them into words.

Speaker-dependent systems are used by stenomask reporters. Such systems are trained to understand pronunciations, inflections and accents and can run much more efficiently and accurately because they are tailored to the speaker. This is analogous to the way a captioning system is trained for a specific stenocaptioner using custom translation dictionaries and phonetics tables. These are the systems that are now in use by court reporters and are likely to be used soon in captioning.

Speaker-independent systems are designed to work for anyone, as long as they're speaking English. To accomplish this, the scientists had to figure out what parts of speech are generic and which ones vary from person to person. A spin-off of this speech-recognition technology is that the speaker-dependent parts have now been programmed into security systems that respond only to a given individual's voice, as shown in movies like *Sneakers*. This is known as *voice recognition.*

Context-sensitive systems increase their accuracy by anticipating or limiting what can be said at any given time. For example, a speech-recognition-based hotel wake-up-call system might ask you what time you'd like to be awakened. It can then assume that whatever you say will represent a time of day. If you say anything else, it will not be able to recognize it. Context-sensitive systems may actually have large vocabularies, but only a small portion of that vocabulary will be activated at a time.

Context-insensitive systems allow you to say anything, anytime. Typically, they have dictionaries in the neighborhood of 20,000 words.

WHAT'S AVAILABLE

Tools for setting up speaker-independent, context-sensitive, voice-based operation of Microsoft Windows-based programs abound. They do everything from running menus to checking selections in dialog boxes. To date, I have seen none that allow dynamic modification (like Total Access Courtroom software, which allows attorneys to add issue codes on-the-fly, or realtime stenocaptioning software, which allows dictionaries to be modified as you go). These systems need all the words and rules to be built in before using the program.

The quality of such tools varies widely. Overall, I have not been impressed. I visited a company marketing a speech-recognition system, and during the demonstration, the company representative took over a dozen tries to get it to accept his telephone number. Understand here that it was only looking for, and accepting, digits, as opposed to the tens of thousands of vocabulary words required for captioning.

Similarly, AT&T has a voice-mail application running with only 10 commands available, one of which is "previous message." In three minutes of trying, I was unable to get it to recognize that command. One time, I said "previous message" and it thought I said "erase all messages." Handy, eh? This is from a company with a huge research facility and a vested interest in making this technology work.

One program that I've tried, for controlling Windows applications, isn't too bad. I went through their demo dialog box and the program selected options fairly accurately based on my spoken commands, as long as there wasn't any text input. It was a hotel demo, where you can call in for towels, pillows, wake-up calls, newspapers, etc. As long as I asked for one of the things on the menu, it was right probably 75 percent of the time. When I entered the time for the wake-up call, it wasn't so hot, which probably explains why I haven't seen it deployed in any major hotels.

ARPA, the U.S. government's Advanced Research Projects Agency, is still sponsoring a lot of research. The best system in their 1995 "contest" achieved 93 percent accuracy with a 20,000-word vocabulary. That's about one wrong word in every 14. It used a minicomputer with 100MBs of RAM (realtime stenocaptioning software will run on a 486 PC with 2MBs of RAM). All of the words used in the test were in the dictionary, so that seven percent error rate represents just a count of *wrong* translations, not words outside the vocabulary. This would be like giving a court reporter a realtime test and saying that "It's OK if the word isn't in your dictionary and it comes out wrong. You'll only be graded off if you write it wrong."

Of course, things have changed since that contest. New speaker-dependent tools allow significantly higher recognition rates, and Pentium III machines are equivalent to those dedicated minicomputers in performance.

Some of the best technology is still batch-oriented rather than realtime. In other words, they use the dictation paradigm, where you speak into a tape recorder or the digital equivalent thereof and it processes it all at once rather than as you do it. Such systems use Unix-based computers with hardware DSPs (digital signal processors) to get the throughput.

Background noise is a killer to these applications. They couldn't handle a newscast where the reporter was standing in a rainstorm, even if they *could* deal with it in the studio.

SO HOW GOOD IS IT?

Overall, I would rate the tools available for speech-based editing as marginally useful. I would rate full-speed realtime speaker-independent speech recognition as a long way from being able to compete with court reporting technology. With the advent of today's more powerful

PCs, the technology has moved from the $20,000 Silicon Graphics workstations onto dual-processor Pentium III machines, which are dramatically less expensive. I asked one vendor (who claims to be the leader in the core technology, as several of them do) when we'd be able to plug a system into a TV newscast and have it create captions in realtime. He said, "Two years." (I don't believe him.) I asked how long before it could get all of the words in the newscast, including live interviews and remotes. He said, "Never."

Speaker-*dependent* speech recognition, as used in the voice writer systems, is here and it's real. Jim Bouck passed his Realtime Verbatim Reporter exam in November 1999. To do so, he had to demonstrate realtime speed and accuracy previously possible only with stenotype.

SHOULD STENOCAPTIONERS FEAR FOR THEIR JOBS?

The main reason opponents of stenotype technology have fought for alternative technologies like tape recording is to eliminate the salary being paid to the court reporter. Voice writing doesn't eliminate that salary. The person running the realtime captioning or CART system isn't using stenotype, but it's still a heavily trained person using an expensive system, so the salary cannot be eliminated.

I foresee both stenotype and stenomask reporters moving into the CART and captioning fields in the future and hopefully working side-by-side. There are a lot of job opportunities out there, and we will have enough trouble finding qualified people to fill them without infighting between proponents of these two competing technologies.

SPEECH RECOGNITION IN CAPTIONING SOFTWARE

As of press time, the realtime stenomask software companies (StenoScribe and AudioScribe) plan to add captioning capabilities to their software, but have not done so yet.

At least two companies have already made attempts to utilize voice-recognition technology to create captioning systems. A company called Blue Feather, from Wisconsin, created a speech-based realtime captioning system, which they demonstrated at the National Association of Broadcasters convention in the early '90s.

I went to Blue Feather's booth at that NAB show and asked to see a demonstration of the system. I was eager to view it in operation, because I had never seen a speech-recognition system that could operate in excess of 120 wpm, and Blue Feather was claiming its system could keep up with a newscast. The company informed me that it was simply impossible to use the system in a crowded, noisy environment like the NAB show floor. I said, "Let's get back here in a corner, take the microphone, and we'll duck under the table. I want to see how this works."

He said, "All right. Try to speak as clearly and distinctly as you can to overcome the background noise, and let's see what we get." I began speaking. I looked at the screen and didn't see anything. I said, "What's going on?" He said, "Keep going, it hasn't got enough yet. It uses contextual information to resolve homonyms; therefore, it always stays at least a sentence behind."

In fact, it stayed 30 seconds behind. I watched several demonstrations, used the system myself for a while, and it stayed, the whole time, around a half-minute behind. The translation quality was quite poor as well, which the company claimed was due to the background noise. To the best of my knowledge, this system has never been deployed in the real world as a realtime captioning system.

The other speech-recognition-based captioning system is called VoiceWriter, and comes from LOBCO in Canada. Unlike Blue Feather, it was announced as an offline captioning system. It was on display at the NAB convention in early 1996. Also unlike Blue Feather, LOBCO simply refused to demonstrate speech recognition on the show floor. "It must have a quiet environment," I was told, despite the current technology in headsets.

VoiceWriter's use of speech-recognition technology is secondary to its function as a nonlinear, offline, caption-editing system. Instead of the traditional method of controlling videotape machines, VoiceWriter uses video that has been "digitized" onto a computer disk. The speech recognition, I was told, is used for operating the system, entering commands and performing editing tasks. Soon, the company said, it would be developed to the point where it was usable for data entry as well.

This is probably the best utilization of speech recognition in the captioning environment that has been attempted to date. Data entry can be performed at any speed and edited for accuracy, unlike realtime captioning, where it must be at full speed and full accuracy as it is done.

Sign-Language Interpreters

Unfortunately, there's often an antagonistic or competitive relationship between sign interpreters and reporters doing CART or captioning. Generally, this stems from a lack of understanding on both sides. The solution, as in so many other cases, is education.

WHAT ARE WE DOING HERE?

This is the first question you and the interpreter need to ask yourselves. At a fundamental level, you both have the same purpose: to enhance communication. This is what can cause interpreters to view you as a threat.

In reality, though, you'll swiftly learn that you are performing different functions.

Deaf people can generally be classified as either prelingually deaf (also called culturally deaf or "capital-D" Deaf) or postlingually deaf. Late-deafened adults fall in the second category.

Those deafened late in life, or elderly people who experience a loss of hearing less than total deafness, usually don't invest the necessary time required to learn ASL. It is estimated that only 10 percent of the 24,000,000 deaf and hard-of-hearing people in the United States know sign language. Captioning serves the other 90 percent.

Postlingually deaf people, especially late-deafened adults, usually have English as their first language. Many don't know sign language at all. They depend on you, and the interpreter is little or no help to them.

Saying that someone is "prelingually" deaf means that the deafness occurred before the person developed linguistic skills and awareness. For these people, sign language is usually their first language and

English their second language. They can easily follow a sign interpreter, because the interpreter is using their native "tongue." Many could have trouble keeping up with the realtime written English you produce and often won't even try.

One exception to this is when people know the wrong sign language. Yes, indeed, there isn't just one sign language. In fact, in the United States, there are two in common usage.

ASL (American Sign Language) is not just a rendition of English; it is a beautiful and expressive language in its own right, one with its own vocabulary, syntax and sentence structure.[1] It is a language that takes years to master. If you provide an ASL interpreter for an event, you are providing a wonderful service for prelingually or culturally deaf people.

SEE (Signed Exact English or Signed Essential English) is a rendering of the English language in signed visual form. It uses English vocabulary, word order and grammar. Many culturally deaf people shun SEE because it is not an offshoot of deaf culture, but it is popular with people who already know English because it is easier to learn.

There are other methods for deaf communication as well, such as cued speech, in which hand motions are used to assist a speechreader in distinguishing between sounds. Once again, no matter whether a deaf person's prime mode of communication is ASL, SEE, speechreading or cued speech, captions can increase their comprehension of an event.

Sometimes, you'll find the prelingually deaf audience reading your captions for another reason. Following an ASL interpreter can be fatiguing. You can't look away, even for a moment, or you may miss something. It requires fixing your eyes on the interpreter, *not* on the speaker, and concentrating for the whole event. Captions keep up to four lines of text on the screen at a time, and CART can keep even more, allowing you to look away for a moment, and then catch up. This does *not* mean that those people would want to give up their sign interpreter, just that your realtime can give them a respite.

---

[1] *ASL is not based on English at all. It is actually derived from a French sign language, so the word order and syntax are loosely based on French.*

WORK TOGETHER

When someone is speaking, you and the interpreter can work independently of each other. When someone is signing, you depend on the interpreter to know what to write. Work closely with interpreters. Exchange cards. Offer to send referrals if the interpreters will do the same. Get to know them, and they won't view you as a threat.

One of the best presentations I was ever involved in was an awards banquet with many deaf attendees and recipients. We set up two cameras, one focused on the person speaking and one on the interpreter. A simple video effects box was used to create a split image with the speaker on the right and the interpreter on the left. This image was fed to the captioning system and then displayed on a big projection screen with captioning on the picture.

Deaf people could choose their own combination of reading the captions, watching the interpreter and lip-reading the person who was speaking. Many deaf groups can't afford an approach like that, but it is absolutely the height of accessibility for those who can.

Be careful of your attitude when you talk to interpreters. They went through a lot of training to become certified, which usually includes deaf studies courses. They probably know the target audience better than you do. Explain how your services work, but don't act superior. Make sure they know that *you* know that many people prefer sign language to realtime and that you don't have a problem working with them.

MONEY

I can't tell you how many times I've had people ask me why captioners and CART reporters cost more than interpreters. You'll be asked this question, too, so have an answer ready. Here are some of the points I always try to make:

- **Interpreters require no equipment.** They don't have to worry about paying for computers, CAT/captioning software, service agreements, steno machines, caption encoders, video projectors and so forth.

- **A four-hour conference requires one captioner or CART reporter,**

but *two* interpreters. Generally they switch off every half-hour or so. Even though the interpreters cost less individually, the cost has to be doubled before comparing.

- **Interpreters can't provide meeting transcripts.**

Chapter 10

The Law

Obviously, any discussion of captioning law has to treat the subject on a country-by-country basis, as laws are set by each country's government. We'll examine these laws by region. *Disclaimer: This section of the book is intended as a general guide to laws concerning captioning. Laws change frequently, and some of the laws described herein may have changed by the time you read this. I am not an attorney. If you need specific legal advice regarding captioning, please consult an attorney.* ***No portion of this book is to be construed, under any circumstances, as legal advice.***

State Laws

To date, there have been few laws mandating captioning enacted by state governments in the United States. One notable exception is Minnesota, which enacted, in 1996, a law concerning educational and government videotapes. (Note that the section is 325I — that's the letter "I" not the numeral "1.")

Minnesota Statutes 1996, Chapter 325I
325I.05 Video captioning.

Subdivision 1. Requirement. A person may not in the ordinary course of business distribute a prerecorded videocassette tape or similar audio-visual material to a videotape seller or videotape service provider unless it is open-captioned or closed-captioned for the deaf and hard of hearing. For purposes of this section, "videotape seller" and "videotape service provider" have the meanings given them in section 325I.01.

Subdivision 2. Enforcement. A person who violates this section is subject to the penalties and remedies provided in section 8.31, except subdivision 3a.

Subdivision 3. Application. This section applies to prerecorded videocassette tapes or similar audio-visual material that:
(1) is primarily produced for sale to educational institutions, training facilities, state or local government agencies, or medical facilities; and
(2) is released or rereleased on or after June 1, 1997, and more than 500 copies are produced in the release or rerelease; or
(3) is produced by a governmental entity for educational purposes.

In South Dakota, Senate Bill 236 had the potential to become the first state law mandating closed captioning. Unfortunately, it was shot down, but it is still worthy of a look here because it was a very short and simple piece of legislation, written to address a specific issue with no extra fluff:

South Dakota SB-236

Introduced by: Senators Daugaard, Flowers, Kloucek, Munson (David), Paisley, and Reedy and Representatives Koetzle, Belatti, Cerny, Fischer-Clemens, Gabriel, Hagen, Lucas, Moore, and Pederson (Gordon)

FOR AN ACT ENTITLED, An Act to require the provision of certain closed captioning and interpretive television services.

BE IT ENACTED BY THE LEGISLATURE OF THE STATE OF SOUTH DAKOTA:

Section 1. Terms used in this Act mean:

1. "Closed captioning," services designed for persons with hearing disabilities that provide a live or prerecorded visual presentation of the sound associated with a given television program. Captioning services are not visible except on a television receiver designed to display them or by use of a specifically installed decoder;
2. "Interpreter services," the relaying of any local news program to the general public through the use of qualified sign language interpreters. The interpreter services are accomplished by simultaneously broadcasting the sign language interpreter's actual person in the same visual

frame as the local news announcer. The sign language interpreter simultaneously signs the contents of the local programmed news as it is spoken by the local news announcer;

3. "Local broadcasting news program," any news program and local broadcasted television programs produced in South Dakota, including sports, weather, emergency, legislation, education, governmental, health, and any other essential program;
4. "Real-time closed captioning," any service similar to closed captioning but specifically used to reference the live captioning of live programs versus the captioning of prerecorded programs. These services are rendered simultaneously on a verbatim basis as a program is being broadcasted.

Section 2.

Notwithstanding §§ 9-35-16 to 9-35-24, effective July 1, 1998, all South Dakota based, local television stations, including South Dakota Public Television, KABY, KDLT, KCLO, KELO, KEVN, KSFY, KPLO, KTTW, and KOTA, shall provide closed captioning, or until closed captioning can be fully implemented in each local television station's broadcast, provide interpreter services, in the production and dissemination of all local news broadcasting programs. However, all South Dakota based, local television stations shall provide real-time captioning on all live local broadcasting news programs as defined in section 1 of this Act no later than July 1, 1999.

There are several fascinating things about this bill,[1] most notably that it recognized the value of realtime captioning. It is widely known that "TelePrompTer captioning" (typically generated by a newsroom computer) leaves much to be desired — a topic covered in more depth elsewhere in this book. This bill would have forced TV stations to use *only* realtime captioning, implicitly declaring all other forms of captioning inadequate for live programming — an opinion I share, and that was written into the latest implementation of the Telecommunications Act of 1996 by the FCC as well.

Another item of note is that this bill contained no "weasel clauses," such as "undue financial hardship." There were no options and no

---

[1] *Aside from the fact that sports programming is considered "essential," which in and of itself says something interesting about the government of South Dakota.*

outs, unlike the infamous Americans with Disabilities Act and Telecommunications Act (discussed later in this chapter).

Lastly, this bill explicitly recognized on-screen sign language interpreters as an option. The use of an inset in the corner of the screen for an interpreter has virtually disappeared, yet this bill would have given stations the option to bring it back. While sign language is by no means equivalent to captioning — each has advantages over the other — it shows that the lawmakers in South Dakota considered the alternatives and decided to make a substantial effort to work with deaf people.[2]

Federal Captioning Laws

In the United States, there are very few laws that explicitly address closed captioning and even fewer that mandate captioning in a way that affects the average citizen on a day-to-day basis. Captioning is appearing more and more frequently in the U.S. Codes, however, a trend that hopefully will continue.

A search through federal law reveals over a dozen code sections that refer to captioning. When referring to one of these code sections, I will use the standard short form citations. For example, "47 USC 611" refers to U.S. Code, Title 47, Section 611. The chapter and subchapter are omitted, as they are not required to find a specific section.

The bulk of the code sections that mention captioning aren't what we think of as laws at all. They represent authorization for federal agencies to provide grant money or consortium money for projects relating to captioning. While this is certainly important (federal money has been responsible for much of the progress captioning has made in the United States), they do not actually mandate captioning. The Telecommunications Act of 1996 is the law that really forces the issue of captioning for everybody.

Code sections 47 USC 330 and 47 USC 303 will be discussed under the

---

[2] *The use of "deaf people" here rather than "deaf and hard-of-hearing people" is intentional. Sign language is a wonderful service for deaf people, but only a small fraction of hard-of-hearing people understand sign.*

heading of "Television Decoder Circuitry Act" later in this chapter. Those two sections do not address captioning per se; they address the decoder that is now included in most TV sets.

Mandatory Captioning

Let's begin by taking a look at a very straightforward code section that specifically mandates captioning:

> **47 USC 611: Closed-captioning of public service announcements**
>
> Any television public service announcement that is produced or funded in whole or in part by any agency or instrumentality of the Federal Government shall include closed captioning of the verbal content of such announcement.

It can't get much clearer than that. This code section does nothing for commercially produced programming, but it shows that the government included itself in the regulation process. It goes on to state that broadcasters are not required to place captioning on public service announcements that the government fails to caption. It is OK for a broadcaster to *unintentionally* leave the captions off of a PSA, but they are not allowed to do it on purpose.

This next code section, 26 USC 9003, is intended for presidential candidates who are looking for government funds for their campaigns (as provided in Internal Revenue Service 26 USC 9006). Once again, we have a law that is clear and unequivocal:

> **26 USC 9003: Condition for eligibility for payments**
>
> **(e) Closed-captioning requirement**
> No candidate for the office of President or Vice President may receive amounts from the Presidential Election Campaign Fund under this chapter or chapter 96 unless such candidate has certified that any television commercial prepared or distributed by the candidate will be prepared in a manner which ensures that the commercial contains or is accompanied by closed captioning of the oral content of the commercial to be broadcast in Line 21 of the vertical blanking interval, or is capable of being viewed by deaf and hearing-impaired individuals via any comparable successor technology to line 21 of the vertical blanking interval.

Surprisingly, this section has no "outs." The candidate must either caption the commercials or receive no money from the Presidential Election Campaign Fund.

Captioning and Education Grants

While there is no law specifically stating that you can't get a grant that involves videotapes unless you caption them, several laws relating to government grants do address captioning. All of the code sections mentioned here are part of Title 20, which covers education-related law.

> **20 USC 1015a: Access and equity to education for all Americans through telecommunications — Application**
>
> (...)
>
> **(a) In general**
>
> Each eligible partnership desiring to receive a grant under this part shall submit an application to the Secretary at such time, in such manner and containing or accompanied by such information as the Secretary may reasonably require.
>
> **(b) Contents**
>
> Each application submitted pursuant to paragraph (1) shall—
>
> (...)[3]
>
> (5) describe the manner in which special services, including captioned films, television, descriptive video and education media for individuals with disabilities, shall be supported;
>
> (...)
>
> **(c) Approval of applications**
>
> (1) In general
>
> The Secretary shall, in approving applications under this part, give priority to applications which describe programs that—
>
> (A) include support for services to make captioned films, descriptive video and educational media available to individuals with disabilities who otherwise lack access to such educational materials;

Here we see that you don't have to caption to get the grant, but that

---

[3] *(...) indicates text not specifically relating to captioning was omitted. This symbol is not included when text is omitted from the beginning or end of the cite.*

you do have to describe what (if anything) you are doing about captioning; if you *do* caption, your grant application will be given priority over others that don't involve captioning. The very next code section reads as follows:

> **20 USC 1015b: Access and equity to education for all Americans through telecommunications — Authorized activities**
>
> Grants awarded under this part shall be used for one or more of the following activities:
>
> (...)
>
> (5) A loan service of captioned films, descriptive video and educational media in order to make such materials available, in accordance with regulations issued by the Secretary, in the United States, for nonprofit purposes, to individuals with disabilities, parents of individuals with disabilities, and other individuals directly involved in activities for the advancement of individuals with disabilities, including addressing problems of illiteracy among individuals with disabilities.

This is more specific. This code section specifically authorizes educational grants for loan services of captioned films. Note that neither Section 1015a nor 1015b has anything to do with broadcast television.

This whole subject of a loan service for captioned films is addressed in much more detail in 20 USC 1452, which is a part of Chapter 33, "Education of Individuals With Disabilities."

> **20 USC 1452: Captioned films, television, descriptive video, and educational media for individuals with disabilities**
>
> **(a) Establishment of loan service**
>
> The Secretary shall establish a loan service of captioned films, descriptive video, and educational media for the purpose of making such materials available, in accordance with regulations, in the United States, for nonprofit purposes, to individuals with disabilities, parents of individuals with disabilities, and other individuals directly involved in activities for the advancement of individuals with disabilities, including for the purpose of addressing problems of illiteracy among individuals with disabilities.

(b) Authority of Secretary

The Secretary is authorized to—

(1) acquire films (or rights thereto) and other educational media by purchase, lease, or gift;

(2) acquire by lease or purchase equipment necessary for the administration of this subchapter;

(3) provide, by grant or contract, for the captioning for deaf and hard-of-hearing individuals and video description for the visually impaired, of films, television programs, and video materials;

(4) provide, by grant or contract, for the distribution of captioned and video-described films, video materials, and other educational media and equipment through State schools for individuals with disabilities, public libraries, and such other agencies or entities as the Secretary may deem appropriate to serve as local or regional centers for such distribution;

Elsewhere in Chapter 33, the issue of financial assistance is raised, and the Secretary of Education is specifically instructed to make captioning of educational materials a reality:

20 USC 1461: Technology, educational media and materials for individuals with disabilities

Financial assistance

(b)(1) With respect to new technology, media, and materials utilized with funds under this subchapter to improve the education of students with disabilities, the Secretary shall make efforts to ensure that such instructional materials are closed captioned.

Chapter 70 of Title 20, "Strengthening and Improvement of Elementary and Secondary Schools," has a section on educational technology product development, which is specifically intended to "support development of curriculum-based learning resources using state-of-the-art technologies and techniques designed to improve student learning; and support development of long-term comprehensive instructional programming and associated support resources that ensure maximum access by all educational institutions."

20 USC 6871: Educational technology product development

(6) Requirements for Federal assistance
Each eligible consortium desiring Federal assistance under this section shall submit an application to the Secretary at such time and in such manner as the Secretary may prescribe. Each application shall include—

(...)

(F) a description of how the product can be adapted for use by students with disabilities, including provisions for closed captioning or descriptive video, where appropriate;

What the government is actually saying here is that companies and organizations may apply to form consortia that include state or local educational agencies, and the federal government may provide funding. The application for this funding must include a description of how captioning might be used, but the funding itself is in no way contingent on captioning.

The "Star School Awards," described later in Section 20, Chapter 70, describe grant provisions for technology-related education. These also specifically address captioning. Much of the grant money is targeted at the development of course materials that may be presented on videotape, and the code section authorizing the grants brings up captioning early on.

20 USC 6894: Technology for education
Star Schools Program — Grants authorized
(h) Closed captioning and descriptive video
Each entity receiving funds under this part is encouraged to provide—
(1) closed captioning of the verbal content of such program, where appropriate, to be broadcast by way of line 21 of the vertical blanking interval, or by way of comparable successor technologies; and
(2) descriptive video of the visual content of such program, as appropriate.

All that section calls for is "encouragement" to provide captioning and descriptive video. The code section describing what grant applications must contain provides a guideline; but, again, it has no teeth.

20 USC 6896: Technology for education

(b) Star school award applications

Each application submitted pursuant to subsection (a) of this section shall—

(...)

(12) describe the activities or services for which assistance is sought, such as—

(A) providing facilities, equipment, training services, and technical assistance;

(B) making programs accessible to students with disabilities through mechanisms such as closed captioning and descriptive video services;

Just like the consortium funding described earlier in Chapter 70, none of the code sections relating to the Star Schools Program actually *require* that material be captioned in order to qualify.

Vocational Rehabilitation

The vocational rehabilitation sections of the Labor Code (Title 29) contain some odd twists. Look, for example, at these excerpts:

29 USC 723: Scope of vocational rehabilitation services

(a) Individual services

Vocational rehabilitation services provided under this chapter are any goods or services necessary to render an individual with a disability employable, including, but not limited to, the following:

(...)

(6) interpreter services for individuals who are deaf, and reader services for those individuals determined to be blind after an examination by qualified personnel under State licensure laws;

(...)

(b) Group services

Vocational rehabilitation services, when provided for the benefit of groups of individuals, may also include the following:

(...)

(4) The use of services providing recorded material for individuals who are blind and captioned films or video cassettes for individuals who are deaf.

For some reason, the people who drafted this law felt that captioned films or videos are important for *groups* of deaf people, but not for *individual* deaf people. By looking at paragraph (a)(6), we can see that our lawmakers felt that deaf people need interpreters. Why they didn't feel that those same individuals needed captions on their training videos is a mystery.

Elsewhere in Title 29, captioned videotapes come up again. This time, it is in the context of research and development projects (grants) related to vocational rehabilitation.

29 USC 762: Research

(a) Federal grants and contracts for certain research projects and related activities

The Director may make grants to and contracts with States and public or private agencies and organizations, including institutions of higher education, Indian tribes, and tribal organizations, to pay part of the cost of projects for the purpose of planning and conducting research, demonstration projects, training, and related activities, the purposes of which are to develop methods, procedures, and rehabilitation technology that maximize the full inclusion and integration into society, employment, independent living, family support, and economic and social self-sufficiency of individuals with disabilities, especially individuals with the most severe disabilities, and improve the effectiveness of services authorized under this chapter.

(...)

(b) Research grants

(1) Specialized research and demonstration activities

In addition to carrying out projects under subsection (a) of this section, the Director may make grants under this subsection (referred to in this subsection as "research grants") to pay part or all of the cost of the specialized research or demonstration activities described in paragraphs (2) through (16).

(...)

(11) Feasibility of establishing center for production and distribution of captioned video cassettes to individuals who are deaf

Research grants may be used to conduct a model research and demonstration project designed to assess the feasibility of establishing a center for producing and distributing to individuals who are deaf captioned video cassettes providing a broad range of educational, cultural, scientific, and vocational programming.

Note how this code section specifically addresses feasibility studies for distribution of captioned videos to individuals.

Captioning on Cable TV

In the eyes of the Federal Communications Commission, and the rest of the government, cable TV systems are rebroadcasters. They are not responsible for the creation of the material on their systems, only for passing through what they are given.

Many people have complained that a particular show isn't captioned, only to find that the TV station or network *had* captioned it. After chasing down the problem, it eventually comes out that the captions were stripped (removed) by the cable TV company.

Why would this happen? Did someone at the station intentionally decide to remove the captioning from your favorite episode of *Home Improvement* today? Not at all. The removal of captions by cable companies is usually a side effect of something else that they are doing. One common culprit is equipment designed to "clean up" a TV signal. As a part of this "cleanup" process, the equipment strips off the entire VBI, which is where the captions are encoded, and regenerates it. The net result is a better-looking picture, but with no captions.

Another culprit is digital compression. When TV programs are transferred through computer equipment, the signal is often compressed to allow more information on less wire. This compression process involves removing redundant or unnecessary information from the signal. Unfortunately, it is all too easy for the captioning data to become classified as "unnecessary."

In either case, what you really want is your captioning back. Is there a way to get it? The answer is a qualified "yes." These two excerpts from Title 47 provide the answer (the italics are mine):

47 USC 534: Carriage of local commercial television signals
(b) Signals required
(3) Content to be carried
(A) *A cable operator shall carry in its entirety, on the cable system of that operator, the primary video, accompanying audio, and line 21 closed caption transmission* of each of the local commercial television stations carried on the cable system and, to the extent technically feasible, program-related material carried in the vertical blanking interval or on subcarriers. Retransmission of other material in the vertical blanking interval or other nonprogram-related material (including Teletext and other subscription and advertiser-supported information services) shall be at the discretion of the cable operator. Where appropriate and feasible, operators may delete signal enhancements, such as ghost-canceling, from the broadcast signal and employ such enhancements at the system headend or headends.

47 USC 535: Carriage of noncommercial educational television
(g) Conditions of carriage
(1) Content to be carried
A cable operator shall retransmit in its entirety the primary video, accompanying audio, and line 21 closed caption transmission of each qualified local noncommercial educational television station whose signal is carried on the cable system, and, to the extent technically feasible, program-related material carried in the vertical blanking interval, or on subcarriers, that may be necessary for receipt of programming by handicapped persons or for educational or language purposes. Retransmission of other material in the vertical blanking interval or on subcarriers shall be within the discretion of the cable operator.

As the italicized passages clearly state, the cable company is required by law to transmit the captions. However, this appears to apply only to local TV stations and educational television. A cable operator who is fully conversant with these laws could well point out that a movie on the Sci-Fi channel doesn't meet either of those requirements.

The Americans With Disabilities Act

The Americans with Disabilities Act, known as the ADA, was a sweeping piece of legislation, covering everything from wheelchair ramps to

Braille labeling. Surprisingly, though, there was very little direct mention of captioning in the ADA.

Of the estimated 44,000,000 people directly affected by the ADA, over *half* of them were affected due to hearing problems, yet the only captioning explicitly mandated by the ADA is for government-funded or government-produced public service announcements.

Captioning is hinted at by a number of other sections in the ADA, most notably the infamous Title II. Section 202 states:

> *Subject to the provisions of this title, no qualified individual with a disability shall, by reason of such disability, be excluded from participation in or be denied the benefits of the services, programs, or activities of a public entity, or be subjected to discrimination by any such entity.*

Earlier in Title II, the term *public entity* is explicitly defined as:

> *(A) any State or local government;*
> *(B) any department, agency, special purpose district, or other instrumentality of a State or States or local government; and*
> *(C) the National Railroad Passenger Corporation, and any commuter authority (as defined in section 103(8) of the Rail Passenger Service Act).*

Note how cleverly the federal government exempts itself from this definition?

Some read this to say that every city council meeting, school board meeting, county supervisor meeting and so on *must* be captioned if it is open to the public. Pushing this point could backfire, however. More than one city has stated that if they are forced to caption all televised meetings, they will simply stop televising meetings.

The Television Decoder Circuitry Act

This bill did more to further the cause of captioning than anything that had come before it, including the ADA. Simply put, the Television

Decoder Circuitry Act mandates that all Americans have access to captions. The actual effects of the Act were more far-reaching than that.

The TDCA (PL 101-431) was enacted in 1990 with the provision that it would take effect on July 1, 1993. It was one of the shortest and clearest pieces of legislation ever to make its way through the federal government — so short, in fact, that it can be included in its entirety right here:

Television Decoder Circuitry Act of 1990

An Act

To require new televisions to have built-in decoder circuitry.
Be it enacted by the Senate and House of Representatives of the United States of America in Congress assembled,

Short Title

Section. 1. This Act may be cited as the "Television Decoder Circuitry Act of 1990."

Findings

Sec. 2. The Congress finds that—

1. to the fullest extent made possible by technology, deaf and hearing-impaired people should have equal access to the television medium;
2. closed-captioned television transmissions have made it possible for thousands of deaf and hearing-impaired people to gain access to the television medium, thus significantly improving the quality of their lives;
3. closed-captioned television will provide access to information, entertainment, and a greater understanding of our Nation and the world to over 24,000,000 people in the United States who are deaf or hearing-impaired;
4. closed-captioned television will provide benefits for the nearly 38 percent of older Americans who have some loss of hearing;
5. closed-captioned television can assist both hearing and hearing-impaired children with reading and other learning skills, and improve literacy skills among adults;
6. closed-captioned television can assist those among our Nation's large immigrant population who are learning English as a second language with language comprehension;
7. currently, a consumer must buy a TeleCaption decoder and connect the decoder to a television set in order to display the closed-

captioned television transmissions;
8. technology is now available to enable that closed-caption decoding capability to be built into new television sets during manufacture at a nominal cost by 1991; and
9. the availability of decoder-equipped television sets will significantly increase the audience that can be served by closed-captioned television, and such increased market will be an incentive to the television medium to provide more captioned programming.

Requirement for Closed-Captioning Equipment

Sec. 3. Section 303 of the Communications Act of 1934 (47 USC 303) is amended by adding at the end thereof the following:

"(u) Require that apparatus designed to receive television pictures broadcast simultaneously with sound be equipped with built-in decoder circuitry designed to display closed-captioned television transmissions when such apparatus is manufactured in the United States or imported for use in the United States, and its television picture screen is 13 inches or greater in size."

Performance and Display Standards

Sec. 4. (a) Section 330 of the Communications Act of 1934 (47 USC 330) is amended by redesignating subsection (b) as subsection (c), and by inserting immediately after subsection (a) the following new subsection:

"(b) No person shall ship in interstate commerce, manufacture, assemble, or import from any foreign country into the United States, any apparatus described in section 303(u) of this Act except in accordance with rules prescribed by the Commission pursuant to the authority granted by that section. Such rules shall provide performance and display standards for such built-in decoder circuitry. Such rules shall further require that all such apparatus be able to receive and display closed captioning which have been transmitted by way of line 21 of the vertical blanking interval and which conform to the signal and display specifications set forth in the Public Broadcasting System engineering report numbered E-7709-C dated May 1980, as amended by the TeleCaption II Decoder Module Performance Specification published by the National Captioning Institute, November 1985. As new video technology is developed, the Commission shall take such action as the Commission determines appropriate to ensure that closed-captioning service continues to be available to consumers. This subsection shall not apply to carriers transporting such apparatus without trading it."

(b) Section 330(c) of such Act, as redesignated by subsection (a) of this section, is amended by deleting "and section 303(s)" and inserting in lieu thereof ", section 303(s), and section 303(u)".

Effective Date

Sec. 5. Sections 3 and 4 of this Act shall take effect on July 1, 1993.

Rules

Sec. 6. The Federal Communications Commission shall promulgate rules to implement this Act within 180 days after the date of its enactment.

Once the TDCA was signed into law, the EIA (Electronic Industries Association)[4] formed a subcommittee (R4.3) made up of businesses with an interest in how the law was to be enacted. The subcommittee was comprised of representatives from TV manufacturers such as Mitsubishi, Sony, Toshiba, Philips and Zenith; prominent captioning companies such as the National Captioning Institute, the Caption Center, VITAC (then known as CaptionAmerica) and Closed Captioning Services; captioning software and equipment manufacturers like Cheetah Systems, CPC, EEG, Teknova and SoftTouch; broadcasters, including PBS, ABC, CBS, NBC and Turner; and other major players.

The EIA subcommittee, with one notable exception, felt that this was the ideal time to remove some of the restrictions that had been present in the captioning standard since the very beginning. This included not being able to place captions in the middle of the screen, being able to place roll-up captions only at the bottom of the screen and a couple of omissions in the character set.[5] Eventually, these enhancements to the de facto standard were put together to form EIA-608, which defines how Line 21 captioning works today.

---

[4] *The EIA later merged with the Consumer Electronics Manufacturers Association, and the name was later shortened to the Consumer Electronics Association.*

[5] *No, they didn't fix the missing letters needed for a full representation of other languages like French and German. They instead replaced the ¼ and ¾ symbols with ® and ™. The other letters are covered in EIA-708, for DTV.*

Meanwhile, Over at Zenith

Even as the EIA was hard at work on the standard, one company decided to show its support for the deaf and hard-of-hearing community by not waiting for the TDCA to take effect. Zenith put televisions with built-in caption decoders into production in early 1992, over a year before the July 1993 deadline imposed in the Act.

The good news is that this put over a million TV sets with caption decoders on the market before the TDCA required it. The bad news is that Zenith didn't wait for the standard to be finalized. In fact, in its haste, the company didn't even fully comply with the existing de facto standard set by the TeleCaption II specification from NCI.

These Zenith televisions had some fairly harmless incompatibilities, like the way they displayed italics. The EIA standard, which was later to be adopted by the FCC, mandates that characters designated as italic be displayed either as true italics or at least as slanted letters. Zenith, rather than adding another whole character set for italics, just displayed italicized captions by changing the color from white on black to black on yellow.

There was also a more significant issue, demonstrating once again how good intentions have the potential for leading one astray. Zenith decided that it would be good to enlarge the caption letters, making them easier to read. This decision had two unfortunate side effects:

First, if the television received a four-line pop-on caption, only three lines of it would be displayed (there wasn't room for the fourth line). While four-line captions are rare, they do occur. One place is in the credits, and that fourth line may well contain useful information, like how to contact the captioning company with suggestions or comments.

Second, the enlarging of the letters changed which portions of the picture got covered by the captions. Offline captioners go to a great deal of trouble (or, at least, they *should*) to assure that the captions don't cover anything important on the picture. This is especially critical with commercials. The company producing the commercial does not want the captions covering the price of the product or the company's phone number. With the Zenith television, the efforts to prevent that from happening could be for naught.

In their defense, however, when the FCC adopted the EIA's recommendations for extension of the standard, Zenith jumped on it quickly. Not only did the company update its sets to work as the standard required, but Zenith did it before it was legally required to do so.

Can we really complain? I don't think so. Over a million people got TV sets with caption capability that otherwise wouldn't have had it at all, and they got them *before* the TDCA mandated it. That's a praiseworthy accomplishment.

Far-Reaching Effects

Remember earlier in the chapter when I mentioned the effects of the TDCA being more far-reaching than just putting decoders in TV sets?

The Television Decoder Circuitry Act raised the level of awareness about captioning to new heights. People who would otherwise never have heard about captioning pressed that "CC" button on their TV remote just to see what it did. This higher level of awareness led to more demand for captioning and to shows being captioned that, otherwise, would not have been.

The TDCA also had effects that stretched beyond U.S. borders. TV companies found it easier in many cases to make a single TV model for everyone instead of making a caption-enabled model for the United States and a captionless model for everyone else. This led to a huge influx of caption-ready televisions in Canada, even though there was no Canadian equivalent of the TDCA.

The TDCA also lowered the cost of delivering captions to the consumer. Mass-market economics shows that you can justify far more engineering expenses when you're manufacturing 18,000,000 units per year of something (the approximate number of TV sets sold in the United States each year) than when you're manufacturing under 100,000 units per year (the approximate number of stand-alone decoders being made each year prior to 1993).

With so much at stake, it didn't take long before several semiconductor manufacturers started making caption decoder chips that could be purchased for a few dollars by TV manufacturers.

Telecommunications Act of 1996

In 1996, the federal government passed sweeping new laws affecting the broadcast and cable industries. The Telecommunications Act of 1996 was complex, and captioning was just one tiny part of it.

Like the ADA, this act itself is not very specific about its mandate to require captioning. It says only that regulations will be implemented to ensure that "video programming first published or exhibited after the effective date of such regulations is fully accessible through the provision of closed captions."

Unlike the ADA, it empowered the Federal Communications Commission to interpret the act and enforce it. This is precisely what happened when the FCC implemented Section 305. The full Report and Order that was issued on August 22, 1997, is a massive and rambling document, with over 300 numbered paragraphs. It does what Congress wanted it to do: It mandates captioning.

Specifically, the FCC's ruling, which took effect on January 1, 1998, provides an eight-year phase-in for captioning of "new" programming (programs that aired for the first time after the ruling takes effect). During the phase-in, the FCC provides these milestones:

- Five hours per day of captioning after two years (January 1, 2000)
- Ten hours per day of captioning after four years (January 1, 2002)
- Fifteen hours per day of captioning after six years (January 1, 2004)

At the end of that eight-year period (as of January 1, 2006), all new programming must be captioned. There is no specific mention of which hours each day must be captioned. Some stations may choose to caption their news, while others caption talk shows or sitcoms.

"Old" programming, which airs before the law takes effect, has only one milestone. After five years (January 1, 2003), 30 percent of pre-rule programming must have captions. After 10 years, that goes up to 75 percent.

Weasel Clauses

Like most laws, the FCC ruling is riddled with exceptions. The FCC provided numerous weasel clauses to allow stations to get out of captioning their programming. No captioning is required at all for:

PROGRAMS IN FOREIGN LANGUAGES

Non-English programming was originally exempted largely because captioning companies bemoaned the lack of non-English realtime captioners. Unfortunately, the FCC failed to see the difference between non-English offline captioning, which is readily available, and non-English realtime captioning, which is quite rare.

In fact, the FCC came back in September 1998 and updated the ruling, stating that Spanish-language captioning is going to be required after all. The phase-in period is delayed from English, with full captioning of new Spanish programming not required until 2010 and old programming in 2012.

In January 2001, the first milestone kicks in for the Spanish-language broadcasters. There is a shortage of stenocaptioners who can write in Spanish, so if you're a native (or fully fluent) Spanish-speaker, learn to write Spanish realtime and you'll be a valuable commodity.

"NONVOCAL" MUSIC PROGRAMMING

Since programs like symphony or instrumental jazz have no words, captioning them doesn't make sense. Note that this does not exempt music with lyrics, such as the vast majority of MTV programming. I, for one, will be pleased to see more captioning on music videos. Maybe we'll finally find out what the words are to "Louie, Louie!"

PUBLIC SERVICE ANNOUNCEMENTS

Public Service Announcements are expected to be addressed in a separate ruling. As we mentioned earlier in this chapter, captioning of government-funded PSAs is already required by the ADA.

SHORT COMMERCIALS

Any commercial less than five minutes in length is exempted. The FCC expects pure market pressure to drive advertisers here. If they don't caption, deaf and hard-of-hearing people don't buy their products.

LATE-NIGHT PROGRAMMING

Captioning is not required on programs aired between 2 a.m. and 6 a.m. Stations that broadcast in multiple time zones can pick any four-hour period in the middle of the night, as long as it doesn't go any earlier than midnight or later than 7 a.m. in any time zone in the continental United States.

PROGRAMMING FROM "NEW NETWORKS"

Any broadcast network less than four years old as of when the rules took effect is completely exempt from these rules until 2002. In other words, any broadcasters that started after January 1, 1994, have an extra two years. They don't have to start captioning until 2002, but then they must caption at the same level as older networks.

SMALL VIDEO PROGRAMMING PROVIDERS

Any video programming provider with less than $3 million per year in gross revenues is completely exempt. If the broadcaster is owned by a larger company, only the sales of the broadcaster are counted, not its parent company. For example, if a billion-dollar company owns a tiny TV station, it is the revenue of the TV station that counts, not the big company that owns it.

UNDUE ECONOMIC BURDEN

We heard these words in the ADA as well. No broadcaster will be required to spend more than two percent of its annual gross revenues on captioning. To put this in perspective, consider a station that makes $3 million per year. This is the smallest station that would be required to caption. The station may not be forced to spend more than $60,000 per year on captioning, which would be barely adequate to pay for a couple of newscasts per day.

HOME VIDEO

The FCC ruling applies only to broadcast television, not to videotapes or DVDs of movies, like those you'd rent for home viewing.

Quality

The FCC was willing to step up to the plate and require that the caption *signal* be of high-enough quality for your caption decoder or TV set. It was not willing to define quality requirements for the caption content.

The FCC correctly identified this as a two-edged sword. If it did not set certain quality standards, then a station can deliver virtually illegible and unusable captions and claim to meet the requirements. If it did set quality standards, then the FCC becomes embroiled in a never-ending stream of arguments concerning whether the captioning on a particular program is "good enough." The FCC chose to avoid that particular pitfall and allow the industry to regulate its own caption content quality.

The Reverse Weasel

One obvious negative potential of the new ruling was predicted and planned for. Under the new law, a station is required to have roughly 25 percent of its programming captioned as of January 1, 2000, and 50 percent by January 1, 2002. What if the station *already* captions 30 or 40 percent of its programs? Does this mean it could cut back dramatically and build back up when required?

Thankfully, no. There is a "no backsliding" clause in the ruling that prohibits a video program provider from reducing its level of captioning. To quote directly from the FCC ruling, "We also will require video programming providers to continue to provide closed captioning at a level substantially the same as the average level of captioning that they provided during the first six months of 1997, even if the amount of captioned programming exceeds that required under the benchmarks."

To Realtime or Not to Realtime

During the public comment phase of the FCC ruling, many broadcasters complained about the cost of realtime captioning compared to the virtually free process of connecting their TelePrompTer system to the caption encoder. Granted, that leaves about half of the typical newscast uncaptioned, but it's cheap and easy.

The FCC originally stated that newsroom computer captioning,[6] such as the aforementioned TelePrompTer scenario, is an acceptable way to caption a newscast. Of course, if only half of a one-hour newscast has captions, then only a half-hour will count toward the station's total captioning quota.

---

[6] *The FCC originally called this "Electronic News Room (ENR)" captioning, but changed the terminology because of trademark issues.*

There was a massive public outcry opposing this ruling. The deaf and hard-of-hearing population consider newsroom computer captioning to be clearly inferior to realtime captioning. In response, as of January 1, 2000, the major network stations (ABC, CBS, FOX and NBC) in the top 25 markets are required to use realtime captioning for their newscasts.

So what's a market? The country is divided into broadcast areas, roughly defined by the households within antenna range of major cities. Nielsen, the same company that calculates ratings for TV shows, estimates the number of households with TV sets in each area and ranks them. The top 25 are:

1. New York
2. Los Angeles
3. Chicago
4. Philadelphia
5. San Francisco/Oakland/San Jose
6. Boston
7. Washington, D.C./Hagerstown
8. Dallas/Fort Worth
9. Detroit
10. Atlanta
11. Houston
12. Seattle/Tacoma
13. Cleveland
14. Minneapolis/St. Paul
15. Tampa/St. Petersburg/Sarasota
16. Miami/Ft. Lauderdale
17. Phoenix
18. Denver
19. Pittsburgh
20. Sacramento/Stockton/Modesto
21. St. Louis
22. Orlando/Daytona Beach/Melbourne
23. Baltimore
24. Portland (Oregon)
25. Indianapolis

This doesn't mean that a TV station in San Francisco isn't allowed to use newsroom computer captioning. It does, however, mean that if that TV station is owned by (or affiliated with) one of the four major networks, then any newsroom computer captioning won't count in determining whether the station meets the FCC's 25 percent test.

Although not specifically addressed in the ruling, the "no backsliding" provision mentioned above may well apply here. The logic is that most deaf viewers find the newsroom computer method unacceptable, thus a station that uses realtime captioning now would not be maintaining "substantially the same" level of captioning if it switched to newsroom computer.

Got a Problem With That?

An unenforced law might as well not be a law. The FCC did put some teeth into its rulings. If you have a complaint about captioning, you must address the problem *in writing* with the network, station, cable company or satellite company and give the company a chance to respond. Only then may you file your complaint with the FCC itself. The FCC reserves the right to impose penalties. One penalty specifically mentioned in the ruling is requiring the video programming provider to caption *more* than the ruling mandates. This is one of the most appropriate penalties ever set forth: If you don't caption enough, you may have to provide extra captioning!

If you see uncaptioned programs on your set at home, how do you know where to direct your complaint? The first stop is the video provider. If you have cable TV or a satellite dish, then the company you write your check to is your video provider. If you get your TV signal from a broadcast station, the station is your video provider. Either way, your video provider is not allowed to take the captions off a program. If the program was originally captioned, but the captions were stripped along the way, complain directly to the TV station, cable company or satellite company.

If the program was never captioned in the first place, then your video provider will tell you who is responsible, and you can go directly to the source.

Hitting Close to Home

"How does this affect me?" you ask. As we build toward virtually all live programming being captioned, we will need to build a pool of qualified captioners many times larger than the existing force. This means job opportunities. Just about every major captioning company in the country is hiring.

As a profession, we have until 2006 to build a work force capable of captioning tens of thousands of hours of live programming every week. We need to make sure there are captioning curricula in our court reporting schools. We need to test and certify captioners. We need to get the word out to the broadcast industry that the National Court Reporters Association is ready to meet the challenge.

As an individual, you need to consider your alternatives. In some ways, captioning relieves you of the burdens of court reporting. There are no transcripts, no arguing attorneys and no 60-mile drives to get to a deposition that canceled and nobody told you. On the other hand, realtime captioning is a stressful and exacting profession, where every word you write is visible to thousands or millions of people immediately, and you don't have the luxury of sending out a clean copy later. An attorney might forgive starting five minutes late because you were caught in traffic. Broadcasters will not forgive missing a portion of a broadcast. Depositions and court sessions usually happen during regular business hours on weekdays. Captioning happens on the 5 a.m. news and the 11 p.m. news.

Emergencies

As of 2000, the FCC is now requiring captioning on emergency broadcasts. The wording does not specifically mandate *closed* captioning — in fact, the FCC explicitly allows subtitles or crawls.

This is a significant ruling, in that it defines a class of programming that is critical to the safety of deaf and hard-of-hearing people, and assures that the key information in the programming will be presented visually as well as aurally.

Canada

The CRTC ("Conseil de la Radiodiffusion et des Télécommunications Canadiennes" in Quebec, or "Canadian Radio-television and Telecommunications Commission" everywhere else in Canada) is the Canadian organization that oversees broadcast television and, therefore, captioning.

In Canada, each broadcaster must be licensed by the CRTC, and that license must be renewed periodically. The CRTC reviews each station's captioning plans carefully before renewing its broadcast license, toward the goal of achieving 100 percent captioning by 2002. In Public Notice CRTC 1995-48, the CRTC announced significantly more stringent captioning rules. The following is taken directly from a CRTC press release:

> Given decreasing captioning costs and new technologies, the Commission believes that most broadcasters should be able to provide full programming service to deaf and hard-of-hearing persons in the near future.

The CRTC then went on to state specific captioning requirements for stations broadcasting in English. In June 1999, the requirements were extended to French-language programming. The following is taken from a CRTC document entitled, "Building On Success — A Policy Framework For Canadian Television."[7]

> **Closed captioning**
> 130. The Commission considers that French-language broadcasters should have requirements for closed-captioning of programming, similar to those applicable to English-language broadcasters. The Commission will discuss the proposed implementation of these requirements in the context of individual licence renewals.
> 131. The Commission's policy on closed captioning is set out in PN 1995-48. Under this policy, television stations earning more than $10 million in annual advertising revenues were required, by 1 September 1998, to caption all local news, including live segments. The policy also

[7] *The entire document is available online on the CRTC Web site at http://www.crtc.gc.ca/ENG/BCASTING/NOTICE/1999/P9997_1.txt.*

requires that all such licensees close caption at least 90 percent of all programming during the broadcast day by the end of individual licence terms. Medium and smaller television stations are respectively expected, or encouraged, to meet the same standards.

132. The Commission notes that English- and French-language television stations historically have not had the same requirements due to the high cost of providing closed captioning for French-language programming. However, the Commission considers that the time has now come for French-language broadcasters to provide more closed captioning. It is confident that market demand will reduce the costs of providing the service.

Chapter 11

Case Studies

Realtime has many applications, and there are hundreds of fascinating people involved in the industry. This chapter is an attempt to introduce you to some of the people who shaped the industry and some of the ways that captioning and CART technology are being used today.

For every person who is mentioned in this chapter, there are dozens of others I didn't mention, not because they aren't worthy, but simply because there isn't enough room.

Some of these profiles come from my earlier book, *Inside Captioning*, and those have been updated to show what has happened since that book was released. Others are new.

Network News

Back when captioning was new (and extremely expensive), only the networks could actually afford to provide realtime captioning of their newscasts. News captioning began with the National Captioning Institute captioning *ABC World News Tonight*. At first, the captioning was done offline and broadcast hours later (open captioned).

Later, ABC began to put multiple typists to work during the 6:30 feed, so that they could broadcast closed captioning on the latest East Coast feed at 7 p.m. This method left large sections of the program uncaptioned, but it was the best available at the time.

Even as this was going on, NCI had a team hard at work developing the technology for realtime captioning of the news broadcasts. Marty Block, the court reporter NCI had chosen to become the first stenocaptioner, recalls: "Day in and day out, new discoveries were made and new ideas were born. It was exciting beyond my wildest dreams. I would spend several hours every day reporting news shows time and time again, building dictionary entries, honing the translation. Most exciting of all, I was the only reporter doing it. I was the first and would be the first forever. What satisfaction and what a challenge."

NCI put realtime captioning on the air first with the live broadcast of the Academy Awards in 1982. It was a smash success. NCI soon hired its second stenocaptioner, Bobbie Showers. Bobbie and Marty worked toward the goal of captioning the *World News Tonight* every night. On October 11, 1982, they met that goal.

In 1985, two more companies went online with realtime news captioning, both doing local news: The Caption Center at WGBH in Boston, Mass., and American Data Captioning (later to become VITAC) in Pittsburgh, Pa.

The Caption Center, working with PBS, is where captioning originated, so it was appropriate that it should get into realtime captioning. ADC was a small start-up company, comprised of Marty Block; two court reporters from Pennsylvania, Joe Karlovits and Ed Fulesday; and two engineers from NCI, Jeff Hutchins and Dave Crane.

By the late 1980s, the United States Department of Education was providing grant money to fund captioning of national news programs. The grant ended up split between three captioning companies. ABC news was captioned by NCI, CBS news by the Caption Center and NBC news by ADC.

The Caption Center and the National Captioning Institute are both nonprofit organizations. ADC was the first of the big for-profit captioning firms.

National vs. Local

What makes network news captioning different from local news captioning? Quite a few things, actually, with one being the level of commitment. There are local stations that have 24-hour, on-call contracts with their captioning firms, but there's nothing quite like the network contracts.

In a visit to VITAC in Pittsburgh some years ago,[1] I was standing in the foyer in front of the caption studios when NBC cut into its regular programming for a news break. NBC's network feed (from the huge VITAC satellite dish) was being displayed on a number of TV sets around the office, and the call went out in seconds: *"Special Report!"*

I quickly stepped out of the way as people went rushing for their stations. In under a minute, the coordinator had taken his post and dialed NBC's caption encoder at its studio in New York. The captioner had slid into her seat and had begun writing frantically. Captions began to appear.

I turned to Joe Karlovits, the president of VITAC, and asked him, "Why the last-minute rush?" He smiled and told me that that's what they got paid for. When NBC airs a special report, there's no time to contact VITAC and warn that it's coming. The special report is put together instantly. VITAC's contract requires it to have people on standby, in the office, around the clock.

When the Persian Gulf War broke out, captioning firms like VITAC went into overtime mode. Stations were providing news around the clock, and the captioning companies were captioning it. All of it. Captioners were putting in long shifts and standby captioners were being called in to give the regular captioners breaks. Virtually nothing was being scripted in advance, so everything was realtime. Steno-captioners switched back and forth all through the day and night. Even when the network wasn't running news, someone had to be there, because the stations could cut back to Desert Storm coverage at any moment.

For a company like VITAC, the equipment investment is immense. From the satellite dishes and encoders to the video, audio and phone line switching systems, everything must be broadcast quality and

---

[1] *This happened almost 10 years before I became an employee of VITAC.*

designed for redundancy. If a captioning studio goes down, the captioning company must be able to instantly switch to another studio. If the company loses power, the auxiliary power system switches in. If the company loses a phone line, backup lines are available. Everything is duplicated: computers, videotape machines, satellite dishes, TV monitors, steno machines and modems.

Today, as new stations go online, the need for national news programming is increasing constantly. CNN captions both the CNN News and the CNN Headline News, one done by VITAC, the other by Media Captioning, based in Carlsbad, Calif. That development alone took network news from tens of hours per week to hundreds of hours per week. Luckily for everyone, the pool of trained stenocaptioners is increasing as well. By 1996, it was estimated that there were over 100 stenocaptioners captioning national and local news programs in the United States alone, and an even greater number writing sports, government broadcasting, religious programming and educational material.

As I write this in the year 2000, that number has more than doubled, and the implementation of the Telecommunications Act of 1996 is increasing the demand for realtime captioners even more.

Local News

Local news is an altogether different level of challenge. The same types of headlines appear that a national newscast would carry, but it is also sprinkled with a heavy dose of local flavor. Why does this represent a different level of challenge? Because, in addition to knowing the spelling of (and being able to write) the names of world leaders, the captioner must know the spelling of, and be able to write, local town, street and landmark names, like Moscone Center, La Cañada College, Dumbarton Bridge, Junipero Serra Freeway and Woz Way.[2]

The need for local news captioning is great. Without it, deaf and hard-

---

[2] *These are actual examples from the San Francisco Bay area. Woz Way is worse than it sounds, because from time to time announcers will explain that it is named after Steve Wozniak, one of the founders of Apple Computer, and then the captioner has to spell* that!

of-hearing people might not know whether the fire on television is threatening their neighborhood or whether the hurricane is headed their way. They won't know when the road they take to work is closed or why every TV channel on the dial is showing a white Bronco cruising down Highway 5 at 45 miles per hour.[3]

After national news captioning had become established, realtime captioning of local news grew slowly. The pool of talented captioners with the requisite equipment was tiny, and the price was high. Relatively few people had caption decoders for their TV sets, and very few people in the broadcast industry had any idea what closed captioning was.

In 1986, two captioners from ADC (American Data Captioning, later renamed VITAC), Chairman Marty Block and President Joe Karlovits, got into a conversation with Judy Brentano, a court reporter from Atlanta, Ga., about captioning local news. Marty and Joe encouraged Judy to join ADC and operate a national captioning branch office in Atlanta.

Judy was a logical choice for them. Marty, known as the father of realtime captioning, and Joe were both members of the Board of Directors of the National Court Reporters Association; and Marty would go on a short time later to become NCRA's President. Judy was every bit as prominent. She was Secretary-Treasurer of NCRA and former president of the Georgia Shorthand Reporters Association, and she would later become President of NCRA herself.

Judy decided that she was going to bring captioning to the South. She and her husband, Mike,[4] operated (and still operate) a deposition firm called Brentano Reporting in Atlanta, which would act as the perfect springboard.

At first, things went forward with Judy and Mike incorporating as ADC-

---

[3] *In case you missed it (you lucky dog, you), this is a reference to the low-speed chase that led to the apprehension of ex-football player and movie actor O.J. Simpson after his ex-wife and a friend were murdered.*

[4] *Just in case I haven't said "President of NCRA" often enough in the last two paragraphs. As I write these words, Mike is preparing to take his own turn as President of NCRA.*

Atlanta. Later on, the focus of the company expanded beyond the original goal of providing regional news captioning, and The Caption Company was formed, replacing ADC-Atlanta.

With a shoestring budget, her first priority had to be education. She targeted WXIA-TV Channel 11 in Atlanta. Realizing that the deaf and hard-of-hearing population around Atlanta was almost half a million people, WXIA eventually made the decision to go forward with captioning and fronted Judy $35,000 for the purchase of equipment.

Equipment

With equipment in hand, Judy still faced a lot of work. Dictionaries had to be built, backup captioners located and trained, and the studio constructed. Since few models existed to work from at that time, much of what Judy did was pioneering. In 1988, WXIA officially went on the air as the South's first station with realtime captioning for their news.

In the beginning, Judy and her staff actually worked at the TV station when they captioned. This has changed over time, and most of the captioning is done from home or from The Caption Company's studios.

In either case, the station has a caption encoder installed in its equipment room, placing captions on the video signal coming out of master control. When the captioners were in the same building, their captioning system was connected to the encoder by a cable. Now, they use a modem and a telephone line to connect from anywhere.

The captioner uses an online captioning system with an array of equipment. Originally, The Caption Company used Xscribe XCS-1 captioning systems, which ran on a proprietary CP/M-based computer, but they later graduated to IBM PC-compatible computers running the CAPtivator Online software from Cheetah Systems.

Aside from the computer, the only equipment required is the steno machine, the modem and the TV sets. Since steno machines are individually adjusted to fit each court reporter, Judy's staff provides their own steno keyboards.

Each captioner uses two televisions, one with captions and one without. That way, the captioner can see her captions on one of the televisions and can use the other to verify that the captions aren't covering anything important on the picture. If they are, a single keystroke on the steno machine moves the captions to a different location on the TV screen.

The second television also provides redundancy. If the primary television breaks down, there's another one there for backup.

Some captioning firms carry the concept of redundancy and backup farther than others. Having a second TV set is only the beginning. Many news captioners have a spare computer, modem and steno machine ready to be swapped in on a moment's notice. It is common for the captioner to use a UPS (Uninterruptible Power Supply) to assure that the system will keep operating for some period of time even in the event of a total power outage.

One captioner, Kevin Daniel, former owner of Bay Area Captioning and now a captioner for VITAC, even went so far as to set up a notebook computer to run from the cigarette lighter adapter in his car, along with a special modem hooked to a cellular phone and a Sony Watchman portable battery-powered television. He can lose power *and* telephone service and still stay on the air.

In areas with cable TV, it is not unusual for captioners to run one of their TV sets from cable and one from an antenna, providing yet another level of redundancy.

Preparing for a Newscast

A news captioner's day begins with a review of the newspapers. This provides spellings of names and places in the news and a "heads-up" about stories that may require more research. A few captioning firms hire people to review stories and highlight words or phrases for the captioner, but most captioners prefer to do it themselves. Nobody knows a captioner's dictionary as well as the captioner does.

As the day progresses, news reporters at the TV station are working on their stories. In a modern newsroom, the reporters will transfer their stories electronically to a newsroom computer system, where the producer, editor and news director can review them.

These stories are arranged on the newsroom computer and edited to fit their time slots. The writing is often hurried, with little concern for spelling and punctuation. After all, nobody actually *sees* the stories in their raw form except the on-air talent reading the TelePrompTer. When new and strange words appear, the reporters or newsroom staff may even add phonetic spellings to assist the anchors in reading it. In WXIA's case, and many other stations around the country, the newsroom computer of choice is Basys.

About an hour before air time, the captioner dials up the Basys system and "downloads" the script files (copies them to her own computer). Then she runs a program that converts them to a format readable by the captioning systems and begins to review them.

Many stories are only the vaguest of outlines, and others won't be completed until minutes before airtime. The captioner scans these stories for new words and phrases, and then deletes them from the script file.

Other stories are complete, and the odds are good that the talent will read them verbatim from the prompter. These stories are carefully edited, preserving the words while cleaning up the spelling and punctuation. When the script file is ready, it is loaded into the captioning system.

Sometimes this process is automated, and sometimes it is almost entirely manual. Some companies have attempted to make general-purpose script-downloading programs to grab the entire rundown from a newsroom computer, but this is a daunting task. Many small, special-purpose programs have sprung up, including one (a DOS program called BScript) that I wrote for my wife, Kathy, and one that I wrote for the company she used to work for (a Windows program called ScriptConverter). As is true of many such programs, neither became a commercial product. They are carefully fine-tuned for one specific application, not for general use. Many captioning companies have developed their own solutions to downloading scripts.

If this process is fast enough, the captioner may have time for one more quick download of the scripts before airtime, which may net one or two more stories for the live-display file.

A few minutes before airtime, the captioner instructs her captioning system to dial up the station's encoder and connect through the modem. Even though the connection has been made, the encoder is carefully left in "pass-through" mode, so that captions on the show preceding the news won't inadvertently be erased or overwritten.

When the news begins, the captioner is ready with a full arsenal: live display (script) files for some stories, realtime for the rest and a collection of stock captions for special cases. Depending on the station, roughly 40 to 60 percent of the newscast can be scripted, and the rest is realtimed.

The stock captions are used for items that stay the same for every newscast, like the closing credits and the re-open (returning from the first commercial).

In the early days of realtime captioning, it was standard practice for each realtime stenocaptioner to have a coordinator, someone who sat through the entire newscast and helped out on the computer keyboard. The coordinator's duties ranged from making additions to the captioner's dictionary to controlling the flow of script files. In recent times, this practice has all but disappeared on a local level. The extra person adds an extra cost that most TV stations aren't willing to bear, and the increased sophistication of captioning software has made it much easier for the captioner to do everything without help.

Branching Out

Judy Brentano is not one to stop and coast when she achieves a goal: She sets a new goal and keeps moving. This has taken her through a phenomenal career, and she has shown no sign of slowing down.

Judy consulted for TV stations in Albuquerque, Denver, Nashville, Orlando, Columbus, Huntsville (AL), Richmond (VA), St. Louis, Tulsa, Dallas, Portland (OR) and Tampa to help them start up captioning. She started a quarterly publication called *The Caption Network Newsletter,* which helped a lot of people get started in captioning, until she ran out of spare time for publishing.

Judy has chaired dozens of committees and subcommittees for various captioning, court reporting and deafness-related organizations, and has poured hundreds of hours into volunteer work. Somehow, she even found time to make an unsuccessful run for the Georgia State Senate.

As Judy branched out, so did The Caption Company. The company has captioned news, meetings, conventions, seminars, talk shows, election coverage, government proceedings and press conferences. Its sports captioning has included baseball (1995 World Series), basketball (Phoenix Suns, Portland Trailblazers and high school championships), and even 102 hours of the 1996 Summer Olympics.

The Caption Company also does extensive work for deaf organizations, including the National Association of the Deaf, the American Society for Deaf Children, Cochlear Implant Club International, Gallaudet University, the Georgia Association for the Deaf, the Junior National Association for the Deaf, the National Deaf Women's Conference, Self-Help for Hard-of-Hearing People and the Southeast Regional Institute on Deafness.

In 1999, The Caption Company returned to its roots when it was acquired by VITAC. After 13 years, Judy's ADC-Atlanta became a part of what used to be called ADC. As I write these words, Judy is heading up a division of VITAC called MetroCaption, which does what Judy has specialized in for all these years: local news captioning.

Educational CART

Cathryn Bauer wasn't your typical court reporting student. At the time she started court reporting school, she already had a bachelor's degree in history, had written two books on acupressure, and had taken extension courses in copyediting, technical writing and printing techniques. Obviously, she believes strongly in having a good general education.

She has a fascination with applications of technology, and during her court reporter training, she realized that realtime could be used to level the playing field for deaf people and provide them with equal opportunities. Growing up bilingual (she's fluent in German) gave her a feeling for what deaf people go through as they balance their native language (ASL) with their second language (English).

Moreover, it got her thinking about late-deafened adults who grew up without knowing sign language. She saw realtime as a way to enhance their communication abilities. At the same time, she hit the speed plateau that so many court reporting students hit and felt that doing CART work for college students would help her to maintain her motivation in school.

Getting Started

When she felt she was ready, Cathryn started to do her homework. She got on the Web and searched for community colleges in her area. Most had Web sites. In each school, she looked for the person in charge of services for disabled students. If she couldn't find someone with such a title, she sent an e-mail to the Webmaster.

She believes that a well-written résumé is extremely important and that it was a key reason she landed her first job: realtiming a general fine arts class. She was surprised to land a job that fast and had to scramble to get ready.

She read books on deafness to try to understand the people she would be working with. To Cathryn, her job isn't just about letting the student know what the professor is saying, it's about *communication.* It's about letting these students contribute to society as well as helping them to learn.

Earlier in this book, I pointed out that one of the major differences between captioning and movie subtitling is that subtitles provide only the dialog, while captions express the entire auditory experience of the movie. Cathryn carries that belief into her CART work.

"The deaf student(s) have the right to know everything going on in the classroom," Cathryn says. She even goes so far as to write "Nobody is saying anything" when the instructor asks a question and there's a long pause with no one answering. "I don't want them to think they're missing something," she explains. These extra comments are generally removed from the transcript when it is prepared.

Although she asks professors for class handouts in advance and reads extensively, she feels that she would have been sunk without a good general education.

Things went well with the fine arts class, and she substituted in a few others before moving on to caption classes in psychology, journalism, history, career planning and biology.

Equipment

Cathryn chose to invest in a topnotch notebook computer with a large, bright screen and to purchase professional CAT software rather than working with free or inexpensive student software. She wanted to make sure that she'd have support if she needed it.

One of the things she realized was that a thorough working knowledge of the equipment was mandatory. When a lecture is about to begin, you can't stop the class to call a technical support line.

She carries backups of everything, including redundant backup copies of her dictionary (where have you heard *that* advice before?), and tries to make contingency plans for everything. One time that she did have a catastrophic failure, her steno machine was not functioning. She managed to make fast last-minute arrangements to get a sign interpreter into the class, and then Cathryn sat in class with her notebook computer and typed notes.

When it comes to equipment, Cathryn says, "Murphy was an optimist. Anything with a circuit board will die sooner or later."[5]

Reaction From Her Colleagues

Cathryn took a lot of criticism for beginning to work in CART while her speed hadn't yet reached the 200 mark. Many professional CART

---

[5] *Personally, I agree with her except for that part about the circuit board. I don't think there were any circuit boards involved the last time I got a flat tire four-wheeling miles from civilization.*

reporters feel that it is inappropriate to begin work before you have the skill level required to at least pass the RPR exam.

"That viewpoint is valid, and I respect their desire to maintain standards," Cathryn responds.

She was very careful to take only work that she felt she could do and put in many extra hours preparing for it.

She feels that she's able to tell if she's in over her head and that she's capable of dealing with the situation. She's had an opportunity to see students who started out with no self-confidence begin to participate in the class, raising their hands and answering questions. She sees the students she realtimes for as people with a lot to offer, and she delights in helping them to join the mainstream and contribute.

Cathryn's Advice to Newcomers

Cathryn is a very vocal and visible person, active in online discussion groups like NCRA's Online Forum. She gets a lot of questions from people who are considering the same career move that she made.

I asked her how she dealt with these calls. Some people she helps. Others she doesn't.

"I will not spend time helping someone get into realtime work unless I hear loud and clear that you have a commitment to helping deaf people," she explains. "The students depend so much on this service that you have to be able to do it or bow out and let someone else do it."

She also advises against jumping into CART when you're in school if you really need the money. As a reporting student, she gets less money than a credentialed CART reporter would receive, and the work isn't steady. "At this point," she admits, "it isn't a secure job in a lucrative profession."

She feels that in educational CART, just like in news captioning, you have to know what's going on in the world: "Read a quality newspaper each and every day — not *USA Today!*" She especially recommends reading the Sunday *New York Times*. As you read, she says, think about what you would do if this material came up in a class.

In her personal reading, there's no subject she won't delve into. She believes strongly in learning how to find answers. Unless pressed hard for time, she prefers to figure out the answer herself, or at least figure out where to find it, rather than taking the easy way and just asking someone.

She considers the Internet the most valuable research tool there is. She has a bookshelf full of reference volumes, including classic references like *Black's Law Dictionary* and *Gray's Anatomy*, but the majority of her research work is done online.

The Internet, of course, is full of bad information along with the good. "That's where a good general education and critical thinking skills come in," Cathryn explains. You have to be able to tell when something just doesn't make sense. If there's any doubt, look for another independent source.

Where to Next?

As of this writing, Cathryn is still in court reporting school and is getting close to taking the CSR and RPR exams. She isn't, however, looking for a traditional career in court reporting.

The side trip that she took into educational CART has become her main path now, and she looks forward to being able to dedicate herself full time to her work rather than sharing time with court reporting school.

Sports Captioning

In the early 1990s, Kevin Daniel and Mary Cox Daniel were both official court reporters, working in the court system of Alameda County, California, and both were looking for something new and challenging to do. With about 20 years of reporting experience each, they were hardly newcomers to the profession.

By 1992, Kevin and Mary were both writing realtime, and Kevin had set up a computer-integrated courtroom in his court so that the judge and attorneys could see the transcript as he wrote it. Some of the new technology used in his courtroom generated enough interest to get the attention of Richard Hart, and a short feature about the technology appeared on his special segment of the local news, called "The Next Step."

Both of the Daniels were perfectionists, constantly competing with themselves and each other. Whenever NCRA added a new credential, husband and wife rushed to see who could secure it first (they both hold CSR, RPR, RMR, RDR and CRR credentials). Mary was learning American Sign Language, simply because she had always been interested in it, and her deaf instructor had been encouraging her to turn her court reporting talents to captioning.

One day, when Kevin was attending the Court Technology Conference in Dallas, Texas, he went out to dinner with Allen Greenly from Cheetah Systems. Allen asked why Kevin hadn't jumped on captioning, and Kevin replied that he wasn't really interested in news. "What about sports?" Allen asked. After all, there were six pro sports teams in the San Francisco Bay area.

That caught Kevin's attention. He and Mary are both die-hard Oakland A's fans. They had been A's season ticket holders for 15 years. In their home, one whole wall of the room known as "Studio B" is a mural of a ballpark, with Kevin and Mary visible in the crowd.

With their new motivation, Kevin and Mary purchased all of the equipment they needed for realtime captioning and spent the better part of a year honing their dictionaries, learning the hardware and software, and building a reputation in the deaf community by volunteering their realtime services.

When they felt they were ready to go, they launched a letter-writing campaign to the Oakland A's and then called the front office to make an appointment. The director of broadcasting, Tom Cordova, agreed to meet with Kevin. Anticipating technical questions and issues, Kevin took along a technical expert.[6]

Kevin really knew how to prepare for a meeting. He and Mary had been practicing A's baseball games for months, and they had prepared a

---

[6] *Modesty prevents me from mentioning who the technical expert was.*

demo tape, writing realtime on the game the night before the meeting. They had researched the demographics, too, and knew exactly how many deaf people there were in the broadcast area covered by the A's.

Taking along a technical advisor on the first meeting was a good move, too. These days, Kevin has no need to take along someone else, as he has developed a comprehensive knowledge of the technical side of captioning. In the beginning, though, the backup was critical.

What Kevin hadn't prepared for was pure serendipity. As it turned out, Tom Cordova was particularly sensitive to issues like captioning, as his wife was losing her hearing at the time. To top that off, Andy Dolich, the A's vice president of operations, had a three-year-old deaf daughter. You might say that Kevin had a receptive audience.

It was the demo tape that closed the deal, though. Soon, Bay Area Captioning was in full swing with a contract to provide the A's with captioning for the full 1993 season, although still as a part-time gig.

Later that year, they had the opportunity to bid for the first contract in the San Francisco Bay area that would provide realtime captioning for every news broadcast a station put out, starting with the "Daybreak" newscast at 5:30 a.m. and ending with the "Nightbeat" broadcast at 11 p.m. They searched their souls and their bank account, then decided to go for it. They quit their full-time jobs in court, accepted the contract with KRON, hired another captioner (Kathy Robson) to round out the team, and Bay Area Captioning was in the big time.

What is it about first broadcasts that brings out the great bloopers? As we saw in Chapter 4, court reporters and stenocaptioners use "briefs" to write long words and phrases in one or two simple strokes. Kevin had created briefs for *health care reform* and *Hillary Rodham Clinton,* which were, unfortunately, similar to each other. He wrote, "President Clinton was in Massachusetts today, telling Hillary Rodham Clinton horror stories."

Later, Bay Area Captioning expanded to five full-time captioners and got contracts with the Oakland A's, the San Francisco Giants and the Madison Square Garden Network (New York Knicks and New York

Rangers) — a total of almost 250 games per year in addition to the KRON news. In 1998, Bay Area Captioning was acquired by VITAC, and Kevin and Mary moved to Pennsylvania, where they both still caption sports.

Captioning a Baseball Game

At first glance, captioning a baseball game seems like it would be much simpler than doing a newscast. Just make sure you have the rosters for both teams in your translation dictionary, and you're ready to go. In some ways, that is true. For example, there are no scripts to deal with. There are no "live remotes" during the newscast, switching to a reporter interviewing who-knows-who about any random topic. You know that the baseball announcers will just be talking about baseball — right?

Well, there are a couple of problems with that model. First, if the baseball announcers talk about baseball, that doesn't necessarily mean that they're talking about the two teams on the field that day. They will give updates from all of the games going on at the time. The captioner will have to be ready to write not only the names of the players in the game they're covering, but the names of any player in any game who might make a great play, any umpire who might make a controversial call, and any coach who might get thrown out for kicking sand on that umpire, not to mention the names of the parks where all the teams play and the owners of all the teams.

Not only that, but sportscasters love to compare today's players to the players of days gone by. You might hear something like "That was the most exciting moment since Willie McCovey hit his 16th grand slam" or "He looks like a young Rick Reushel."

When you add in the unique vocabulary of baseball, with *sliders, bullpens, RBIs, doubleheaders, pinch hitters, knuckleballs* and *innings,* you have stenocaptioners scrambling for their reference books. And if you're captioning sports, you had *better* have reference books. A quick glance at a baseball captioner's bookshelf will show you record books, baseball dictionaries, team rosters, the *Sports Illustrated Baseball Register,* Monette Benoit's book on sports terminology and rule books.

If that hasn't added enough vocabulary, take a look at some of the ways that sportscasters have slaughtered the English language. Ever listen to a football announcer saying, "They defensed well on that play?" All in all, sportscasters are not chosen for their command of the English language, Howard Cosell notwithstanding.

A perfect example of the kind of sportscasting that keeps captioners on their toes came from San Francisco Giants announcer Mike Krukow. When a sponsorship deal changed the name of Candlestick Park to 3Com Park, many locals rebelled and stuck with the old name. Krukow decided to compromise and began calling it "3Comdlestick Park."

To throw the last variable into the mix, let's look at the length of the broadcast. News captioners know to the second when their broadcasts will be over and when they are done working for the day. Sports such as football are rigidly timed, rarely exceeding the three hours allotted for them by the TV stations. Even when a football game goes into sudden-death overtime, there is a time limit imposed.

Baseball, on the other hand, can go on forever. There's no way of knowing, when the game begins, whether it will be a typical broadcast or a repeat of the 25-inning game between Chicago and Milwaukee in 1984 that went on for eight hours and six minutes.

If you love baseball, though, such unforeseen developments just add to the excitement. Kevin once commented that he would be watching the game anyway (remember, he and Mary had season tickets to the A's), and this way he gets *paid* to watch it. The only drawback, of course, is that he can't have a beer until after the game is over.[7]

Local Government

Fremont, California, is that comfortable size that's big enough to be called a city, yet small enough to feel like a town. With a population of 185,000, it is the 100th entry on the list of the 100 largest cities in the United States. In land area, it is the fourth-largest city in California, after Los Angeles, San Diego and San Jose.

---

[7] *And if he* did, *he certainly wouldn't tell* you *about it!*

Much more germane to this case study, however, the city of Fremont, in early 1992, was home to a group of deaf people that wanted access to the city government. As the home of the California School for the Deaf and a Gallaudet University extension, Fremont had a larger-than-average deaf and hard-of-hearing population.

If that didn't make it enough of a prime target to pioneer realtime captioning of city meetings, Fremont was also home to Cheetah Systems (the leading supplier of realtime captioning equipment at the time), Mike Teague (an active and articulate ex-sign language instructor with a deaf wife) and Kathy Robson (a realtime court reporter/stenocaptioner).

Mike Teague and I served on a community scholarship committee together and were talking one day about his wife, Joni, and how frustrating it was, because she was deaf, for her not to be able to understand the city council and Fremont Unified School District Board meetings on cable TV. "It's too bad we can't get those meetings captioned," he said.

Thus it began.

Standing in the parking lot at the New United Motors manufacturing plant after a scholarship foundation trustees' meeting, I explained to Mike how he could get those meetings captioned and what it would cost. Mike came up with a way to finance it, then organized a letter-writing campaign urging the city to institute captioning. He then contacted Mayor Bill Ball and offered to bring a captioning system to a council meeting and demonstrate how it worked. Mayor Ball accepted.

The First Captioned Meeting

At the next meeting, a group of deaf people and advocates showed up and settled in. We connected the equipment to the cable TV "head end" in the council chambers as my wife, Kathy Robson, prepared to do the captioning. To make the maximum possible impact, the captioning equipment was set up for open captioning and broadcast to both the council chamber and the cable system so that everyone could see it. The audience had the big projection TV system in the council chambers, and the mayor and council members had their own video monitors.

Mike spoke briefly, outlining what captioning was about and what we were going to do, while Kathy captioned everything he said. The mayor and council were glued to their screens. Mike then made way for Joni. Despite being deaf since birth, she is very articulate and understandable; and she gave an impassioned speech about what captioning means to a deaf person. The impact on those who heard her speak was incredible. I explained how the technology worked and how this could be set up on an ongoing basis. Mike explained his idea for financing the captions.

The mayor and council asked questions, all of which Kathy captioned so that Joni and the deaf audience members could follow along. Councilmember Gus Morrison, who became Fremont's mayor two years later, spoke of the large deaf population in the city and the duty that the city had to its citizens. The presentation was a resounding success.

Never underestimate the impact of actually seeing what captioning looks like. Obviously, we'll never know what would have happened that day had the mayor and council members not been able to see that live demonstration, but everyone involved agrees that it was a major factor in the decision to move forward.

Paying for the Captioning

Mike Teague showed up at that meeting with a unique idea for funding the captions. "Have you ever looked at your phone bill," he asked the council, "and noticed there's a surcharge on it to pay for the California Relay Service that allows deaf and hard-of-hearing people to utilize telephones? Why not do the captioning that way?"

He explained that there would have to be an up-front equipment and software purchase by the city, which would cost about $15,000. He then went into the actual costs of captioning the meetings. He calculated the average length of the city council and school board meetings, multiplied that by the number of meetings in a year, and multiplied *that* by the average hourly cost of a captioner. He then added in the cost of an annual maintenance agreement on the equipment and arrived at the cost to caption one year's worth of meetings — approximately $30,000.

At that point, the city of Fremont had about 35,000 households subscribing to cable TV. By adding *seven cents per month* to their cable TV bills, this service would be paid for without having any ongoing need to touch the city's budget.

The contract between the city and TCI Cablevision did, indeed, have a clause allowing the city to add riders to the cable bills. The money, always the hardest part of a new city program, was taken care of.

Moving Forward

The city council assigned the city's PIO (Public Information Officer), Karen George, to handle the research. She confirmed all of the facts and got excited about the idea of doing the captioning. Now, the captioning cause had the final necessary ingredient: an advocate within the system.

Karen organized the requests for bid and put together the specifications and requirements. There would be one vendor chosen to supply the equipment and one to provide the captioning services. Cheetah Systems provided Karen with a list of almost 100 court reporters in the Greater San Francisco Bay Area that had either done realtime work or expressed an interest in it. The requests for bids went out.

When the bids were in, Karen pulled all the numbers together. Mike Teague's plan would work! She presented her findings to the city council, along with recommendations for vendors. The city council voted unanimously to begin captioning all city council and school board meetings. A CAPtivator Online system was purchased from Cheetah Systems, and captioners were chosen to do the captioning work.

Initially, the team consisted of Kathy Robson to caption the city council meetings and Kevin Daniel to caption the school board meetings. After the first year, Kevin withdrew to put his focus into sports and news captioning (see the sports captioning profile earlier in this chapter), and Kathy took over the entire contract.

Certainly, the ADA (Americans with Disabilities Act) played a large part in the decision to implement captioning. The city attorney reviewed the ADA provisions requiring equal access to local government and decided that the city would be at risk by not captioning.

The TDCA (Television Decoder Circuitry Act) had been enacted, but it was not due to take effect until the middle of 1993 — almost a year down the road. Still, it meant that if the city started captioning, virtually everyone would have a way to view the captions, even those on a tight budget. This, too, influenced the decision.

Breaking New Ground

On November 17, 1992, the city of Fremont became the first city in the United States to offer realtime captioning for every telecast city council and school board meeting. The first regular meeting to be captioned was turned into a celebration. A reception was held outside the city council chambers, and Fremont's deaf and hard-of-hearing population was invited to attend.

A new television was installed next to the podium where audience members stand when they address the council. The captions on this television served as a way for deaf and hard-of-hearing citizens to read questions asked of them by the council or city staff. Sign interpreters, as well, were offered for those who needed them.

For the first time, the deaf and hard-of-hearing population of Fremont could actually understand everything that was going on at a city council meeting (well, at least as well as *anyone* can understand what goes on at a city council meeting). Not only that, between the captions and the sign interpreters, they could *participate* in a city council meeting.

Of course, no matter how much preparation goes into a meeting, something will always come up that you didn't think of. For Kathy, it was right at the beginning of the meeting — the Pledge of Allegiance. When the Mayor asked everyone to rise for the Pledge, her upbringing told her to stand up and place her right hand over her heart. Her captioning training told her to sit down and write it for the deaf people.

She realized during her split second of indecision that almost everyone watching would know the words to the Pledge of Allegiance, and she had already written what the mayor said, so she chose to stand.

The mayor and city council really got excited about what they were doing. Mayor Ball asked Kathy how long she could go without a break. She said that she could really use an opportunity every two hours or so to stand and stretch and shake out her fingers. He became very good at checking the clock before starting something lengthy, as well as asking her how she was doing. She even taught him the ASL signs for "Break, please" so that she could signal him when there was a short pause.

A deaf man approached Kathy during a break, took her hand and said, "You've changed my life." Those simple words changed her life.

As these words are written, over seven years later, Kathy and her team still caption the meetings (including the Planning Commission now), and the city maintains its reputation for concern about *all* of its citizens, not just the ones who can hear.

Preparation

When jumping into a job like this, it's important to be ready for it. When Kathy Robson started captioning for the city of Fremont, she had been a court reporter for almost 10 years. She had her state CSR license and an RPR certification from the National Court Reporters Association. Later, she was to become one of the first 55 reporters to receive the CRR (Certified Realtime Reporter) certification.

Kathy has been active in the profession, as president of the Bay Area General Reporters Association and as a member of her national and state associations. She has spoken on captioning and realtime at both a local and national level. Skill level was not an issue.

The translation dictionary was.

A court reporter builds up a dictionary of words that occur in court (or, in Kathy's case, depositions). This dictionary can get lengthy. It doesn't help much, however, when the mayor says, "Now, we're going to discuss JoNelle Zager's proposal to place new signs in the Irvington Business District and in Centerville, near Mowry Avenue."

Preparation for captioning municipal government consists of two phases. First, before taking the job, you do broad-brush dictionary building. Kathy had a marathon session with her computer, all the information packets on the city that we could get from the Chamber of Commerce and a city map. In went street names, names of districts, large businesses, prominent businesspeople, landmarks (parks, nearby hills and mountains, transit systems and so forth). In went the names of the city council, the planning commission, school board, all of the senior city staff, the police chief, the fire chief, the county supervisors, the officers and directors of the Chamber of Commerce, the names of the boards and commissions, the names of the *members* of the boards and commissions, and the names of all the schools in town. The dictionary swelled.

Phase two happens for every single meeting. A courier would bring the agenda to her door four days before the meeting (nowadays, Kathy gets agendas from the city's Web site). She goes through the agenda, looking for names she might not have. Proclamations and ordinances are entered and prepared as scripts so that she can feed them verbatim using live display, no matter how fast they are read.

Kathy also makes a point of checking the newspapers the day before a meeting and the day of the meeting. A seemingly insignificant issue on the agenda, if written up in the newspaper, can generate a disproportionate amount of public attention. If something is mentioned in the paper, it's worth a bit of extra research. If someone is quoted in the newspaper, the name goes in her steno dictionary.

Of course, there are always surprises. Fremont, at the time, had sister cities in Australia, the Azores, Japan, the Philippines and Mexico. Fremont's Sister City Committee had been discussing the possibility of adding Jaipur, India, as a sixth sister city. A delegation from Jaipur made a visit to Fremont and decided at the last minute to visit a city council meeting.

As Kathy was getting ready for the meeting, she noticed quite a few people taking their places in the audience, many of whom appeared to be of Indian descent, but didn't think much of it. Fremont is a diverse community with a large Indian/Pakistani population. She was totally taken off-guard when the first group stood up during oral communications (when any citizen may address the council) and announced that they were from Jaipur, India.

Kathy had never heard of Jaipur and had no idea how to spell it, and over 30 people got up to talk about making Jaipur a sister city for Fremont.[8] Again, it just goes to show that a stenocaptioner must be prepared for anything.

When looking at a captioner's hourly pay, always remember, an hour of captioning is not an hour of work. There is preparation time in advance and time afterward to review the transcript and look for problems so that those same problems might be avoided next time. This is why Kathy can consistently get translation rates of 99.8 percent or 99.9 percent at meetings that go from 7 p.m. until late in the evening.

The U.S. Senate

In early 1990, the United States Senate put out an RFP (Request for Proposal) for a company to provide gavel-to-gavel captioning of all Senate proceedings on C-SPAN II. The RFP went out through the Department of Education, and there were no responses.

That's right. Not one single captioning company was willing to put in a bid for what the Senate required. After the bid deadline had passed, NCI (the National Captioning Institute) did contact the Senate; but by that time Jeri Thomson, the assistant secretary of the Senate, had already begun thinking about alternatives. Specifically, she wondered if the captioning could be done in-house.[9]

When Ms. Thomson began the process of researching equipment suppliers, she checked with the court reporters who produce the *Congressional Record* (known as the Senate floor reporters) to see what equipment they used. They had computer-aided transcription systems

---

[8] *Were you paying attention back in Chapter 1 (The History and Theory of Realtime) when we had the embarrassing digression? This is what we were talking about.*

[9] *Well, I suppose it would have to be "in-Senate," since "in-House" would have other implications in the federal government.*

from Xscribe, so she contacted Xscribe to see if it had realtime captioning software.

As it turned out, Peter Jepsen, Xscribe's captioning specialist in the field, happened to be in the Washington, D.C., area at the time, so he was asked to extend his trip and visit with the Senate.

Peter was certainly no stranger to setting up captioning operations. He first entered the field when, in 1983, he was recruited by Marty Block to join the Canadian Captioning Development Agency. At the time, he had been a court reporter for about seven years, looking for an opportunity to get involved in this new field of realtime TV captioning. Marty got in touch with him and convinced him to make the move from Minnesota to Ontario.

While working at CCDA, Peter was integrally involved in the development of one of the early realtime captioning systems, which was based around the Xscribe XEC-3 court reporting system. The chairman of Xscribe, Bert Mawhinney, visited CCDA, saw this hybrid system and fell in love with it. He hired the programmer who developed the system, Rod MacPherson, right away and hired Peter shortly thereafter.

At the time of his visit to the Senate, Peter had been with Xscribe for about three years. He had spent most of that time on the road, helping people get going in the captioning business and, of course, selling them their equipment. He kept up his own realtime captioning skills and remained active in the National Court Reporters Association.

The Senate officials were impressed with Peter's skills and pleased that they could use an existing vendor. The deal they cut with Xscribe included both captioning systems and Peter's consulting services, and Peter set to work building the Senate captioning operation and staffing it.

Soon, Peter saw a once-in-a-lifetime opportunity, and, in May 1991, he left Xscribe to become the director of the U.S. Senate Office of Captioning Services.

Captioning the Senate

Four captioners currently work in the U.S. Senate Office of Captioning Services, which is still managed by Peter Jepsen. They switch off on 30-minute shifts, working out of two captioning studios deep in the bowels of the Senate building.

When I visited the captioning offices at the Senate, it was quite an exciting experience. I had been visiting with a Senate aide who had worked in that building for two years, and even *he* had to call Peter for directions to reach the captioning office.

We traveled down elevators and through a maze of corridors on the Terrace level of the Senate building, eventually finding our way to the captioning office. Several desks were arranged in an anteroom, with plenty of TV monitors here and there. Behind the anteroom were the two captioning studios where the work is done.

Each studio has captioning equipment and TV equipment aplenty and multiple sources of input. A complex switching system allows the captioners in both studios (only one is active at a time) and the anteroom to switch between C-SPAN, C-SPAN II, outside sources like CNN, and various in-house video and audio feeds, showing different camera angles and using different microphones.

The sound system in the Senate is carefully designed with layers of backup, so that even a catastrophic failure of the system still leaves an independent collection of boom microphones operational. The captioning office can tap into all of these audio and video systems.

Each studio can accommodate two captioners, even though only one of them works at a time. The working captioner's partner may need to scamper from the room on a moment's notice to find the spelling of an unknown name. Where do they go? According to Peter, "The first spot is usually the day's newspapers, followed by a call to the library." Thank goodness for librarians!

Unlike Kathy Robson's experience with the city of Fremont, these captioners receive no material in advance — no scripts, no copies of bills, no proclamations, no agendas. Everything must be written in realtime.

When asked how they can prepare for their day of captioning, Peter's response was, "Stay current with current events — it's about all you *can* do." Peter and the other captioners have to keep up with the newspapers and TV news, as well as goings-on in the White House and down the street at the House of Representatives.

Only once in the last three years has Peter had to caption a Senate bill, in its entirety, as it was read out loud. It wasn't fun. In 10-minute shifts, the clerks took turns reading. Obviously, they wanted to get it over with, so they read as fast as they could. Captioning somebody who is speaking that fast is a difficult enough task as it is, a task made even more difficult by the reality that most people cannot speak *clearly* at a high reading rate. Did I already mention that it wasn't fun?

Again, I asked Peter if there was a way to get this information in advance and script it. Surely they had access to a computer hooked up to the Internet where they could pull the text of the bills from THOMAS, a legislative Web site maintained by the Library of Congress,[10] which contains a wealth of information about pending legislation.

Peter patiently explained that the latest amendments and proposed amendments won't *be* in THOMAS when the bill is read on the floor. Amendments won't necessarily even be typed. They may well be handwritten on a paper napkin from the Senate cafeteria.

Communication is fairly limited with the floor reporters who produce the *Congressional Record.* Their task is very different, and their approach to that task is very different.

The floor reporters take down what is being said on the Senate floor, but their transcript is not displayed to the public in realtime. They have the luxury of transcribing it after the fact and editing for accuracy, along with the extra bonus that senators will sometimes drop off a copy of a speech to make their lives easier. The senators, of course, want to make sure that their speeches appear clean, accurate and cogent in the *Congressional Record.*

---

[10] *THOMAS can be found at http://www.thomas.loc.gov. It is a great resource for any research related to U.S. lawmaking.*

The floor reporters are also faced with a difficulty that the captioners don't face. The senators are allowed to review and edit the transcripts before they go into print in the *Congressional Record.*

The Senate captioners mostly get in touch with the floor reporters to check on spellings and compare notes. For the most part, they go their separate ways. Until recently, the two groups weren't even located on the same floor of the Senate building.

Communication is even more limited between the captioners covering the Senate on C-SPAN II and the captioners covering the House of Representatives on C-SPAN, largely because C-SPAN isn't captioned in-house (or should that be "in-House"?), but is contracted out to the National Captioning Institute, which isn't located close to Capitol Hill.

The Captioners

Obviously, you have to be a good captioner to work for the U.S. Senate. Peter sets a high standard and expects a lot from his people. Accurate writing at high speed isn't enough, though.

Stamina and the ability to work under conditions of extreme pressure are absolutely essential qualities for those who caption the Senate. When the session is drawing to a close for the year, the days can get very long. If the Senate floor is open and active until midnight, the captioners must be there until midnight, still as accurate and fast as they were first thing in the morning, which explains part of the rationale for the 30-minute shifts worked by the Senate captioners. Avoiding long consecutive periods of captioning allows them time to catch up on some quick dictionary maintenance and, more importantly, have time to stretch, take a walk down the hall, grab a cup of coffee or a snack, and hit the steno keyboard refreshed when the next shift comes up.

To work for the Senate also requires an intense interest in the affairs of the nation. In order to be prepared for anything a given senator might say, Senate captioners must constantly update their knowledge concerning current events, both on a local and national scale. Translation dictionaries must be constantly updated and maintained, so that everything will come out as the captioner intended.

Senate captioners must also be able to think fast on their feet. The dictionary must be filled not only with words and phrases, but with word *parts.* When the name of a town is mentioned, the captioner must be able to write a root word and quickly add *-ville* or *-town* or *-ton* or *-burg* or *-burgh* to produce a correct (or near-correct) spelling. Similarly, the dictionary must be filled with name parts, including endings like *-son* and *-vich* and *-ski.* Like news captioners, the Senate reporters, in their writing, must be able to distinguish between *Kathy, Cathy, Kathie, Cathi* and all of the other possible variants of each name.

Being a Senate captioner is very hard work, but the people who do it love it. Not only that, it looks pretty darned good on a résumé.

Church Captioning

Closed captioning is known as a way for deaf people to watch television, but can it be used in a church or synagogue as well? Absolutely!

Closed captioning is a way to expand a ministry not only to deaf people, but to many hard-of-hearing people (especially the elderly) and to people just learning English as a second language.

It is a common misconception that closed captioning is only for deaf people. In fact, you will often hear it referred to as "closed captioning for the hearing-impaired." In reality, it is a much more general aid to understanding oral communications.

Even in the best of churches, the acoustics in the sanctuary aren't perfect because there are a lot more criteria to the design of the sanctuary than just sound. It isn't only the deaf and seriously hearing-impaired people who sometimes have trouble understanding what is being said. Elderly people often develop loss of hearing within just one register, meaning that they may be able to hear and clearly understand a woman's speech, but not the deeper voice of a man.

Captioning provides, on a normal TV monitor or projection television, the text of the sermon so that people can watch both the face of the person speaking *and* the words being spoken. This close-up of the minister helps truly deaf people with their "speech reading," which involves reading lips, expressions, gestures and body language.

People learning English as a second language are helped as well, because when they first hear an unfamiliar word, they can look at the screen to see how it is spelled and possibly recognize it from their reading. It is easier for them to follow written English, where they don't have to worry about accents and pronunciation. They are likely to recognize in print names of people and places from the Bible, which they may never have heard spoken.

Offering captioning in a church better serves the existing congregation *and* spreads the Word to those who aren't being reached today. The age group that most wants and needs to hear the sermons is the elderly. These are people who may be embarrassed that they don't hear as well as they used to, and this may lead them to either sit in the pew, not comprehending the sermon, or simply not to attend services at all.

When word gets around about captioning, it attracts new members to the church. Elderly parishioners bring their friends. Deaf people spread the word through their community. People learning English are better able to understand the service because of these captions, and they, too, spread the word to their compatriots.

A Real-Life Example

The Second Baptist Church of Houston, Texas, is a large church, with over 20,000 members on its rolls, making it the largest church in Houston and one of the nation's largest. Each service seats up to 5,000 people at once. In 1996, the church decided that realtime captioning would be a valuable addition to its services. The church put the word out that it needed a captioner and found one right in its own congregation.

Mark Kislingbury had been a court reporter for about 13 years. He is certified in Texas and Iowa and holds an impressive array of credentials from NCRA, including the RPR, RMR and CRR. His speed can be attested to by his placement in court reporter speed contests. He won first place in the Texas speed contest in 1995 and 1996, and took fifth in the national contest those same two years. In 1999, he won the first

National Realtime Competition with an accuracy of 99.1 percent (the next-best score was 97.4 percent), and tied for first place in the literary portion of the speed contest.

When asked whether he felt all of those credentials were necessary for a captioner, Mark responded, "Credentials are not necessary. However, if one is not skilled enough to pass the CRR, one should probably not be providing closed captioning or realtime — at least not for pay."

Mark began adding Christian and Bible terminology to his steno dictionary almost from the beginning of his court reporting career, anticipating a future opportunity to combine his personal beliefs with his realtime skills. This vocabulary has helped him surprisingly often, as words like *Genesis, testament, apostle, prophet* (as opposed to *profit), ecclesiastical, thy, thou shalt, thine, proverbs, Moses, Israel, Damascus, Assyria, Babylon, Jerusalem, Eden, Sodom and Gomorrah, Messiah, Pharisees, devil, demon* and *Lucifer* creep into political and legal speech.

As Mark began working more with deaf and hard-of-hearing people, he began volunteering his services for groups like the Center for Hearing and Speech and SHHH (Self-Help for Hard-of-Hearing People). This culminated in the call from his church to caption its services.

How it Works

The staff at Second Baptist decided that realtime captioning would be too distracting if it was visible to the entire congregation, so it is currently shown on a 27-inch television monitor on one balcony. Mark captioned everything during the service, the text being displayed as four-line roll-up captions at the bottom of the screen.

Unlike some other church captioners, Mark didn't receive, in advance, a copy of the sermon, so he had to be prepared for whatever came up. This is where his realtime skill came in. A particularly important part of that skill is dealing with names he doesn't know. Without a list of the people being baptized, he needed to guess at the spellings of names; and he had to generate those spellings, nearly instantaneously, from his steno machine.

Mark did get lyric sheets for hymns and songs that the choir and soloists sang, a crucial consideration, as it can be very difficult to understand the words to songs sometimes.

Captioners (and churches) can have divergent opinions regarding Bible readings. Some, like Mark Kislingbury, have translation dictionaries so comprehensive and well crafted that they can write Bible quotes verbatim in realtime; others simply write the book/chapter/verse citation and let each individual look it up. This approach is difficult, because no one can read from two sources at the same time.

A third approach is to load prepared script files containing the Bible text. Scripts like these are available with some captioning systems. The set of Bible scripts I put together for Cheetah's system included over 1,100 files (one for each chapter of each book) and occupied about 4.5MBs of disk space on the captioner's computer.

The structure of these Bible scripts allows a captioner to quickly call up a specific chapter. For example, to display Leviticus 19:14 ("Thou shalt not curse the deaf, nor put a stumbling block before the blind"), the captioner would simply open the script file for Leviticus, Chapter 19, and skip down 14 verses.

When Mark captioned the service, he worked in the control room with the AV technicians. He wore headphones to reduce distraction and to receive better sound quality. This is a fairly standard practice in the larger churches; smaller churches tend to put the captioner down in front, close to the deaf and hard-of-hearing people who are actually using their captions.

Another practice that varies from church to church is recording the captions. A videotape recorder can be set up to capture exactly what is being displayed in the sanctuary, so that deaf and hard-of-hearing people who were unable to attend the service, or who wish to watch it again, can have a tape with captions. With some editing and cleanup work, the caption file on the computer can also be turned into a transcript of the service, although this is rarely done.

Other Uses for a Captioning System in Church

Few churches are fortunate enough to have a Mark Kislingbury in their congregation. In the absence of a stenocaptioner, can a church still gain something of value from a captioning system? Certainly!

Many preachers prepare their sermons in advance on a word processor. The word processor files can be loaded into a captioning system before the service, and a captioner without realtime skills can use live display to feed out the text as the preacher speaks.

Obviously, such a procedure can't completely replace live realtime captions. I haven't met a minister yet who, during the sermon, actually follows a script word for word. The deaf and hard-of-hearing people would miss all of the extemporaneous speaking if all they had was a script. *But they still have something.* If you can't afford steak and lobster, should you skip dinner? No, you should eat what you can afford and hope for the steak and lobster soon.

One part of a church service that is verbatim is the hymns. These can be entered into the system in advance and fed out as captions — another useful service to the hearing people in the congregation.

When something is going on that isn't scripted, any good realtime captioning system will permit "electronic notetaking," which allows a typist to enter a summary of what is happening. It isn't verbatim, but it gives people an overview of what is going on. There are also specialized C-Print systems that allow a typist to use abbreviations and macros to increase typing speed, although I've never seen one that outputs captions.

Another useful capability of online captioning systems is automatic caption feed. When nothing is going on in the sanctuary, the captioning system can be set to feed out church announcements or other useful information at a predefined reading rate, adding even more value to the concept of a captioned TV monitor in the church lobby.

Most people who arrive late wait for an appropriate moment before entering the sanctuary so that they don't disrupt the service. Similarly, parents with crying children will often take them into the lobby. A captioned monitor in the lobby lets these people follow what is going on, even when the piercing cries of a baby fill their ears.

Oops!

Do bloopers happen in church like they do on television?[11] Of course they do! My favorite blooper happened at Willow Creek Community Church in South Barrington, Ill. I was there for the inaugural kickoff of closed captioning for their services. The captioner was going on the air in the church for the first time; and if this didn't make her nervous enough, she had a collection of "visiting dignitaries" watching everything she did.

The church has a number of large projection screens, one of which was displaying the captions. The service began. Everything looked great. The captioner had prepared carefully, and she had all the appropriate terminology in her translation dictionary. Everything came out great, that is, until one misfingering turned the pastor's "Let us sing together" into "Let us *sin* together."

Where Next for Mark?

In addition to captioning every service for the Second Baptist Church of Houston, Mark went on to caption TV newscasts and major events, both in person and on the Internet. He captioned the Dove Awards (Christian music awards) live from Nashville, Tenn., and also captioned the Houston Rockets using the giant screen at The Summit in Houston, Texas.

Mark has also captioned some very high-profile people on the Internet, including Microsoft Chairman Bill Gates doing a new product announcement and Apple CEO Gil Amelio welcoming Steve Jobs back to the fold at Mac Expo 1997. He recently relocated to West Virginia and continues to make use of his CART and captioning skills.

A real treat for Mark, who is currently approaching a Master rating in chess, was captioning the big chess rematch between world champion Garry Kasparov and IBM's "Deep Blue" computer, live on the Internet, in May 1997.

---

[11] *See the collection of online bloopers in Chapter 4.*

Does Mark feel that he's ready to move on to something other than captioning in his church? In his words, "What could be more important than not only writing the spoken word, but the spoken Word, to those who cannot hear? I am translating the Word of the Lord to those who, without the technological 'magic' of captioning and the gift of accuracy that God has given me, would never be able to hear a sermon preached."

That pretty well sums it up.

Bilingual Captioning

Captioning in one language is difficult. Captioning in more than one language raises the difficulty level to a whole new plane.

Depending on whether you are looking at online (realtime) captioning or offline captioning, entirely different issues arise. With offline, the captions are typically prepared in one language and then translated to another. Quite a few captioning firms employ bilingual caption editors so that they can produce videos with two languages.

Training films are one prime candidate for multilingual captioning, and movies are another. Ted Turner, who purchased the rights to many classic movies for his cable TV empire, has made a big business out of captioning English-language movies in Spanish and selling them in Latin America. At one point, three different large captioning firms were working on movies for Turner, each providing several titles per week.

The vast majority of realtime captioning in the world is done in English. Obviously, there are places where other languages are required and a few places that require more than one.

Spanish-language captioning will be required in the United States for some broadcasts starting in 2001, and Canada implemented rules in 1999 requiring French-language captioning.

In recent years, the CBS show *60 Minutes* has begun broadcasting every show with English captions on CC1 and Spanish captions on CC3.

Spanish and English in Puerto Rico

Fernando Altamirano is quite familiar with the problem alluded to above. Fernando was, for many years, a federal court reporter in Puerto Rico. While the court system is ostensibly English only,[12] Spanish is the native tongue for many of the residents of Puerto Rico.

Originally a native Mexican, Fernando is fluent in Spanish; consequently, his court reporting translation dictionary was peppered with Spanish words and phrases. He could not, however, using the theory he had learned, write pure Spanish. The stenotype keyboard is phonetic in nature, and there is no way to represent some of the sounds in Spanish using traditional English stenotype theory. Also, certain sounds would produce differently spelled words in Spanish and English, preventing them from coexisting in the same dictionary, such as *cañon* and *canyon*, *sí* and *see*, or *Pancho* and *poncho*.

Fernando took up the challenge and created a Spanish-language theory on his own, using the same stenotype keyboard, but treating some of the keys differently. Since it was difficult to jump back and forth between his new Spanish theory and the English theory that he had been using, he also developed a complementary English theory that was very similar to his Spanish system. This allows him to use both.

Fernando now operates a small school in San Juan, where he is teaching his Spanish stenotype theory, and he performs realtime captioning for two TV stations in Puerto Rico.

A couple of thousand miles north of Puerto Rico, another bilingual problem exists: the Canadian province of Quebec.

French and English in Canada

At the captioning firm of Nathanail & Waite, in Toronto, Ontario, partner Valerie Waite had been asked, for years, about realtime captioning in French. Valerie and her partner, Rena Nathanail, had never had the means to tackle the problem. In 1990, the business split up. Rena took half the customers, moved to western Canada and started her own

[12] *Puerto Rico is, after all, a territory of the United States.*

firm. Valerie took the other half of the customers and continued operation in Toronto as Waite & Associates.

Shortly thereafter, Valerie attended the NCRA annual convention, where she met a court reporter by the name of Claire Yelle. Claire lived in Montreal and reported in French.

Claire and Valerie talked about the difficult problem of performing realtime in French. A company in France did produce a stenotype machine, the Grandjean, which was available in Canada, but didn't have the extensive support and realtime tools that the American machines had. The Grandjean keyboard and stenotype theory were not designed with realtime in mind, and it was difficult to produce clean, error-free captions.

Claire set out to solve the problem by developing a French-language theory for the American-style stenotype keyboard. Once the theory was developed, she began to teach it at LaSalle College in Montreal. Valerie was standing by to hire three of Claire's first graduates.

Valerie is, herself, a captioner. Like most realtime captioners, she started her career as a court reporter, where she began building up the collection of alphabet soup that follows her name (Valerie Waite, CSR, CRR, RPR, CM). She joined the CCDA (Canadian Captioning Development Agency) in 1986; less than two years later she and Rena Nathanail had their own captioning firm.

Valerie has served two terms as president of the Chartered Shorthand Reporters Association of Ontario and worked on task forces, committees and advisory boards relating to captioning and services for deaf and hard-of-hearing people.

Waite & Associates has had many opportunities to use French captioning, but one of the most widely viewed occurred in May 1996. In May of every year, there is a week designated "Caption Awareness Week" in Canada. Many programs are shown open-captioned that week so that more people can see and appreciate captioning.

Valerie was given the opportunity to caption the Canadian Parliament that week, in both English and French. Finding the captioners[13] was not difficult. Parliament meetings always use United Nations-style translators, so getting both English and French audio feeds was not hard. Orchestrating the captioning and setting up the equipment was another issue entirely.

Having one captioner writing in English on one captioning system and another captioner writing in French on another captioning system would seem to be quite straightforward. Just hook up two caption encoders and go, right? Not quite. The problem is that a caption encoder, when it lays down new captions, *replaces* existing captions in Line 21. Only one of the languages would survive.

Valerie called her captioning software vendor, Cheetah Systems, and was connected to the product manager for CAPtivator Online, a software engineer by the name of David Blanchette. David, recognizing that there was a tight deadline, proposed a simple solution: He would create a custom program for this application, which would take the output from two CAPtivator Online systems, merge them together and feed them into a single caption encoder.

David set out to create this special captioning system for multilingual realtime, and he delivered it to Valerie in time for Caption Awareness Week. The caption merger works like this:

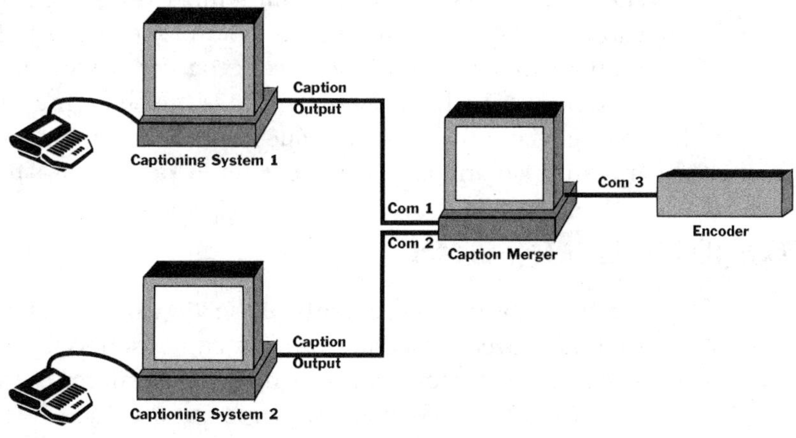

---

[13] *Or captionists, as they are usually called in Canada.*

Two captioners, one writing in English and one writing in French, produce the realtime captions for the proceedings. Each captioner has a captioning system, and each captioning system sends out captioning data as though it were feeding an encoder.

In reality, though, the two captioning systems feed the Cheetah caption merging system that David Blanchette created. This system interleaves the captions, carefully placing one set of captions on CC1 and the other on CC2, and sends the merged caption data to the Line 21 encoder, which puts it on the video. The viewer can then choose "Caption 1" to read English or "Caption 2" to read French.

Today, you would be better off choosing CC1 and CC3, as the recommended practices from the EIA suggest not putting two languages in the same caption field.[14]

This same concept has been implemented on-site at government conferences and hearings with Canadian ministries. Two large video screens are set up, both showing the same picture. The Waite & Associates team writes French captions onto one of them and English captions onto the other.

Of course, a job doesn't have to be bilingual to be challenging, and the challenge is what Valerie likes best. Her favorite work is sports; lately, she's been doing cricket tournaments. Unlike a football or baseball game, cricket tournaments can go on for eight to 12 hours. This requires that two captioners work together, switching off every hour or two. One of the biggest challenges is the changing cast of announcers. In one recent tournament, Valerie had announcers with, respectively, Indian, Irish and Jamaican accents. What a contrast!

Captioned Theater

Increasingly, many segments of the viewing audience are *expecting* that mainstream TV shows will be captioned. When a new movie is released, deaf people who wish to see it wait for the video release, for they know that, when it *does* come out on video, it is virtually certain

---

[14] *CC1 and CC2 are in field 1, while CC3 and CC4 are in field 2.*

that it will be captioned. What about live theater, though?

That question bothered Roy Brown. Roy, an Englishman transplanted to Connecticut, is one of that rare breed who is both an ASL sign interpreter *and* a realtime court reporter/stenocaptioner. Owing to his ASL skills, his church was using him, every Sunday, as an interpreter. Additionally, he was serving as an interpreter for the productions of the Connecticut Gay Men's Chorus.

As Roy worked more with CGMC and with the Connecticut chapter of the Association of Late-Deafened Adults, he came to realize that there are many deaf or hard-of-hearing people who do not know sign language. As valuable as his ASL interpreting was, it simply couldn't help those people.

As an experiment, he brought his CAPtivator Online realtime captioning software to a CGMC production. A Sony Hi-8 camcorder was set up, and an EEG DE352 character generator connected to the captioning system provided the open captions.

The captioning was placed at the bottom of the picture, and the video was projected onto a screen above the audience, about two-thirds of the way back in the theater. Roy received the complete script ahead of time, so that the production could be captioned using live-display. Obviously, there was some ad-libbing, and the musical director spoke briefly before the show. Using Roy's stenocaptioning skills, those portions were captioned in realtime.

At the end of the production, a couple of women approached Roy and, with tears of joy, thanked him because they had *finally* found a way to enjoy theater productions again. In fact, the captioned production was very well received by *all* of the members of ALDA and SHHH (Self-Help for Hard-of-Hearing People) who attended. As a consequence, captioning has continued at CGMC productions ever since.

Now, rather than the single projection television with captions on the bottom of the video picture, CGMC uses four TV monitors daisy-chained from the video output, placed in the seating area of the audience, and the captions are placed at the top of the video picture, so that they are less likely to be hidden by the head of that tall person who inevitably sits *directly* in front of you.

Roy's story differs from most captioners in that he started out as a sign interpreter. When asked whether this made his captioning better, he responded, "Knowledge of ASL, I don't believe, helps one to be a better captioner. A knowledge of the deaf/Deaf[15]/HOH communities is very important to any captioner, and ASL skills are very beneficial in providing ease of communication with the Deaf community."

This brings up a key issue. Many captioners and CART (communication access realtime translation) reporters who have done work for deaf groups find themselves, because they can't sign, unable to communicate easily with the people for whom they work. The captioner, of course, can always use the captions to talk with another person. There are times, though, when you don't *want* the contents of your private conversation projected onto a 40-foot screen at the front of an auditorium.

As more stenocaptioners and court reporters come to this realization, ASL seminars are becoming common at court reporting conventions. More and more captioners are learning at least basic signs for "Please," "Thank you" and "My name is Tess." That last one, of course, turns out to be much more useful, and less embarrassing, if your name actually *is* Tess.

Roy's captioning work has led him into a couple of high-profile captioning jobs, like the production of *Victory Canteen*, which commemorated the 50th anniversary of the end of World War II at the Shubert Theatre ("Birthplace of the Nation's Greatest Hits") in New Haven.

He was also a part of one of the largest interactive realtime-captioned events on the Internet, which took place at the National Guard Armory in Hartford, Conn. The event was Connecticut's Net Day, known as ConneCT 96, which celebrated the connection of the state's schools to

---

[15] *The deaf community is split into several segments. The prelingually deaf people refer to themselves as "culturally deaf," or simply "Deaf" with a capital D, as a way of distinguishing themselves from hard-of-hearing and postlingually deaf people.*

the Internet.

In addition to the roughly 500 people present at the Armory, the ConneCT 96 celebration included live captions and graphics broadcast to K-12 schools throughout the state. An estimated 6,000 students and teachers attended via the Internet.

The most significant aspect of the presentation that day, however, was *how* that captioning was used. Roy sat up near the front of the Armory, where a stage was arranged with three huge video-projection screens. During the main presentation, the governor and various other government officials, both state and federal, talked about the significance of the new Internet connectivity and then accepted questions from the audience.

As the governor called for questions, he alternated between the local audience and the students out on the Internet. Students connected via the Internet could type in their questions and send them to the event moderator, who collected them for the governor. When he called for a question from the Internet, the next question in the queue was forwarded to a huge projection display above the screen, as well as to a smaller monitor in front of the governor. His response, just like everything else that was being said, was captioned by Roy; and the text appeared on both the projection screen and the remote attendees' Internet screens. The great significance of this is that deaf students from American High School were able to participate in this event *exactly like hearing students*. They received the same text and sent their questions in exactly the same way. For at least that one day, they were not treated as if they were handicapped, disabled or different. They were just people, like everyone else.

Chapter 12

Resources

Software and Hardware Vendors

This section provides the last known contact information for companies mentioned in this book as of press time. Obviously, things change, and some of these entries may be incorrect or out-of-date. Some companies failed to respond to the survey that I sent out or to telephone calls. Usually, the Web is the best place to begin a search in that case. Check my Closed Captioning FAQ (www.robson.org/capfaq/) for updated information.

Advantage Software
online and offline captioning software, CAT software
925 Central Parkway
Stuart, FL 34994
Tel: 800/800-1759 (United States); 561/288-3266 (international)
Fax: 561/288-1737
E-mail: gseely@eclipsecat.com
Web: www.eclipsecat.com

AristoCAT
CAT software
423 Northeast Clay Avenue
Bend, OR 97701
Tel: 800/727-4786
Fax: 541/389-2417
E-mail: sales@aristocat.com
Web: www.aristocat.com

ATI Technologies
caption grabbers
33 Commerce Valley Drive East
Thornhill, Ontario, Canada L3T 7N6
Tel: 905/882-2600
Fax: 905/882-2620
E-mail: sales@atitech.ca

AudioScribe Inc.
CAT software for voice writers
401 Audubon Blvd., Suite 212b
Lafayette, LA 70503
Tel: 800/869-0569 or 318/232-3430
Fax: 318/237-6232
E-mail: sales@audioscribe.com
Web: www.audioscribe.com

Cheetah Systems Intl.
online and offline captioning software, CAT software
40 North Swan Road, Suite 112
Tucson, AZ 85711
Tel: 800/829-2287
Fax: 520/722-1699
E-mail: swsales@caption.com
Web: www.cheetahsystems.com

Computer Prompting & Captioning Co. (CPC)
online and offline captioning software
1010 Rockville Pike, Suite 306
Rockville, MD 20852
Tel: 800/977-6678 or 301/738-8487
TTY: 301/738-8489
Fax: 301/738-8488
E-mail: info@cpcweb.com

The Corby Group
steno accessories and supplies
P.O. Box 329
Springfield, NJ 07081
Tel: 800/255-5040
Fax: 800/788-2729
Web: www.corbyco.com

EEG Enterprises
encoders and other broadcast equipment
1 Rome Street
Farmingdale, NY 11735
Tel: 516/293-7472
Fax: 516/293-7417
E-mail: vbi@eegent.com
Web: www.eegent.com

Evertz Microsystems
encoders and other broadcast equipment
3465 Mainway
Burlington, Ontario, Canada L7M 1A9
Tel: 905/335-3700
Fax: 905/335-3573
BBS: 905/335-9131 (available 24 hours)
E-mail: sales@evertz.com
Web: www.evertz.com

EZ-CAT
CAT software
817 Villa Gran Way
Fenton, MO 63026
Tel: 800/328-9228

Gigatron Software Corporation
CAT software
2805 McGaw Ave.
Irvine, CA 92614
Tel: 800/909-9199
Fax: 949/261-5147
E-mail: gscsales@gsclion.com
Web: www.stenocat.com

GlobalCAT
online captioning software, CAT software
1425 Main St., Suite 215
Ramona, CA 92065
Tel: 760/788-4555 [1]
Fax: 760/788-0165
E-mail: support@globalcat32.com
Web: www.globalcat32.com

---

[1] *GlobalCAT's area code is changing to 442 after November 2000.*

Image Logic
offline captioning software
6807 Brennon Lane
Chevy Chase, MD 20815-3255
Tel: 301/907-8891
Fax: 301/652-6584
BBS: 301/652-6584
E-mail: webmaster@imagelogic.com

Link Electronics
encoders and other broadcast equipment
2137 Rust Ave.
Cape Girardeau, MO 63703
Tel: 573/334-4433
Fax: 573/334-9255
E-mail: sales@linkelectronics.com
Web: www.linkelectronics.com

Mixed Signals Technologies (formerly Ultech)
encoders and other broadcast equipment
28 C Great Hill Road
Seymour, CT 06483
Tel: 203/735-5805 (Orders: 888/360-0010)
Fax: 203/735-6653
E-mail: mail@ultechvideo.com
Web: www.ultechvideo.com

Mycap USA
decoders
1123 E. Dominguez St., Unit E
Carson, CA 90746
Tel: 800/692-2788

Norpak Corporation
encoders and other broadcast equipment
10 Hearst Way
Kanata, Ontario, Canada K2L 2P4
Tel: 613/592-4164
Fax: 613/592-6560
E-mail: info@norpak.ca
Web: www.norpak.ca

Pengad
steno accessories and supplies
P.O. Box 99
55 Oak Street
Bayonne, NJ 07002
Tel: 800/631-6989
Fax: 800/631-2329
E-mail: pengad@compuserve.com

ProCAT
online captioning software, CAT software, steno keyboards
5126 Clareton Dr., Suite 260
Agoura Hills, CA 91301
Tel: 800/966-1221 (United States); 818/879-5600 (international)
Fax: 818/879-5620
E-mail: sales@procat.com
Web: www.procat.com

RapidText
online captioning software
1801 Dove Street, Suite 101
Newport Beach, CA 92660
Tel: 949/399-9200
TTY: 949/399-9273
Fax: 949/399-9216
E-mail: rapidtxt@rapidtext.com
Web: www.rapidtext.com

Robson Technologies Inc.
steno keyboards
18815 Glen Ayre Drive
Morgan Hill, CA 95037
Tel: 408/779-8008
Fax: 408/782-7132
E-mail: gemini@robson.org
Web: www.cyberdawg.com/gemini/

SoftTouch
encoders, decoders, caption grabbers
6196 Oxon Hill Road
Oxon Hill, MD 20745-3100
Tel: 301/749-1484
E-mail: SoftEncode@aol.com
Web: www.softtouch-inc.com

StenoScribe Inc.
CAT software for voice writers
P.O. Box 839
Abilene, TX 79605
Tel/Fax: 800/456-3290
E-mail: info@stenoscribe.com
Web: www.stenoscribe.com

Stenovations
CAT software
Suite 300
606 Virginia Street East
Charleston, WV 25301
Tel: 800/626-7228
Fax: 304/346-8376
E-mail: jjackson@stenovations.com
Web: www.stenovations.com

Sunbelt Industries Technologies Group
caption grabbers
83 S. 30th Avenue
Jacksonville Beach, FL 32250
Tel: 904/249-5577 (main)
Tel: 800/870-2039 (sales)
Fax: 904/241-1853
E-mail: sunbelt@sunbeltindustries.com

Stenograph LLC
CAT software, steno keyboards, accessories and supplies
1500 Bishop Court
Mount Prospect, IL 60056
Tel: 800/228-2339 (United States); 847/803-1400 (international)
Fax: 847/803-1097
E-mail: sales@stenograph.com (U.S. sales)
judywolf@stenograph.com (international sales)
Web: www.stenograph.com

Ultech (See *Mixed Signals*)

Product Cross-Reference

It can get confusing digging through a list of products and trying to figure out where to find more information. This section lists products by name and shows which company makes the product. Some of these products are no longer manufactured, but are included here for historical or research purposes.

This is *not* a comprehensive list of products. It is only a reference to help you find the manufacturer of a product when the manufacturer's name is not obvious from the product name.

CAT/CART/Text-Entry Software

Product	Manufacturer
Case CATalyst	Stenograph
CATnip	Stenovations
DigitalCAT	Stenovations
Eclipse	Advantage
OpenWrite 32	Gigatron
Premier Power	Stenograph
RapidText	RapidText
RapidWrite	Stenograph
RiTE	ProCAT
SCAT	Stenovations
SpeechCAT	AudioScribe
StenoCAT	Gigatron
Techlennium	StenoScribe
TurboCAT	Cheetah
Winner	ProCAT

Captioning Software

Product	Manufacturer
AccuCap	Advantage
CAPtivator Offline	Cheetah
CAPtivator Online	Cheetah
PostCAP	Cheetah
RapidCaption	RapidText

Stenotype Keyboards, Accessories and Supplies

Product	Manufacturer
AccuWriter	Digitext
Fon'iksWriter	ErgoFon'iks
Flash Writer	ProCAT
Gemini	Robson Technologies
Legit'i'Mate	AssemblyFAB
MeritWriter	VertiCAT/AssemblyFAB
Optimate	AssemblyFAB
ProWriter	ProCAT
Transcriptor X	Stenograph (was BaronData)
SmartWriter	Stenograph
StenoRAM	Stenograph (was Xscribe)
StenoWriter	StenoCAT
Stentura	Stenograph
TurboWriter	Cheetah Systems
UltraTilt Tripod	Corby
Vision	Stenograph (was Xscribe)

There are dozens of steno keyboards that are no longer manufactured, so they are not listed here.

Captioning/CART Web Sites

Caption TV
www.captiontv.com
A device to censor obscene language from captions.

Captioning Helps a Student Get the Big Picture
www.edc.org/FSC/NCIP/Captioning_Sitcom.html
A viewer's perspective on captioning.

CARTWheel
www.machineshorthand.com/CARTWheel.htm
An organization of and for providers of CART services.

Cathryn Bauer's Educational CART Pages
www.mindspring.com/~cathryn/deafframes.htm
A must-read for anyone considering offering CART services in a school setting.

The Closed Caption FAQ
www.robson.org/capfaq/
Over 100 common questions and answers about closed captioning, with dozens of pages of related documents, articles, laws, dissertations and other information.

The Closed Captioning Web
www.captions.org
An excellent collection of captioning advocacy and consumer information by a deaf woman named Jamie Berke.

Digital Television Closed-Captioning (DTVCC) Home Page
www.avio-systems.com/dtvcc/home.html
The Electronic Industries Association working group (R4.3 WG1) that developed EIA-708, the standard for captioning on DTV.

ETFC — Caption TV Orientation Project
www.deafexpo.org/ctop.htm
The "Deaf Expo" people help you to choose a television with captioning.

FCC Disabilities Issues Task Force
www.fcc.gov/dtf/
This portion of the FCC Web site is dedicated to captioning and related issues, including TTYs and Telephone Relay Services.

Gary Robson's Articles About CART and Captioning
www.robson.org/gary/writing/captioning.html
Columns, articles, papers and seminar transcripts for anyone who hasn't had enough of me after reading this book.

Joe Clark's Captioning Articles
www.interlog.com/~joeclark/ccbibl.html
A dozen or so articles from someone who's been following — and commenting on — TV captioning in Canada for over 20 years.

The Media Access Mailing List
www.interlog.com/~joeclark/axxlist.html
An Internet mailing list dedicated to closed-captioning, audio description, Web, CD-ROM and multimedia access, and other Media Access issues.

MultiLingual Media Inc.
www.mlmedia.net
Instant translation of captions into other languages.

NCRA: The National Court Reporters Association
www.ncraonline.org
Look for articles and news, as well as the NCRA Online Forum discussion area.

ReporterCentral
www.reportercentral.com
A Web site dedicated to the latest in news, reference materials and career information about court reporting and closed captioning.

SAMI
www.microsoft.com/enable/sami/default.htm
The Synchronized Accessible Media Interchange file format from Microsoft

can be used for captioning of multimedia files.

Supertext: The Australian Caption Gopher
gopher://gopher.slnsw.gov.au:70/11/DRA/About/captions
This gopher contains information about Supertext, teletext and general captioning information in Australia.

TVGuardian: The Foul Language Filter
www.tvguardian.com
A V-Chip alternative from Principle Solutions Inc. that filters out offensive language while you watch television or videos.

Video Captioning and Language Learning
http://sunyfact.buffalo.edu/cit95/papers/CIT95-PA.SHEA
Research paper by Peter Shea.

Bibliography

- *The Court Reporter's Guide to Cyberspace*
  Gary Robson and Richard A. Sherman
  CyberDawg Publishing 1997
  ISBN 0965151808

- *DVD Demystified*
  Jim Taylor
  McGraw-Hill 1998
  ISBN 0070648417

- *Fashionable Realtime for Steno Writers*
  Denis Thievin
  Wanderlust Publishing 1999

- *Inside Captioning*
  Gary Robson
  CyberDawg Publishing 1997
  ISBN 0965960900

- *An Introduction to Court Reporter Technology*
  NCRA 1997
  ISBN 1881859215

- *Real-Time Writing: The Court Reporter's Guide for Mastering Real-Time Skills*
  Tammie Shedd, Karen Finkelstein and Darlene Parker of the National Captioning Institute

- *Television Engineering Handbook*
  McGraw-Hill
  ISBN 0070047790

- *Video Demystified*
  Keith Jack
  Independent Publishers Group (Computer)
  ISBN 187870723X

- *Writing Naked: Principles of Writing for Realtime and Captioning*
  Kevin Daniel and Mary Cox Daniel
  NCRA 1999
  ISBN 1881859509

- *The Court Reporter Reference Series from CRRBooks*
  Monette Benoit and Emmett Donnelly

  The ADA, Civil Rights, Affirmative Action, Business, Convention Handbook
  ISBN 1881149072

  The Politics, Elections, Government, Military, Criminal Handbook
  ISBN 1881149080

  The Universal Religions, Ethics, Philosophy Handbook
  ISBN 1881149129

  The Sports, Olympics, Security, Terrorism Handbook
  ISBN 1881149056

  The Environment, Weather, Sciences, Geology Handbook
  ISBN 1881149064

  The REALTIME Vocabulary Workbook
  ISBN 1881149021

Glossary

-A-

AARP American Association of Retired Persons. An organization for people aged 50 and over.

ACC Australian Caption Centre, headquartered in Sydney, New South Wales.

acute accent An up-rising accent mark placed over a letter, as in á. Known in French as an "aigu" accent.

ADA Americans with Disabilities Act

AEA American Electronics Association

ALDA The Association of Late-Deafened Adults. An organization created by and for postlingually deaf people, most of whom lost their hearing later in life. It addresses issues not faced by those deaf since birth.

ANSI American National Standards Institute

ASCII American Standard Code for Information Interchange. ASCII is a way, inside a computer, of representing characters in binary format. An extended form of ASCII is used in personal computers. The character set used by Line 21 caption encoders/decoders is similar to, but *not* the same as, ASCII.

ASL American Sign Language

aspect ratio The ratio of the width to the height of an image. Typical NTSC video has a 4:3 aspect ratio, which means it is one-third wider than it is high. DTV can be either 4:3 or 16:9, which is the movie "widescreen" format.

ATV Advanced Television. Now called DTV (digital television).

autofeed Captioned data that is pre-entered in the computer, which allows the text to be displayed automatically and at a predetermined speed.

-B-

BASYS A popular newsroom computer system with TelePrompTer and closed-captioning output options.

baud rate A measurement of transmission speed, named for J.M.E. Baudot. At low transmission speeds, baud rate is equivalent to bits per second (see *bps*), but at higher speeds they diverge quickly.

Baudot A character system similar to ASCII, which actually predates ASCII. It is still used in TTYs. Like the baud rate, Baudot is named for French inventor J.M.E. Baudot.

BBC British Broadcasting Corporation

Betacam A half-inch professional video recording format developed by Sony that offers very high quality. It is portable, so it is easy to use for ENG. Not to be confused with the old consumer Betamax format.

Betamax (More commonly just called "Beta.") A home (consumer) half-inch videotape format developed by Sony as early competition to VHS. (It lost that competition.)

bit A contraction for "binary digit." A bit is the smallest unit of information that a computer can hold. A bit has only two possible values: on and off (usually represented as 0 and 1 or true and false).

BNC Bayonet connector for coaxial cables. Typically, BNC connectors are used in professional video equipment, rather than the RCA connectors or F connectors used in home video equipment. BNC connectors slide on to a post and then twist to lock in place, using one pin on each side of the post.

bps Bits per second. A measurement of transmission speed that is often (incorrectly) called *baud rate.*

bug A logo placed in the corner of the screen by a TV station or network. Also used by programmers and hardware engineers to refer to a problem in a system.

byte Eight bits. A byte is the basic unit of measurement for data storage in a computer. It can hold either one character or a number between 0 and 255. Anything more than that would be byting off more than it could chew.

-C-

CAB Canadian Association of Broadcasters

CAL-TVA Californians for Television Access. A coalition in the San Francisco Bay Area that deals with captioning and emergency broadcasting issues. The member organizations include deaf organizations, captioning firms, broadcasters and various government entities (state and federal).

Caption FAQ A document containing frequently asked questions about closed captioning. The Caption FAQ resides at http://www.robson.org/capfaq/. It is maintained by that Gary Robson fellow.

CART Communication access realtime translation. Usually used to differentiate realtime text shown on a computer screen from realtime captions shown on a video image. CART utilizes the same stenocaptioning skill set that captioning uses, but is usually used for live (in-person) events for deaf and hard-of-hearing people, especially in schools and meetings.

CATV Cable television. The acronym comes from the original name for cable TV: Community Antenna Television.

CBC Canadian Broadcasting Corporation

CCITT Commité Consultatif International de Telecommunications et Telegraphy (in English, the International Telegraph and Telephone Consultative Committee). CCITT is a standards committee that makes technical recommendations about communications equipment, both voice and data. It is now a part of ITU (the International Telecommunication Union), a United Nations agency.

CCP Certified Captioning Professional. A captioning certification exam given by the Deposition Reporters Association in California.

CD Compact disc. A four-and-three-quarter-inch (12cm) digital optical disc format. The term "CD" is usually used if the disc contains only music, and "CD-ROM" is used if the disc contains data.

CD-R A CD-ROM that can be written by a special type of drive that you can use on your computer at home or in the office. It can be written precisely once and never erased.

CD-ROM Compact Disc Read Only Memory. A CD used for computer data, which can hold about 650 megabytes.

CD-R/W A rewriteable CD-R. You can write it once and then erase it and write it again a limited number of times. Unlike CD-Rs, these cannot be used in normal CD-ROM drives or CD players.

CEA Consumer Electronics Association. The group that merged with EIA and now produces standards for closed captioning (see *EIA* for more information).

cedilla The "hook" under the letter ç in French and Portuguese to specify that it is pronounced as an *s* rather than as a *k*, as in *façade* or *français*.

CEMA Consumer Electronics Manufacturers Association. Now called CEA.

character A letter, number, space or symbol. For example, the phrase "I'm feeling 100% better!" contains 24 characters (not counting the quotes). In a computer, a single character is usually stored in one byte (eight bits).

character generator A device that draws text onto a TV picture. Character generators are used for subtitling and open captioning and also for creating other text, such as credits, titles and the names of people appearing on a news show.

check tape A copy of a videotape made for preview or approval of edits and/or captions. Check tapes are usually on lower-end (less expensive) tape formats like S-VHS or even VHS.

chrominance or **chroma** The part of a video signal that carries color information. "Chrominance" is the "C" in "Y/C," the format used for Super-VHS (the "Y" is for "luminance"). Chrominance includes hue and saturation, but not brightness.

Chyron A leading manufacturer of character generators. They are so pervasive that the word Chyron has nearly become synonymous with character generator.

circumflex accent A caret-shaped accent placed over a letter, as in ô.

closed captioning Captions that are encoded (hidden) in the blanking interval of the TV signal. They are invisible without a decoder.

CLVS Certified Legal Video Specialist. A certification offered by NCRA for people who videotape legal proceedings.

CM Certificate of Merit, a credential awarded by NCRA or NVRA that requires higher skills than the basic RPR or CVR. NCRA's CM is now known as the RMR.

component video A video signal separated out on several wires. Typically, the signal is either broken out into colors ("RGB" for "Red, Green, Blue") or into chrominance (color) and luminance (brightness) signals.

composite video A complete video signal on a single wire.

computerized notetaking The use of a fast typist to simulate realtime by typing a summary of events as they happen. These notes can be displayed as standard captions, just more slowly.

C-Print A method of computerized notetaking that doesn't use captioning equipment or stenocaptioners. Similar to CART, C-Print uses typists with a collection of macros and abbreviations to increase their effective typing speed. It provides a summary of important (in the mind of the C-Print operator) points rather than a verbatim or near-verbatim transcript.

crawl Text that scrolls horizontally across the TV screen, usually at the bottom. Crawls are often used for emergency notification, breaking news stories or financial data. Crawls are created by character generators.

CRP Certified Realtime Professional. A realtime court reporting certification exam given by the Deposition Reporters Association in California.

CRR Certified Realtime Reporter, given by NCRA, designed to test writing and technical skills relating to realtime court reporting and captioning. The test consists of setting up realtime computer equipment and writing literary dictation at speeds ranging from 180 to 200 words per minute. The examinee is graded on the accuracy of the test as written in realtime. The final portion of the test involves copying the unedited file to a 3.5-inch floppy diskette in ASCII format.

CRT Cathode ray tube. A traditional video display, like the kind found in most TV sets and desktop computer monitors.

CRTC Canadian Radio-television and Telecommunications Commission (that's the Conseil de la Radiodiffusion et des Télécommunications Canadiennes to our friends in Quebec). This is the group that oversees TV broadcasters in Canada — the approximate equivalent of the FCC in the United States.

CSR Certified Shorthand Reporter, a state certification differing from state to state. In California, it consists of writing and transcribing four-voice Q&A testimony at speeds up to 225 wpm and includes a written examination relating to court reporting duties.

CV Curriculum Vitae. An accomplishment-based summary of professional experience, similar to a résumé.

CVR Certified Verbatim Reporter, the base certification offered by NVRA for stenomask reporters.

Cyrillic The alphabet used for writing Russian. Cyrillic is named for Saint Cyril, who developed the alphabet in the ninth century.

-D-

D1 A component format for digital videotape recording. D1 is of very high quality and very expensive.

D2 A composite format for digital videotape recording. Like D1, it is of very high quality and very expensive. There are several D2 caption encoders available.

data-recovery decoder A caption decoder designed to be connected to a computer. For example, an offline captioning system can be connected to a data-recovery decoder to allow it to capture existing captions from a videotape and modify them rather than starting from scratch.

DB-9 connector A connector with pins in two rows, used for serial port connections or older video (EGA, CGA, MDA) connections.

DB-15 connector A connector with three rows of pins, used for VGA video connections. DB-15 connectors are the same physical size as DB-9 connectors, but with an extra row of pins squeezed in.

DB-25 connector A connector with two rows of pins, used for serial and parallel port connections. DB-25 connectors are the same height as DB-9 and DB-15 connectors, but substantially wider.

decoder A device that displays closed captions "hidden" in the VBI. Originally, "decoder" referred to an external box. It can now also refer to the chip built into the TV set.

default What your software does if you don't tell it otherwise. If, for example, all new files are called "newfile" until you specify otherwise, then "newfile" is called the default file name.

descriptive video service A voice-over on an auxiliary channel, such as SAP, containing a description for blind people of what's going on in a video program.

diacritical An accent mark placed over a letter, such as an acute, grave, circumflex or dieresis.

dieresis A double dot placed over a letter, as in ü. Also called an umlaut. Also spelled diaeresis.

DIN connector A round connector with pins arranged inside the circle. DIN connectors are used for S-Video connections, as well as for mouse and keyboard connectors.

disc or **disk** A circular flat storage medium. Usually "disc" is used for audio and video, while "disk" has been used in the computer industry. The convergence of the two is leaving us, once again, unsure of how to spell anything. *Compact disc* is always spelled with a c" while *floppy disk* (as in *diskette*) and *hard disk* are always spelled with a *k*.

dropframe timecoding Omitting frame numbers in SMPTE timecodes every so often to compensate for the fact that there are 29.97 frames in a second rather than 30. This is rather like the way leap years are handled on the calendar.

DSS Digital Satellite Service. The little satellite dishes that folks are using these days in place of the big 8–12' dishes that you always used to see in areas with poor TV reception or no cable.

DTV Digital Television. The new super high-resolution TV format being phased in in the United States.

DVD A high-capacity laser disc format. Various sources report that it stands for "Digital Video Disc" or "Digital Versatile Disc."

DVD-ROM The computer version of a DVD. A DVD-ROM holds about seven times what a CD-ROM holds.

DVE Digital Video Effects generator. This is a device used by video-production facilities to achieve flashy transitions and screen effects. DVE shows up in this captioning glossary in large part because most DVE devices regenerate the VBI, thus destroying any captions that exist on the picture unless some special bypass device is being used.

Dvorak keyboard An alternate typewriter keyboard layout to replace QWERTY. The Dvorak layout was designed to speed typing by placing the most commonly used letters in the home position and arranging letters so that any given finger is unlikely to be used for two successive letters. Wherever possible, keys alternate from one hand to the other.

DVS See *descriptive video service.*

-E-

EBU European Broadcasting Union. EBU is an organization, but the term is mostly encountered when talking about the 25-frame-per-second PAL timecoding standard.

ECI European Captioning Institute in Peterborough, United Kingdom.

EIA Electronic Industries Association. The EIA is the standards group responsible for captioning standards in the United States. The EIA has merged into CEMA, which then changed its name to CEA, all as part of a plot to keep us on our toes.

encoder A device that "hides" captions in the VBI.

endless loop A program that keeps doing the same thing over and over without stopping. See *loop, endless.*

ENG Electronic News Gathering

-F-

F connector The screw-on connector for coaxial cables that is commonly used for antenna or cable TV hookups in consumer (home) electronics, as opposed to the BNC connector used in professional (studio) equipment.

FAQ Frequently asked questions. Many sites you visit on the Internet will have FAQ files available, and I recommend that you always read it first. This file will explain everything you ever wanted to know about the area or resource you are visiting. Probably more than you ever really wanted to know.

FCC Federal Communications Commission. The organization in the United States that oversees broadcast television and radio.

field Half of an interlaced TV frame. A full frame of video is built by transmitting every other line and then making a second pass to fill in the blanks. In captioning, we refer to Line 21, field 1 as the place where most captioning data is stored (CC1, CC2, Text1 and Text2). Line 21, field 2 can be used for more caption and text data (CC3, CC4, Text3 and Text4), or for XDS data.

frame One of the many still pictures that, when shown in rapid succession, make up a moving video picture. In the United States, using NTSC video, we see one frame of video every 30th of a second. In other parts of the world, using PAL or SECAM, they see one frame every 25th of a second.

-G-

Gallaudet University for deaf and hard-of-hearing people, located in the Washington, D.C., area. Interesting factoid: Gallaudet originated the "huddle" in football as a way to prevent the other team from "listening in" when the quarterback signed the next play to the rest of the team. Now, doesn't that make this whole glossary worthwhile?

gigabyte or **GB** 2^{30} bytes, or roughly a billion bytes (Using the American definition of "billion." That's a thousand million to the Brits in the crowd). You can think of it as 1,024 megabytes.[1] Gigabytes are becoming the typical unit of storage for computer hard disks, although systems exist now that go up to the next larger unit: the terabyte.

grave accent A down-sloping accent mark placed over a letter, as in è.

-H-

HBI Horizontal blanking interval. Yes, there's an HBI to go with the VBI. The HBI is the space in the video signal between the end of one line of video and the beginning of the next. The HBI is considerably smaller than the VBI.

hertz (Hz) Usually used in technical discussions, as in "my head hertz after talking about video formats." OK, just kidding. A hertz is the standard unit of measurement for frequency, named for physicist Heinrich Hertz. One Hz is equivalent to one cycle per second. In the United States, our video signal is 60Hz, which means it cycles 60 times per second. Each cycle contains one field. Two fields make a frame, so our video is 30 frames per second.

---

[2] *My goodness! You actually looked this up. You must really want to know. OK, a gigabyte is actually 1,073,741,824 bytes.*

HoH Hard-of-hearing. The preferred term for someone with some level of hearing loss less than that required to be considered completely deaf.

HTML HyperText Markup Language. HTML is the native language of the World Wide Web, used to encode the billions of Web pages that await your perusal. It is also the basis for SAMI, a captioning format for the Web and CD-ROM world.

-I-

interlaced video Displaying each frame of video in two passes (fields), with each pass displaying every other line. In other words, with interlaced video (used in NTSC, PAL and SECAM), the electron gun in the TV set scans from the top of the screen to the bottom twice for each frame, drawing the even-numbered lines in one pass and the odd-numbered lines in the other. This is done primarily to reduce flickering, to allow for more stable pictures and to confuse people reading books like this one.

internet (lowercase "i") Usually used in the context of "an" internet, as opposed to "the" Internet. An internet (short for "internetwork") is a network of networks. Any structure made up of a set of computer networks connected together.

Internet (capital "I") In the context of "the" Internet. This is the global collection of networks and internetworks that interconnects virtually all of the major e-mail systems and online services in the world.

ISO International Standards Organization. A consortium that defines many of our transmission and storage formats.

ITV Interactive Television, where the viewer becomes more than just a passive observer and actually participates in the TV program.

ITV Link An Internet address (URL) embedded in the closed-caption data to connect a TV program to a Web site.

ITVA The International Television Association

-J-

JPEG Joint Photographic Experts Group. This is a standards group, working under ISO, to define standards for compression and storage of still pictures. Most of the photo-quality pictures you'll find on the Web are stored in JPEG format, as it provides very good quality in a fairly small amount of space. You can use JPEG format to compress a photographic image to about one-twentieth of its original size before you start to notice the colors degrading.

-K-

kanji The Japanese "alphabet" of symbols, derived from Chinese characters.

katakana Another Japanese writing system (see *kanji),* often used for writing words borrowed from other languages.

kilobyte or **KB** 1,024 bytes. Why 1,024? Well, although *kilo* means *thousand* in the metric system, its meaning was modified slightly when adapted to the binary world. In the metric system, we want even numbers of tens. One thousand is 10^3 (1 followed by 3 zeros). In binary, a thousand becomes a rather awkward number.[2] A much more useful number in a computer is 2^{10}, which comes out as 1,024. Aren't you glad you asked?

kilohertz or **kHz** One thousand cycles per second. See *hertz.*

-L-

LCD Liquid crystal display. The type of screen used in most notebook computers. LCDs are flat, lightweight and require much less power than traditional CRT displays.

LCD panel A computer display designed to sit on an overhead projector and project onto a wall or screen. LCD panels are usually about a foot square and an inch or so thick.

LCD projector A video projector that uses LCD technology to form the image. Unlike an LCD panel, an LCD projector is self-contained and does not require an overhead projector. Some LCD projectors have floppy drives and can show PowerPoint-type presentations without having a computer attached.

ligature Two letters written together, like the *ae* in *encyclopædia.* Ligatures are a typesetting phenomenon in English, but are actual letters in some other languages.

Line 21 The 21st line of the VBI, where closed-captioning data is stored and transmitted.

linear editing Editing from a standard analog videotape. It is called "linear" because all the frames are arranged along the tape in a line. To get from a frame near the beginning to a frame near the end, you must scan across all of the frames in between. Compare this to nonlinear editing.

Listserv A program that manages Internet mailing lists. The Listserv program is so popular that it came to be used as a generic term for a mailing list. See *mailing lists.*

live display Hand-timing captions from a script during live programming. Used when somebody is reading from a script or a TelePrompTer.

---

[2] *It's 1111101000, if you really must know.*

loop, endless A program that keeps doing the same thing over and over without stopping. See *endless loop.*

LTC Longitudinal (or "Linear") Time Code. The form of SMPTE timecode that can be stored on an audio track. Some tape formats, such as S-VHS, have a longitudinal track reserved for LTC.

luminance or **luma** Brightness of the TV signal. Luminance is what "Y" stands for in "Y/C," the format used for Super-VHS ("C" stands for "chrominance"). "Why, oh why," I hear you cry, "would they use a Y for luminance instead of an L?" Good question, grasshopper. The NTSC standard for color video images uses a set of equations that represent each color as a point in a three-dimensional space, represented by X, Y and Z coordinates. The Y value contains no chrominance information, so even though the X and Z coordinates from this system aren't used, "Y" stuck as a symbol to represent luminance.

-M-

mailing lists Similar to Usenet newsgroups, except that the discussion takes place using e-mail rather than a news server. Conversing via mailing list means that every comment or question transmitted to a mailing list goes to everyone else on that list, whether they want it or not. Most mailing lists utilize a Listserv. See *Usenet.*

mask reporter A court reporter who records proceedings by repeating everything into a special microphone with a surrounding mask to reduce ambient noise. The recording device can be a traditional tape recorder, digital recording on computer or speech recognition.

misstroke A misfingering on a stenotype keyboard.

megabyte or **MB** 2^{20} bytes, or roughly a million bytes. It's actually 1,024 kilobytes, which works out to be precisely 1,048,576 bytes, should you care. If you're that curious, you might also want to check out the next larger unit of measurement, the gigabyte. Megabytes are the typical unit of storage for RAM in a computer.

megahertz or **MHz** One million cycles per second. See *hertz.*

MPAA Motion Picture Association of America. The organization that created the movie rating system (G, PG, PG-13, R, NC-17 and X) used in the United States.

MPEG Motion Picture Experts Group. MPEG is used to refer to both the ISO committee which came up with the standard for digital storage and compression of video and audio signals and to refer to the standard itself. There is an MPEG-1 and a newer MPEG-2.

-N-

NAB National Association of Broadcasters (United States)

NAD National Association of the Deaf. A national organization of, and for, deaf people.

NCAM National Center for Accessible Media. An R&D organization formed by the Corporation for Public Broadcasting and WGBH in Boston. NCAM researches and develops technologies that create access to public mass media.

NCI National Captioning Institute. A large not-for-profit captioning company in Virginia that provides captioning services. NCI also created the TeleCaption line of caption decoders.

NCRA The National Court Reporters Association. Despite the name, NCRA has members from around the world, though the vast majority of its approximately 30,000 members are in the United States and Canada.

newsgroups Ongoing discussion groups on the Internet (well, on Usenet, actually) devoted to a particular topic. Newsgroups tend to have names like alt.television.fanclubs.startrek.original.tribbles. OK, I exaggerated slightly, but there are over 25,000 of them, and the number is increasing every day. See *Usenet.*

newsreader A program that enables you to read Usenet news. Up until recently, people used specialized programs to read newsgroups, but now the capability is built into many Web browsers (such as Netscape and Microsoft Internet Explorer).

NewStar A popular newsroom computer system with TelePrompTer and closed-captioning output options.

nonlinear editing An editing system without tape. The video is loaded onto a computer hard disk, where it can be accessed randomly. In other words, you can skip from any frame anywhere in the video to any other frame, without having to "fast-forward" through all of the frames in the middle. This saves a lot of time fast-forwarding and rewinding. It requires a large hard disk.

NTSC National Television Systems Committee. The term *NTSC* is used to refer to the EIA committee that came up with the TV format we use in the United States today and to refer to the format itself. The NTSC format was developed to provide a way to place color information on a TV signal while remaining compatible with black-and-white televisions. The format was adopted by the FCC in 1953.

The NTSC format, the standard format used throughout North America, uses 525 lines of video at 60Hz (30 frames per second, interlaced). See also *PAL* (most of Europe) and *SECAM* (France and the old

USSR).

NVRA National Verbatim Reporters Association. The main association for mask reporters in the United States.

NWPC National Working Party on Captioning. An Australian group established to facilitate communication between the consumers of captioning and the providers of the service. The NWPC also acts as a consumer lobbying group for captioning.

-O-

O&O Owned and operated. A TV station owned by its network.

offline captioning Captioning done on a videotape in a studio. This does not require a realtime stenocaptioner.

online captioning Captioning done on-the-fly, as something is happening, typically a live event or newscast. Captions can be realtime, live display, autoscroll or computerized notes.

open captioning Captions that are visible as subtitles on the TV picture, do not require a decoder and cannot be turned off.

-P-

paint-on captions Captions being drawn a letter at a time anywhere on screen.

PAL Phase alteration line. PAL is the color TV standard format throughout most of Europe (pretty much everyone except France, which uses SECAM). It is higher resolution than the NTSC used in North America, using 625 lines of video instead of 525, but it has a lower frequency (50Hz interlaced, yielding 25 frames per second).

PAL-M A 525-line version of PAL used in Brazil.

pel or **pixel** Short for picture element, which refers to a single image-forming dot on a video screen.

phone plug A connector often used for professional audio accessories like headphones and sometimes microphones. Not considered as “high-end” as the XLR connector. Not to be confused with a phono plug.

phonetic translation Converting strokes that aren’t in a steno dictionary into something more closely resembling English rather than displaying them as raw steno.

phono plug See *RCA connector.* Not to be confused with a phone plug.

pop-on captions Captions appearing all at once anywhere on a TV screen.

post-production Working from videotape or film (offline), as opposed to working with live camera (online).

POTS Plain old telephone service. Used to refer to ordinary phone lines (as opposed to dedicated lines or ISDN).

PPV Pay-per-view

PSA Public Service Announcement

-Q-

QWERTY The QWERTY keyboard is the most common typing keyboard for languages using Latin alphabets, such as English. It is named for the first six keys in the top row. The Dvorak and steno keyboards both support higher typing speeds than the QWERTY keyboard.

-R-

RAM Random-access memory. The dynamic memory in a computer where your programs and documents are when they're in use. RAM is erased every time you turn off the computer, unlike disks, which represent a more permanent storage medium.

RCA Connector used for home video and audio equipment. Also called a phono plug (not to be confused with a phone plug).

RDR Registered Diplomate Reporter certification, offered by NCRA, designed to test a broad range of knowledge associated with court reporting, captioning and related subjects. The highest certification currently attainable, the examinee must already have at least an RMR just to take the RDR exam.

realtime The translation of spoken words to written text on a screen, as they are spoken. This requires a court reporter or captioner using a steno keyboard, computer and translation software.

RGB Red, Green, Blue (for component video signals on three wires).

RGB/Sync Red, Green, Blue with synchronization signal (four-wire video).

RMR Registered Merit Reporter certification, offered by NCRA. The skills portion consists of writing and transcribing testimony at 260 wpm, jury charge at 240 wpm and literary dictation at 220 wpm. It includes a written test relating to court reporting duties. This certification used to be known as the CM.

roll-up captions Captions that scroll up a word or a line at a time.

RPR Registered Professional Reporter certification, offered by NCRA. The skills portion consists of writing and transcribing Q&A at 225 wpm, jury charge at 200 wpm and literary dictation at 180 wpm. It includes a written knowledge portion relating to court reporting duties.

RS-232 The transmission standard used for most serial communications from computers. The serial (or "COM") ports on your computer are most likely RS-232 compatible and are typically DB-9 or DB-25 connectors.

RS-422 A transmission standard designed for longer distances than RS-232. For that reason, it is often used in broadcast equipment like tape decks that may be quite a distance from the control system. RS-232 and RS-422 are not compatible, although adapters are available.

RTNDA Radio and Television News Directors Association

RVR Realtime Verbatim Reporter. This is the certification given by NVRA to mask reporters ("voice writers") who can produce realtime output at high accuracy.

-S-

safe area TV manufacturers make the case around the TV set cover part of the edge of the picture tube. This is done for aesthetic reasons, to compensate for differences in manufacturing processes from time to time, or factory to factory, and so that when the tube gets old and the picture starts to shrink, you don't see a black border around it. The safe area (or "safe title area") is defined as the portion of the picture that is guaranteed to be visible on all televisions. Captions have their own safe area, which is even smaller than the safe title area.

SAMI Synchronized Accessible Multimedia Interchange. SAMI was announced by Microsoft in June 1997 and is intended to be the standard format for encoding closed-captioning information in multimedia (video, audio and animation) files on CD-ROMs and the World Wide Web.

SAP Second Audio Program. An auxiliary audio channel on the TV subcarrier used for either a second language or descriptive video service for blind people.

SECAM An underwater camera (just kidding!). SECAM stands for Sequential Couleur Avec Memoire (sequential color with memory). Other sources list it as Système Electronique Couleur Avec Memoire, or "electronic system for color with memory." SECAM is the French color TV standard, also adopted in the old USSR. It uses 625 lines of video at 50Hz interlaced (25 frames per second), like PAL does. See also *NTSC*, the North American standard.

SGML Standardized General Markup Language. SGML is the basis of HTML, which is the language used for Web page creation. SGML is also the basis of SAMI, which is a standard captioning format for Web and CD-ROM multimedia.

SHHH Self Help for Hard-of-Hearing People. A national organization of, and for, deaf and hard-of-hearing people.

SMPTE Society of Motion Picture and Television Engineers. SMPTE developed, among other things, the standard for timecoding that is used by most broadcast and captioning equipment.

speech recognition A computer system that can automatically convert speech to text. See *voice recognition* and *voice writers.*

stenocaptioner Someone who can perform realtime captioning using a stenotype keyboard.

stenotype keyboard or **stenotype machine** A keyboard using "chording" (a system of pressing more than one key at a time) to allow much faster writing than a traditional QWERTY or Dvorak keyboard.

stroke A combination of one or more keys pressed all at one time on a stenotype keyboard. One stroke usually represents one syllable or word.

subtitling In the United States, subtitling refers to open captions created with a character generator. In the United Kingdom, subtitling is a synonym for captioning.

Supertext Captions produced by the ACC. Supertext is a registered trademark of the Australian Caption Centre.

Super-VHS A half-inch videotape format with resolution and color handling superior to standard VHS. Super-VHS is better than most consumer (home) video and is considered the low end of professional-quality video equipment.

S-VHS Abbreviation for Super-VHS.

S-VHS-C (S-VHS compact) A smaller S-VHS cassette designed for use in small camcorders. S-VHS-C tape cassettes can be played in a standard S-VHS tape deck using an adapter.

S-Video See *Y/C video.*

-T-

TBCM See *time base corrector.*

TCL Television Crossover Link. This is an obsolete term for an Interactive TV Link, or ITV Link.

TDCA Television Decoder Circuitry Act. This piece of legislation, which took effect in July 1993, mandates that every TV set 13 inches or larger manufactured for sale in the United States must have a caption decoder chip in it.

TDD Telecommunication Device for the Deaf. This term has fallen out of favor, and TDDs are more commonly known now as TTYs.

TDI Telecommunications for the Deaf Inc. Although TDI functions principally as an advocacy group for equal access via telephone (using TTYs), it has also been involved in captioning issues. TDI publishes a directory of TTY numbers.

TeleCaption Home caption decoder manufactured by NCI.

Teletext Captioning standard used in the United Kingdom and parts of Europe.

Television Crossover Link This is an obsolete term for an Interactive TV Link, or ITV Link.

TER Total error rate. This is how captioners measure their accuracy. It involves counting words in a selection of caption text and marking errors to find a ratio.

terabyte or **TB** 2^{40} bytes, or roughly 1,012 bytes (that's a trillion to the Americans or a billion to the British). While you don't see terabyte disks in your PC yet, large Web sites (search engines, video servers, etc.) do have terabytes of storage. If someone asks you what a terabyte actually is, you can just tell them it's 1,024 gigabytes, or 1,099,511,627,776 bytes. Got it? You can also memorize the next largest measurement, the petabyte, which I've never actually been able to find a way to slip into a sentence at a cocktail party.[3]

text mode Caption-like text transmitted in Line 21, which covers all (or at least half) of the screen when displayed.

tilde A wavy line (~) placed over a letter, as in ñ.

time base corrector (TBC) A device used for cleaning up video signals. A TBC produces stable, high-quality images, but can also wipe captions from the VBI while doing it.

timecode Unique time identifier stamped on each frame of video. SMPTE defines two ways of storing timecodes: LTC goes on a linear (audio) track, and VITC goes in the VBI.

TTY The "text telephone" used by deaf and hard-of-hearing people. This basically consists of a keyboard connected to an old-style Baudot modem, so that two people can connect TTYs to their telephones and type messages to each other.

---

[3] *You're not actually expecting me to tell you what a petabyte is, are you? You are? OK, it's 1,125,899,906,842,624 bytes. I hope you're happy!*

-U-

U-Matic An old, professional three-quarter-inch videotape format. There is an updated version called U-Matic/SP.

umlaut The double dot over vowels in German, as in München, and French, as in Noël. Also called a dieresis.

Usenet A huge message-based bulletin board system. Usenet is divided into thousands of different newsgroups, which are roughly the Internet equivalent of CompuServe's forums. There are currently over 18,000 newsgroups focusing on particular areas of interest. You subscribe to those that look interesting to you, and you participate by simply reading the messages of others, or you can elect to post your own messages to a newsgroup. If you do not wish to continue to receive postings from a particular newsgroup, you can easily unsubscribe. It does not cost anything to subscribe to newsgroups, thus proving beyond a reasonable doubt that you very often do get exactly what you pay for.

-V-

VBI Vertical blanking interval. The 21 "blank" lines of video picture between the bottom of one frame and the top of the next. Line 21 of the VBI is where closed captions are stored.

VCR Video cassette recorder

VHS Video home system. The most common tape format used for consumer videotapes, developed by Matsushita and JVC.

VHS-C VHS compact. A smaller VHS cassette designed to use in small camcorders. Using an adapter, VHS-C tape cassettes can be played in a standard VHS tape deck.

VITC Vertical interval timecode. The form of SMPTE timecode that can be stored on the VBI.

voice recognition A computer trained to recognize the identity of a person by his or her speech patterns. This is usually used in security systems and is very different from speech recognition.

voice writer Someone who creates real-time text by speaking into a trained speech recognition system.

VTR Videotape recorder. This acronym is more common with professional, broadcast and studio equipment than VCR, which is usually reserved for consumer (home) electronics.

-W-

wpm Words per minute. A measurement of caption speed. The theoretical maximum that can be stored on Line 21, field 1 is approximately 600 wpm. The actual maximum is lower than that.

-X-

XDS Extended Data Services. Data packets carried in field 2 of Line 21, containing information like time of day, network name, program name, National Weather Service alerts, parental guidelines ("V-Chip") information and so forth.

XLR Three-pin connector for "balanced" audio cables. Typically, XLR connectors are used in professional audio/video equipment such as microphones, rather than the RCA connectors used in home video equipment. Among its advantages are that it locks in, so that it can't fall out by accident.

XML Extensible Markup Language. A file format, based on SGML and HTML, that uses tags for adding nontextual information. A variant of XML, called Legal XML, is being developed for court and deposition transcript exchange.

-Y-

Y/C video The component video signal used in the Hi8 and S-VHS videotape formats. Y/C transmits luminance and color portions separately, using multiple wires. Also known as S-Video.

Index